BLACK HARLEM AND THE JEWISH LOWER EAST SIDE

SUNY series in Multiethnic Literature

Mary Jo Bona, editor

BLACK HARLEM AND THE JEWISH LOWER EAST SIDE

narratives out of time

EDITED BY
CATHERINE ROTTENBERG

STATE UNIVERSITY OF NEW YORK PRESS

Cover photograph: Berenice Abbot, *Pike and Henry Streets, Manhattan,* March 6, 1936. Used with permission of the Photography Collection, Miriam and Ira D. Wallach Division of Art, Prints and Photographs, The New York Public Library, Astor, Lenox and Tilden Foundations.

Printed in the United States of America

For information, contact
State University of New York Press, Albany, NY
www.sunypress.edu

Production, Laurie D. Searl
Marketing, Michael Campochiaro

Library of Congress Cataloging-in-Publication Data

Rottenberg, Catherine.
Black Harlem and the Jewish Lower East Side : narratives out of time / Catherine Rottenberg.
p. cm. — (SUNY series in multiethnic literature)
Includes bibliographical references and index.
ISBN 978-1-4384-4521-2 (hardcover : alk. paper)
ISBN 978-1-4384-4522-9 (pbk. : alk. paper)
1. American literature—Minority authors—History and criticism. 2. Harlem Renaissance. 3. African Americans—New York (State)—New York—Relations with Jews. 4. Jews—New York (State)—New York. 5. Lower East Side (New York, N.Y.)—Intellectual life—20th century. 6. New York (N.Y.)—In literature. I. Title.
PS153.M56R67 2012
810.9'920693—dc23 2012005002

10 9 8 7 6 5 4 3 2 1

CONTENTS

ACKNOWLEDGMENTS

I would like to thank each and every one of the contributors for their infinite patience, hard work, and wonderful essays. Their graciousness when I became a nudge, their willingness to revise at my request, and all that I have learned from their work has made this project more than worthwhile. I would also like to thank Henry Louis Gates Jr. and Hasia Diner for their enthusiastic responses to my requests to republish their essays.

A year at the Frankel Institute for Advanced Judaic Studies at the University of Michigan planted the original seeds for this project. I am particularly grateful to Anita Norich and Deborah Dash Moore for creating an intimate, informal, yet productive environment for all the inaugural fellows. The conversations with Barbara Mann and Julian Levinson were invaluable to me. And Lila Corwin Berman has become a dear friend and long-distance interlocutor.

The Department of Foreign Literature and Linguistics at Ben-Gurion University has made my day-to-day working environment amazingly welcoming and supportive. I would not have been able to complete this volume without the many (and there were many) pep talks by my colleagues, especially Yael Ben-Zvi, Barbara Hochman, and Eitan Bar-Yosef. The Gender Studies Program has also been a great place to work. Special thanks go to Niza Yanay for her unwavering support and for her brilliant insights; to Amalia Ziv for her many challenges to my normativity and for her friendship, and to Nitza Berkovitch for all of the conversations, constructive comments, and incredible help over the years.

This volume could not have been possible without the continued support and encouragement of Amritjit Singh and Stephen Knadler—two of the most generous scholars I know, whose research has had a great influence on my own. I would also like to thank the anonymous reviewers for their productive comments, Beth Bouloukos for making the publication process so seamless, and Mary Jo Bona for her faith in the project from the very beginning.

Finally, I would like to thank my partner, Neve Gordon for his willingness to help at every step of the way—and the way has been long and the steps many.

* * *

Henry Louis Gates's chapter "Harlem on Our Minds" first appeared in *Critical Inquiry* (24, no. 1, 1997) and is reprinted here by permission of the author.

Hasia Diner's chapter "Texts of Memory" is a shortened version of a chapter that originally appeared in her book *Lower East Side Memories: A Jewish Place in America*, copyright 2000 Princeton University Press, 2002 paperback edition. Reprinted by permission of Princeton University Press.

Chapter 2 draws on material from Catherine Rottenberg, "Affective Narratives," *Journal of American Studies* 44, no. 4, 777–93, copyright Cambridge University Press, reproduced with permission.

INTRODUCTION

Black Harlem and the Jewish Lower East Side

Catherine Rottenberg

Harlem and the Lower East Side: two world-famous neighborhoods in New York City that evoke not only a rich history but also a particular ethnic or racial narrative. Most Americans can likely conjure up which ethnic or racial group has "belonged" to which space.[1] In fact, these spaces—one downtown and one uptown on Manhattan Island—have become almost synonymous with the history of African Americans and Jewish Americans in the Progressive Era and Jazz Age. This is at least a little odd since blacks and Jews did, of course, live in many other places—in other cities, in small towns, and in rural settings. Nevertheless, these two urban neighborhoods have, over the past one hundred years, accrued symbolic significance.

Indeed, Harlem and the Lower East Side are unique in the way they have been imagined and represented in U.S. popular culture in general and in the imagination of African Americans and Jewish Americans more particularly. It is impossible to recount the history of U.S. Jewry or discuss the emergence of Jewish American literature without emphasizing the importance of the Lower East Side in such narratives. The same is true of Harlem with respect to black history, especially if one is interested in the African American literary and artistic traditions. It is extremely difficult, moreover, to think of any other U.S. "ethnic" group that has so closely identified and been identified with any one specific neighborhood, or, as Hasia Diner has so aptly argued, with one "particular chunk of space."[2] There are many Chinatowns, Little Italys, and Greek towns, but there is only one Harlem and only one Lower East Side. The various and striking parallels between the emergence and appropriation of "Black Manhattan" and the "Jewish East Side" quite simply call out for a comparison between the representations of these two spaces, which, over the course of the twentieth century have become iconic. Yet, despite the many similarities between their "imaginings," this is the first volume to take on the task of placing the two urban neighborhoods in conversation with one another.

HARLEM AND THE LOWER EAST SIDE: THE CREATION OF URBAN ENCLAVES

The area in lower Manhattan that would eventually be called the Lower East Side had had a Jewish presence long before the first wave of Eastern European Jews arrived on its streets. Beginning in the early nineteenth century, Jews from Bavaria, the Rhineland, and other (what would later become) German provinces immigrated to the United States, and some settled in the vicinity of lower Manhattan. During the 1830s the area went by the name of Little Germany due to the numerous Christian and Jewish German speakers who lived there. It was only following the tidal wave of Jewish immigration from parts of Eastern Europe that a certain swath of lower Manhattan—south of Fourteenth Street and north of Fulton, nestled between Broadway and the East River—began to be perceived of as a specifically "Jewish" place. Approximately two and a half million Eastern European Jews arrived in the United States between 1880 and 1920, and the majority of these immigrants settled in the few square miles of city space on the east side of Manhattan's southern tip.[3]

The first decades of the twentieth century consequently witnessed the emergence of a rich cultural landscape on the Lower East Side. Although the neighborhood was never entirely Jewish, the overwhelmingly presence of Jews within such a circumscribed and densely populated area helped to create the popular perception—both inside as well as outside the Jewish community—that it was indeed a "Jewish" place. Amidst the poverty of the crowded tenements and the seemingly omnipresent sweatshops, the hundreds of thousands of Jews who lived in this urban enclave espoused and developed diverse ideological and religious commitments: from anarchism and Zionism to Yiddishism and Orthodox Judaism. Moreover, these immigrants managed to build, within a relatively short time, an impressive array of visible and highly developed institutional networks, including trade unions, synagogues, and settlement houses, such as the still-operational Educational Alliance. Another towering Lower East Side institution was the *Jewish Daily Forward*, the most influential Yiddish newspaper of the era, which operated out of the tallest building in the area and dominated the immediate skyline. This period also spawned the "golden age" of the Yiddish theater. Sanford Sternlicht documents that, at the height of the Yiddish theater's popularity in 1920, there were at least eighteen individual Yiddish theaters dotting the streets of the neighborhood.[4] In addition to the flourishing of journalism, theater, and other creative arts during the early part of the twentieth century, the Lower East Side also laid claim to the first major Jewish American fiction writers, Abraham Cahan and Anzia Yezierska. These authors, both of whom spent much of their own lives in the neighborhood, not only portrayed life on the "Jewish East Side" but also drew their creative inspiration from its chaotic and eclectic cultural makeup.

The mass black movement to Harlem began a few decades after the Jewish settlement of the Lower East Side and was part of the Great Migration of a half-million African Americans who left the South for northern cities between 1910 and 1920. When blacks started to settle in the northern reaches of Manhattan at the turn of the century, Harlem was an upper-middle-class white residential suburb that had recently begun to see the arrival of upwardly mobile "ethnic" immigrants. Railroad and subway development eventually led to land speculation in the area, and a subsequent housing bust pushed previously reluctant white real estate owners to sell or rent property to African Americans. As blacks moved into the area, the white residents, especially the more established and wealthier Harlemites, quickly moved out. Historian Gilbert Osofsky notes that already prior to World War I the neighborhood had become "the largest colony of colored people in similar limits in the world."[5]

More famous than its Jewish counterpart for its artistic outpouring during the 1920s, Harlem rapidly gained a reputation as the African American cultural capital. The Jazz Age saw the emergence of what would later be coined The Harlem Renaissance—a period of unprecedented African American creativity in literature and the arts. And, as an increasing number of migrating African Americans chose New York City as their preferred final destination, Harlem also became the headquarters for some of the most influential national African American social and political organizations, including the NAACP and its magazine *The Crisis*, which served as one of the major venues for African American writers and intellectuals. These were also the years in which many of the most prominent artists, writers, and political leaders lived and worked in Harlem—people such as W. E. B. DuBois, James Weldon Johnson, Nella Larsen, Jessie Fauset, and Marcus Garvey, the controversial leader of the "Back to Africa" movement.

It is important to remember, however, that though Harlem remained at the heart of African American cultural life for many years to come, already by the mid-1920s what had once been an affluent white suburb had become an overcrowded, poverty-ridden, and racialized urban enclave.[6] Indeed, for many scholars, the 1935 Harlem riots mark the end of the "renaissance" period and the beginning of a significant transformation in the way this urban space was perceived in the U.S. popular imagination: from the symbol of African American achievement to the emblem of black inner-city problems.[7]

Recent scholarship has made two central and convincing claims about the African American and Jewish American relationships to these metropolitan neighborhoods. One is that both communities have developed a powerful affective relationship toward Harlem and the Lower East Side respectively. The second is that these two neighborhoods have gained exemplar status, one that allows these spaces to "stand in" for *the* black or *the* Jewish U.S. experience in the twentieth century.[8] And yet, despite a series of interdisciplinary studies that investigate why Harlem *or* the Lower East Side has come to figure so prominently in the psyche of African Americans or Jewish Americans, hardly any work comparing the two iconic enclaves has been carried out. Moreover, given the current spatial turn in literary studies, an emphasis on the spatial dimension of African American and Jewish American identity formation—rather than these groups' affective links to a particular place—is long overdue. *Black Harlem and the Jewish Lower East Side* aims to begin filling in these lacunae by placing canonical—and less canonical—African and Jewish American novelists who wrote about these urban spaces in dialogue with one another.

Since the publication of Hasia Diner's seminal *In the Almost Promised Land: Jews and Blacks: 1915–1935* and later Emily Miller Budick's *Blacks and Jews in Literary Conversation*, an increasing number of works—literary, sociological, and historical—have been carried out on what Adam Zachary Newton has memorably termed "blackjewishrelations."[9] Among the numerous cultural histories examining the fraught relationship between African American and Jewish Americans, Cheryl Greenberg's *Troubling the Waters: Black-Jewish Relations in the American Century* stands out. In the last five years, a number of excellent cross-ethnic literary studies, such as Dean Franco's *Ethnic American Literature: Comparing Chicano, Jewish, and African American Writing*, and Martin Japtok's *Growing Up Ethnic: Nationalism and the Bildungsroman in African American and Jewish American Fiction* have also been published. Still other work, such as Eric Sundquist's encyclopedic study *Strangers in the Land: Black, Jews, Post-Holocaust America* has sought to compare post–World War II African American and Jewish American literature by looking at the specific political, cultural and sociohistoric contexts of each tradition's emergence. This impressive and constantly growing body of scholarly work suggests that, today, comparative Black-Jewish Studies has become a field in its own right within U.S. Multiethnic Studies.

Perhaps not surprisingly, much of the comparative work in Black-Jewish Studies has concentrated on the way in which these two communities have represented each other in literature (e.g., Budick), how they have formed and/or torn asunder alliances at particular historical junctures (e.g., Greenberg), or how each community's identity and self-representation have been linked one to the other (e.g., Japtok). Another interesting and more recent comparative angle—exemplified in Franco's book—has centered on what might be called a dialogic multicultural approach that attempts to unsettle the nationalist-based or other "essentialist" assumptions of the field. While *Black Harlem and the Jewish Lower East Side* builds on these path-breaking studies and perhaps comes closest to Martin Japtok's emphasis on how these two groups have represented *themselves* in and through literature, this book aims to use notable literary texts in order to introduce the *spatial dimension* into the ongoing discussion about the relationship between and the self-representation of African Americans and Jewish Americans in the United States.

This volume accordingly continues and expands upon existing Black-Jewish scholarly studies. Its unique approach and contribution consist of its comparative envisioning of Harlem and the Lower East Side, each of which has been absolutely central in the cultural memory of these two communities as well as in helping shape modern and contemporary notions of African Americanness and Jewish Americanness. Tapping into the growing interest in comparative ethnic studies, the book also shifts away from essentialist models of ethnic studies and underscores the spatial aspect of black and Jewish self-fashioning, while contending that the process of each group's ethnic or racial identity formation has been linked in complex ways both to the relationship between the two groups and to the urban spaces each group has called its own. Through a comparative study that accentuates the spatial dimension by juxtaposing depictions of the Lower East Side with Harlem, we begin to see just how important particular spaces have been in negotiating U.S. identity. And, though this volume focuses exclusively on blacks and Jews, its claims, I believe, have concrete implications for Multiethnic Studies more generally.

While each article in the volume discusses one period or specific authors, all of the articles in this collection offer a spatially informed reading of African American and/or Jewish American literature. Some of the chapters, such as Meredith Goldsmith's and my own, engage directly with comparative readings of Harlem and the Lower East Side. However, other chapters, such as Cherene Sherrard-Johnson's and Adam Meyer's, read only one author or literary tradition through the lens of space. Each chapter critically engages with the impact of space on the identity formation of the two communities, but it is the volume as a whole that carries out the broader comparative work. This approach, where essays alternate between a comparative and single neighborhood/author perspective, allows for a breadth of scholarship without forfeiting in-depth investigations of each space. The comparative chapters map out how the representations of Harlem and the Lower East Side dovetailed as well as diverged one from the other, while the chapters that focus on one tradition or author reveal the contradictions and complexities that characterized the depiction of each of these neighborhoods. Taken together, the volume offers the first truly comprehensive overview of how "Black Harlem" and the "Jewish East Side" have been represented over the course of the twentieth century in African American and Jewish American literature.

There is another—and perhaps less obvious—spatially informed framework that organizes this volume and links the various chapters together. All of the essays address, in their own way, two central questions: one relates to the social production of space and the other to how space, in turn, helps produce social subjects. More specifically, the first question queries *why* these urban spaces have come to stand in for *the* twentieth-century Jewish American and African American experience. What is it about Harlem and the Lower East Side's "social production" that has facilitated the transformation of these spaces into icons? This first question assumes, of course, that the literary depictions of these neighborhoods, these imaginative fashionings and negotiations of space, are not simply passive or reflective of already existing places, but rather—as Edward Soja has taught us in a different context—have themselves helped to engender the way in which these communities have thought about, explained, experienced, and indeed created and recreated Harlem and the Lower East Side over time.[10]

The second question, no less important and inextricable from the first, is informed by the notion that space is constitutive of identity and relates to what the literary representations can tell us about how these city spaces have affected the positioning of Jewish Americans and African Americans in relation to dominant U.S. society. In other words, socially produced space, in its turn, helps to shape how groups know, narrate, and experience themselves, and the way they are identified and experienced by others. Therefore, examining the way the representations of Harlem and the Lower East Side have changed over time can help us understand the shifting position and self-understanding of U.S. Jews and blacks over the past century.

HARLEM AND THE LOWER EAST SIDE AS SITES OF CULTURAL MEMORY

There is widespread agreement among social and cultural historians of American Jewry that the Lower East Side has become a site of intense emotional investment for Jewish Americans and that, in the post–World War II era, there has been a certain sacralization of this neighborhood.

Historian Beth Wenger, for example, claims that as increasing numbers of Jews left the Lower East Side in the 1920s and 1930s they developed a sentimental relationship to it. The neighborhood helped to frame their collective experiences as American Jews, helped them to make sense of change, as well as to create a narrative history and a physical context for locating Jewish American communal origins. American Jews have, in other words, claimed the Lower East Side as their originary site of cultural memory, "embracing it as the Plymouth Rock of American Jewish history."[11]

U.S. Jewry has come to perceive the Lower East Side as the site of lost and retrieved origins and, as such, this place has become sacrosanct. It has, over the years, become suffused with both mystique and nostalgia. By evoking its name, by identifying with it, Jewish Americans can both stake a claim in a common Jewish American history and in a dominant Jewish American narrative, one that tells the story of poor immigrants who rose out of the quintessentially Jewish American ghetto and managed to enter mainstream middle-class U.S. society. Just as importantly, the neighborhood has come to represent authenticity, a place where Jews could be truly themselves. In the minds of many contemporary U.S. Jews the Lower East Side lays claim to a purer and more authentic Judaism, one that has to a great extent been lost or at least diluted.[12] These Jewish Americans, then, attempt to tap into if not reclaim this authenticity by appropriating the neighborhood as their own.[13]

Turning to Harlem, one immediately notices a difference. Scholars do not and cannot talk about cultural memory in the same way for the simple reason that Harlem as a site of crowded black urban life did not disappear over the course of the twentieth century. The process of iconization of this neighborhood, then, cannot be limned in the same terms as the Lower East Side, since the sacralization of the Lower East Side for Jewish Americans has meant the making sacred by having left it as well as through a certain memorialization and reconstruction of a neighborhood that no longer exists in present reality. Hasia Diner reminds us that the memory of the Lower East Side assumed its power not only from the Jewish sojourn there but more importantly from the drama of exodus from it.[14] And, yet, as scholars such as Dorothea Lobbermann have convincingly pointed out, Harlem still signifies as a crucial "memory place" for African Americans.[15] Harlem, then, represents something else in the popular imagination, and its status as the symbol of black American experience has evolved through a different path.

Although its transformation into an iconic space cannot be limned in the same terms, Harlem—like its Jewish counterpart—has over time become a place associated with cultural exemplarity and a site of intense emotional investment. Beginning with the Harlem Renaissance and continuing all the way into the present, Harlem has continuously been invoked and served as a catchphrase or even catchall for African American life, both in scholarship and in literature. In the 1970s, the prominent African American historian Nathan Irvin Huggins claimed: "Throughout the world, and throughout this century, Harlem has *been* Afro-American life and culture."[16] Several decades before this declaration, Harlem had already been famously described as "the Mecca of the New Negro" and as a "prophetic space,"[17] and these epithets were reiterated in fiction and nonfiction alike, thus indicating that the neighborhood has also been suffused—at least during particular periods—with a certain sacrosanctity. Thinking about the title of John Henrik Clarke's edited volume of short stories: *Harlem: Voices from the Soul of Black America*, one immediately notices the conflation of Harlem with "Black America," while the use of the term *soul* can be seen to gesture toward the endurance of an identification of Black Manhattan with some aspect of sanctity.[18] These are just a few examples that demonstrate that Harlem has indeed been invested with sacredness—not because of black sojourn and exodus, but rather because of the promise this space once generated and, as many of these essays propose, continued to engender throughout the past century.

This urban enclave began to signify incredible optimism during the late Progressive Age and into the Jazz Age, representing the possibility of producing a rich African American culture against the odds created by a bleak history of slavery, oppression, Jim Crow, and poverty. This space also came to represent—again, during particular periods—the possibility of living out certain aspects of the American Dream. Harlem, like the Lower East Side for Jews, has been the place that African Americans embraced as the Plymouth Rock of African American history—at least in terms of the escape from the persecution of Jim Crow and the place where blacks could practice hitherto unknown cultural freedoms.

However, as many of the articles in this collection forcibly remind us, Harlem as metaphor has been Janus-faced, since alongside its promise, it has simultaneously been inscribed as a site of intense anguish that has not been transmuted over time into mere nostalgia or mystique. Harlem can thus be understood to stand in for a dual modality in the minds of African Americans: one modality is full of promise and hope, while the other is full of despair. There is, in other words, a deep ambivalence in the very iconicity of Harlem, an ambivalence that hardly exists in the contemporary representations of the Lower East Side. Unlike its Jewish counterpart, whose sacralization has produced a narrative of linearity—from ghetto to middle class, with some nostalgic loss and sadness on the way—Harlem's sacralization has not been the result of a "progressive," one-way, and linear story, since the possibility this space symbolized always dovetailed with desperation. The story Harlem points to is zigzagged and jagged-edged.

In order to begin giving an account of why these parallel processes of iconization have differed so markedly, this volume traces the ways in which Jews and Blacks in the United States have imagined, fashioned, and understood Harlem and the Lower East Side over the course of the twentieth century. Incorporating the insights of sociologist Pierre Bourdieu, the supposition throughout this volume is that a group's positionality in social space is constitutive not only of the group's habitus but also of the kinds of narratives communities construct about themselves and their "place."

Scholars such as Karen Brodkin and Matthew Jacobson have convincingly argued that even though "Jewishness" was still framed within a discourse of race during the Jazz Age, it was to undergo a radical sea change as the century progressed: namely, Jewishness was slowly morphed from a racial category into something that would later be articulated as "ethnicity." "Blackness" by contrast, continued to be linked to a series of *racial* characteristics, and the definitional power of the black-white divide only increased over time. Indeed, it was this reinforcement of the black-white divide that helped Jews—who had been interpellated as off-white subjects—jockey successfully for a position as normative and white Americans. Jewish American white ethnic identity formation has been, then, fundamentally dependent on the prior racialization of African Americans and on the specific operations of the black-white divide, which—interestingly enough—is itself a spatial metaphor. It could also be argued that in the United States, ethnicity and the creation of an "ethnic" rather than a "racial" identity have been intimately linked to minority groups' ability to move across different spaces. In other words, spatial movement—both horizontally, in terms of being able to enter and exit certain places relatively freely, and vertically, in terms of climbing up the class ladder—has been key to the de-racialization of particular minority groups, such as the Jews. By sharp contrast, the black-white divide prevented this kind of spatial mobility for African Americans during much of the twentieth century.

Harlem and the Lower East Side—as real and imagined spaces—have been two crucial sites through which Jewish Americans and African Americans have negotiated and renegotiated their diverging social positions as well as their gendered, racial, and class identities. Examining the (re) production and (re)presentation of these two neighborhoods thus becomes crucial for understanding the coalescing of modern and contemporary, individual as well as collective, Jewish African and African American identity. Through its shifting focus, *Black Harlem and the Jewish Lower East Side* shows how these identities have been forged in the crucible of space.

VOLUME'S TRAJECTORY

Henry Louis Gates Jr. opens the volume with a panoramic overview of the emergence of Harlem as cultural icon. Gates argues that while the Harlem Renaissance was the second African American literary renaissance, it was the New Negro writers who were, in fact, responsible for imagining and promoting this New York City neighborhood as *the* site of the black cultural sublime. Tracing the other renaissances that emerged in the wake of the New Negro one, Gates underscores how the invention of Harlem as the cultural metaphor for black America presents a certain paradox that many of the articles in this volume touch upon: it was precisely as Harlem was turning into the great American slum that influential intellectuals and "race leaders" such as Alain Locke and James Weldon Johnson were touting this black urban space as "the Mecca" of the New Negro and "the greatest Negro city in the world." What this, in turn, suggests is that Harlem, as a metaphor for black life in the United States, has functioned to suture a certain tension—the tension between the myth and hope on the one hand and Harlem's social reality on the other. Teasing apart the ambivalence at the heart of the iconicity of Harlem is therefore key to unraveling the kind of cultural work—the elisions and disavowals—that this process of sacralization of Harlem has accomplished.

Following Gates's cue and beginning the comparative work of the book, in the second chapter I trace the representations of Harlem and the Lower East Side back to the early-twentieth-century canonical novels of Abraham Cahan, Jessie Fauset, Nella Larsen, and Anzia Yezierska. I outline how in both the African American and Jewish American narratives the protagonists' relationship to Harlem and the Lower East Side is portrayed as being informed by a complex dynamic of attraction and repulsion. Yet in each case the source of the ambivalence as well as its manifestations are different. In the African American novels, the ambivalence toward Harlem manifests itself in racialized terms where the positive and the negative pull of the neighborhood are inextricably linked to Harlem being perceived of as "black" space. For the African Americans protagonists, in other words, the problem with their ghetto and their position in society is construed primarily through the prism or race. In the Jewish American narratives, by contrast, the ambivalence toward the Lower East Side, especially in its negative manifestation, is much more class-inflected and is not directed at the perceived "Jewishness" of the neighborhood. I argue that these differences—which emerge from an investigation of the common trope of ambivalence—are significant and can help us to account for the diverging significations of Harlem and the Lower East Side as the twentieth century progressed.

As the 1920s waned, Harlem solidified into the largest black urban ghetto in the United States, and Jews moved out of the Lower East Side in increasing numbers, authors Jessie Fauset and Tess Slesinger began exploring "alternative spaces" in which their female characters could forge less scripted gender, ethnic, and class identities. Juxtaposing Jessie Fauset's *Plum Bun* with Tess Slesinger's vastly understudied *The Unpossessed*, in chapter 3 Meredith Goldsmith shows how racially identifiable urban enclaves—such as Harlem—are limned as too conservative for the novels' upwardly mobile minority female characters, especially in terms of dominant gender norms. More specifically, femininity in these "racialized" enclaves is portrayed as reinforcing either "genteel" heteronormative coupling or maternity. The protagonists in *Plum Bun* and *The Unpossessed* therefore explore the emancipatory potential of Greenwich Village, hoping that a different—or "third"—space will allow them to escape the oppressive gender norms of the more clearly ethnically marked areas. Ultimately, and tragically perhaps, both novels underscore how the Village fails to serve as a constructive setting for the development of an emancipated ethnic female subjectivity.

During the 1930s and 1940s, Jewish presence in the quintessentially Jewish American ghetto steeply declined. Consequently, the Lower East Side tended to fade into the background of the fictional landscape, only—as Hasia Diner argues in chapter 8—to reappear in full force in the 1950s. By contrast, African Americans continued to pour into Harlem during the mid-century, which, in turn, ensured that Harlem never really dimmed in the popular or fictive imagination. In chapter 4, Cherene Sherrard-Johnson takes us back to Harlem via the writings of Ann Petry. Through a multilayered investigation of Petry's fiction and nonfiction, Sherrard-Johnson argues that these various texts simultaneously reinforce and pose a challenge to the popular conception of Harlem as either ghetto or the originary site of African American revival, renaissance, and possibility. On the one hand, in her nonfiction, Petry seems to incorporate and emphasize the dual "nature" of the neighborhood space by contrasting vignettes of urban blight with those of society ladies and famous Harlem residents. On the other hand, in her fiction, she reminds us how the urban space of Black Manhattan has always been profoundly influenced by norms traveling from the South and the white suburbs. The New Negro and other Afrocentric conceptions of the black community, then, have always been informed by other spaces and places. More specifically, by contrasting Petry's famous *The Street* with her less famous *Country Place*, Sherrard-Johnson traces how middle-class black female gentility—associated with the New Negro Woman of the Harlem Renaissance—traveled and transmogrified from country to city and vice versa.

Providing yet another crucial comparative perspective to the question of iconicity, Cheryl Greenberg reads *Call It Sleep*—the last of the early classic Jewish fiction in which the Lower East Side features prominently—alongside James Baldwin's first novel *Go Tell It on the Mountain*. Greenberg claims that the symbolic setting of each novel has not only helped guarantee its canonical status, but that the striking similarities between the two texts' trajectories can help scholars to understand more fully the many parallels between the way that Jews and blacks have imagined and fashioned themselves through space in the United States. The essay outlines how both communities have understood their identity as shaped by their marginalization—spatial and otherwise—and how they have constructed a comparable historical narrative of persecution, struggle, and perseverance. Greenberg persuasively argues that *Call It Sleep* and *Go Tell It on the Mountain* are profoundly informed by these "founding" group narratives, which, in turn, makes these novels particularly useful sites for exploring the specific way in which the black and Jewish experiences have intersected, reflected as well as differed from one another.

In chapter 6, Adam Meyer challenges the neat bifurcation of Harlem as black and the Lower East Side as Jewish. His essay not only gestures toward the continued Jewish presence in Harlem, but also focuses on a genre that has yet to receive critical attention in comparative Jewish American and African American literary studies: namely, the novel about liberal Jewish educators in Harlem schools. Following the narrative trajectories of various novels that sketch the careers of these young and ideological teachers, Meyer reveals their striking similarity: The teachers begin with missionary zeal, are soon forced to confront the harsh realities of their pupils and eventually to deal with the death of one of their pet students; this traumatic event, in turn, leads to a tempering of their idealism but, perhaps paradoxically, a redoubling of their determination to remain and teach in Harlem. In the novels, it is important to note, the neighborhood is not presented as mixed or multiethnic space; rather, the Jewish protagonists are consistently described as entering all-black space. In the end, however, Meyer argues that it is the Jewish protagonists' inability to confront their own privilege as liberal educators—as representatives of the white mainstream who can come and go as they please—that helps to undermine their own effectiveness as reformers.

In chapter 6, then, Adam Meyer consequently underscores one fraught aspect of the "jewishblackrelations" that Cheryl Greenberg touches upon in her chapter. As Greenberg demonstrates, the potential for cooperation and the bridging of differences between these two relatively visible minority groups have not only existed throughout the twentieth century, but that potential has been realized during certain junctures in modern and contemporary U.S. history. However, the very different positions of Jews and African Americans in the post–World War II era made any alliance between the two minority groups laden with potentially explosive fault lines. As Meyer suggests, one of the fault lines has been the extraordinary success of Jews in the United States.

Magdalena Zaborowska's essay continues the focus on Harlem and examines James Baldwin's oeuvre, arguing that, throughout Baldwin's career, he portrayed Black Manhattan as both a source of artistic inspiration and a prison for the black body. Opening with his early nonfictional essay "The Harlem Ghetto," Zaborowska traces the centrality of this neighborhood in the creation of Baldwin's aesthetics and ethos. If Harlem is depicted as a place of destructive social forces, it is also a place that offers African Americans uncanny chances for spiritual and artistic liberation. This paradoxical juxtaposition of harsh social realties with possibilities of a better, racially and ethnically mixed future becomes a pattern in Baldwin's work, and this pattern is particularly marked in his later fiction. Zaborowska argues that *If Beale Street Could Talk* is pivotal for understanding Baldwin's developing aesthetic and political vision. Not only is the novel told from the perspective of a young black woman, who, against all odds, carves out a temporary space of love and hope for herself, but it also presents an alternative future for those who are willing to transgress gender, race, and class lines. This novel, then, underscores with particular force how modern African American identity has been shaped—circumscribed but also transformed—by the double-edged legacy of Harlem.

Providing a final frame for the volume, and complementing Gates's opening chapter by concluding with the same kind of panoramic overview, this time of Harlem's Jewish counterpart, Hasia Diner argues that the post–World War II era has spawned "a Lower East Side memory culture." This memory culture has not only reimagined but re-created the Lower East Side, transforming it into the most potent signifier of Jewish American authenticity and traditionalism. Beginning with the publication of Sydney Taylor's wildly popular children's book *All-of-a Kind Family* in 1951 and continuing in the 1960s with the republication of "lost" immigrant novels set on the Lower East Side, the neighborhood took on increasing significance in the American literary imagination. On the one hand, the increasingly powerful memory culture ensured the enthusiastic reception of these novels, while on the other the novels themselves served to (re)enforce the neighborhood's iconic status, demonstrating yet again how the social produces space. Diner concludes by analyzing a fascinating new fictional genre, the Lower East Side romance novel, which emerged in the 1980s. If the popularity of these contemporary novels are any indication, the production of the Lower East Side as *the* site of Jewish American origins and *the* Jewish American sacred space has been extravagantly successful.

Bringing together prominent and young emerging scholars, *Black Harlem and the Jewish Lower East Side* engages in spatially informed readings of twentieth-century Jewish American and African American literature.

This book thus offers new approaches to Jewish American and African American literary criticism, and, I hope, will urge us to think about how individual and collective modern and contemporary U.S. Jewish and black identity formation has occurred in relation to specific iconic spaces.

NOTES

1. Throughout the introduction, "race" will be used to describe African Americans and "ethnicity" will be used to describe Jewish Americans. Although Jewish Americans were still considered a "race" in the early twentieth century, today they are clearly "white ethnics." For more on the distinction between race and ethnicity, and its genealogy, see Catherine Rottenberg "Race and Ethnicity in *The Autobiography of an Ex-Colored Man* and *The Rise of David Levinsky: The Performative Difference.*" *MELUS* 29, no. 3–4: 307–23.

2. Hasia Diner, *Lower East Side Memories* (Princeton: Princeton University Press, 2000), 50.

3. For a very short history of the Lower East Side prior to the 1880s, see Diner, *Lower East Memories*, 46–47.

4. Sanford Sternlicht, *The Tenement Saga: The Lower East Side and Early Jewish American Writers* (Madison: University of Wisconsin Press), 44–48.

5. Gilbert Osofsky, *Harlem: The Making of a Ghetto: Negro New York, 1890–1930* (New York: Harper and Row, 1963), 122–23.

6. Ibid.

7. See Dorothea Lobbermann "Harlem as a Memory Place: Reconstructing the Harlem Renaissance in Space," in *Temples for Tomorrow: Looking Back at the Harlem Renaissance*, ed. Genevieve Fabre and Michel Feith (Bloomington: Indiana University Press, 2001), 211.

8. See, for example, Hasia Diner, Jeffrey Shandler, and Beth Wenger, eds., *Remembering the Lower East Side* (Bloomington: Indiana University Press, 2000); and Lobbermann, "Harlem as a Memory Place."

9. Adam Zachary Newton, *Facing Black and Jew* (Cambridge: Cambridge University Press, 1999), 10.

10. See Edward Soja, "Thirdspace: Expanding the Scope of the Geographical Imagination," in *Human Geography Today*, ed. Doreen Massey, John Allen, and Philip Sarre (Oxford: Polity Press, 1999), 260–79.

11. "Introduction" in *Remembering the Lower East Side*, 2, 6.

12. See Diner, *Lower East Side Memories*, 8, 27.

13. The edited volume *Remembering the Lower East Side* as well as Hasia Diner's *Lower East Side Memories* document the "reconstruction" of this urban space. Through the creation of the Tenement Museum, the opening of restaurants meant to produce a certain turn-of-the-century aura, and of a variety of tours, there has been a concerted effort to make the Lower East Side "real" again.

14. Diner, *Lower East Side Memories*, 20.

15. See Lobbermann, "Harlem as Memory Place," 210–13.

16. Nathan Irvin Huggins, *Revelations: American History, American Myths* (New York, Oxford University Press, 1995), 21; emphasis added.

17. See, for example, Alain Locke's "The New Negro," in *The New Negro*, ed. Alain Locke (New York: Simon and Schuster, 1997), 7.

18. John Henrik Clarke, ed., *Harlem: Voices from the Soul of Black America* (New York: Signet, 1970).

ONE

HARLEM ON OUR MINDS

Henry Louis Gates Jr.

> The real fever of love for the place will begin to take hold upon him. The subtle, insidious wine of New York will begin to intoxicate him. Then, if he is wise, he will go away, *any* place—yes, he will even go over to Jersey. But if he be a fool, he will stay and stay on until the town becomes all in all to him; until the very streets are his chums and certain buildings and corners his best friends. Then he is hopeless, and to live *elsewhere* would be death. The Bowery will be his romance, Broadway his lyric, and the Park his pastoral, the river and the glory of it all his epic, and he will look down pityingly on all the rest of humanity.
>
> —Paul Laurence Dunbar

> It was loving the City that distracted me and gave me ideas. Made me think I could speak its loud voice and make the sound human. I missed the people altogether.
>
> —Toni Morrison

The idea of a black renaissance has a long and curious history in American culture.

Writing in *Lippincott's Magazine* in 1889, an anonymous reviewer, lamenting the absence of the Great American Novel, predicted that a truly sublime American literature would be created not by a man but by a woman, and an African American woman at that:

> Fate keeps revenge in store. It was a woman who, taking the wrongs of the African as her theme, wrote the novel that awakened the world to their reality, and why should not the coming novelist be a woman as well as an African? She—the woman of that race—has some claims on Fate which are not yet paid up.

This artist, the reviewer went on to predict, would emerge at the forefront of a bold new movement in the arts, a veritable renaissance in blackface. With Toni Morrison's receipt of the 1993 Nobel Prize in literature and the unprecedented number of black artists at work in so many genres today, it is difficult not to recognize the signs that African Americans are in the midst of a cultural renaissance.

Today's African American renaissance is the fourth such movement in the arts in this century. It is also the most successful and the most sustained. The first occurred at the turn of the century. In 1901, the black Bostonian William Stanley Braithwaite, a distinguished critic and poet, argued that "we are at the commencement of a 'negroid' renaissance . . . that will have as much importance in literary history as the much spoken of and much praised Celtic and Canadian renaissance." At the end of a full decade of unprecedented literary productions by black women—who published a dozen novels and edited their own literary journal between 1890 and 1900—and precisely when the poet Paul Laurence Dunbar, the novelists Pauline Hopkins and Charles Chesnutt, and the essayists W. E. B. DuBois and Anna Julia Cooper were at the height of their creative powers, a critic in *The A. M. E. Church Review* in 1904 declared the birth of "The New Negro Literary Movement," likening it, as had Braithwaite, to the Celtic renaissance.

It was Booker T. Washington who first hoped to institutionalize the cultural and political force of this New Negro. In 1900 Washington enlisted several of his fellows (including his nemesis, DuBois) to construct an image unfettered by the racist burdens of the past, a past characterized by two and one-half centuries of slavery and nearly a half-century of disenfranchisement, peonage, black codes, and legalized Jim Crow—not to mention the vicious assault on Negro freedom and political rights enacted in literature, in theater and on the vaudeville stage, and throughout the popular visual arts, in the form of a blanket of demeaning stereotypes of deracinated, ugly, treacherous, hauntingly evil Sambo images. At the beginning of the century, families could encounter these images throughout their homes from the time they turned off their alarm clocks in the morning and sat down to their egg cups or tea cozies, napkin rings or place mats at breakfast, to the time they spent in the evenings playing parlor games, reading advertisements in magazines, or addressing U.S. government postcards. Such an onslaught of stereotypes, reinforced subliminally in advertisements and on trading cards, in pulpits on Sundays, and even in the law, demanded resistance and an organized response. "We must turn away from the memories of the slave past," Washington demanded, no doubt with this proliferation of negations of black humanity in mind. "A New Negro for a New Century," he argued, would be the answer.

This New Negro movement, which took at least three forms before Alain Locke enshrined it in the Harlem Renaissance in 1925, drew its artistic inspiration from across the Atlantic in Europe. First, Anton Dvořák in the early 1890s declared spirituals America's first authentic contribution to world culture and urged classical composers to draw upon them to create *sui generis* symphonies. A decade later, Pablo Picasso stumbled onto "dusky Manikins" at an ethnographic museum and forever transformed European art, as well as Europe's official appreciation of the art from the African continent. Picasso's *Les Demoiselles d'Avignon* (1906–07)—the signature event in the creation of cubism—stands as a testament to the shaping influence of African sculpture and to the central role that African art played in the creation of modernism. The cubist mask of modernism covers a black Bantu face. African art—ugly, primitive, debased in 1900; sublime, complex, valorized by 1910—was transformed so dramatically in the cultural imagination of the West, in such an astonishingly short period, that the potential for the political uses of black art and literature in America could not escape the notice of African American intellectuals, especially DuBois, himself educated in Europe and cosmopolitan to the core, and Locke, the Harvard-trained philosopher, who went to Oxford as a Rhodes scholar in 1907, the year after Picasso stumbled uncannily onto the African sublime, and who studied aesthetics in Germany in the heady years of the modernist explosion. If European modernism was truly mulatto, the argument went, then African Americans could save themselves politically through the creation of the arts. This renaissance, the second and most famous in black history, would fully liberate the Negro—at least its advanced guard.

The Harlem or New Negro Renaissance was born through the midwifery of Locke, who edited a special issue of *Survey Graphic* magazine entitled "Harlem: Mecca of the New Negro" in March 1925, which was followed by the 446-page anthology *The New Negro: An Interpretation*, replete with illustrations by the German expressionist Winold Reiss and the African American Aaron Douglas. Writers such as Langston Hughes, Jean Toomer, Countee Cullen, Jessie Fauset, and Zora Neale Hurston—the fundaments of the black canon today—came of age at this time, leading the *New York Herald Tribune* to announce that America was "on the edge, if not already in the midst, of what might not improperly be called a Negro renaissance." Locke liked the term, too: part 1 of his anthology is called "The Negro Renaissance." Locke even urged young black visual artists to imitate the European modernist, so heavily influenced by sub-Saharan African art. "By being modern," Locke declared, with no hint of irony, "we are being African."

For Locke and his fellow authors, the function of a cultural renaissance was inherently political: the production of great artworks, by blacks, in sufficient numbers, would lead to the Negro's "reevaluation by white and black alike." And this reevaluation would facilitate the Negro's demand for civil rights and for social and economic equality. Stopped short by the 1929 stock market crash, which hurt the white patrons upon whom the Renaissance was so dependent, the Renaissance writers (a tiny group, numbering perhaps fifty), whom Locke thought of as "the Negro's cultural adolescence," were never able to nurture black art to its formal adulthood, nor were they able to usher in the new world of civil rights through art.

The third renaissance was the Black Arts movement, which lasted from 1965 to the early seventies. Defining themselves against the Harlem Renaissance and deeply rooted in black cultural nationalism, the Black Arts writers saw themselves as the artistic wing of the Black Power movement. Writers such as Amiri Baraka, Larry Neal, and Sonia Sanchez saw black art as fulfilling a function, primarily the political liberation of black people from white racism. Constructed on a fragile foundation of the overtly political, this renaissance was the most short-lived of all. Yet many of the artists who have come of age in the decades since were shaped or deeply influenced by this period. By 1975, with the Black Arts movement dead (Baraka had become a Marxist in 1973), Black Studies departments in peril, and a homogenized disco music on the rise, many of us wondered if black culture were not undergoing some sort of profound identity crisis. A decade later, however, black writers, visual artists, musicians, dancers, and actors would enter a period of creativity unrivaled in American history.

Critics date the current renaissance variously, some tracing its origins to the resurgence of black women's literature and criticism in the early eighties, especially in the works of Ntozake Shange, Michele Wallace, Alice Walker, and Toni Morrison. These women and their successors were able, simultaneously, to reach a large, traditionally middle-class, white female readership plus a new black female audience that had been largely untapped. The growth of this community of readers has resulted in an unrivaled number of novels by and about black women since 1980, as well as an unprecedentedly large African American market for books about every aspect of the black experience. While it is always arbitrary to try to date a cultural movement, it seems reasonable to note an upsurge in black creativity in 1987, the year in which August Wilson's *Fences* premiered on Broadway and Toni Morrison published her masterpiece, *Beloved*. Both would receive Pulitzer Prizes. In that same year, PBS aired Henry Hampton's *Eyes on the*

Prize, the six-part documentary of the civil rights era; Cornell scholar Martin Bernal published *Black Athena*, a bold revisionist history that locates the origins of classical Greek civilization in Africa. As Nelson George says in his *Buppies, B-boys, Baps and Bohos: Notes on Post-Soul Black Culture*, T-shirts with slogans such as "Black By Popular Demand" and "It's A Black Thing, You Wouldn't Understand" spread across the nation from predominately black colleges. Moreover, the rap revolution was well under way at about his time. Meanwhile, Spike Lee and Wynton Marsalis were establishing themselves as masters of film and jazz. Since that year, the production of cultural artifacts in virtually every field and genre has been astonishing.

The grandchildren of DuBois's "Talented Tenth," those who were able to profit from the affirmative action programs implemented in the late sixties that are facing such a harsh onslaught today, have thus for the past decade been in the midst of a great period of artistic productivity, much of it centered in New York. The signs of cultural vibrancy are unmistakable: in dance, Bill T. Jones and Judith Jamison; in literature, Toni Morrison and Terry McMillan, Walter Mosley and John Edgar Wideman; in drama, August Wilson; in poetry, Rita Dove; in opera, Anthony Davis and Thulani Davis; in jazz, Wynton Marsalis and Cassandra Wilson; public intellectuals such as Cornel West and bell hooks, Greg Tate and Lisa Jones; the visual artists Martin Puryear and Lorna Simpson; the rap musicians Public Enemy and Queen Latifah; the filmmakers Spike Lee, Julie Dash, and John Singleton—the list is stunningly long. From television to op-ed pages, from the academy to hip-hop, never before have so many black artists and intellectuals achieved so much success in so very many fields. Do their efforts amount to a renaissance?

"It depends on how you define 'renaissance,'" Cornel West has argued. "The rebirth by means of a recovery of classical heritage, I wouldn't call it that. What we do have, however, is a high-quality ferment, a proliferation of a variety of new voices that are transgressing the boundaries in place. These artists exhibit a certain kind of self-confidence, a refusal to accept the belief that they have to prove themselves. Artists such as Wright and Baldwin clearly wrestled on a different terrain."

A different terrain, indeed. Since 1968, when the civil rights movement, a century old, ended so abruptly with the murder of Dr. King, affirmative action and entitlement programs have *dramatically* affected the black community's collective economic health. Not only has the size of its middle class quadrupled since 1968 but, according to the 1990 census, almost as many blacks between the ages of twenty-five and forty-four are college graduates as are high school dropouts, whereas "just twenty years ago, there were five times as many black high school dropouts as college graduates in the workforce," as Sam Roberts reported in the *New York Times* on June 18, 1995. Between 1970 and 1990, moreover, the percentage of blacks who had attended some college increased from 9.1 percent to 33.2 percent, of those graduating from college from 5.1 percent to 11 percent, the highest in history, and of those with some postgraduate work from 1.2 percent to 4.1 percent. By 1989, one in seven black families were middle class (earning $50,000 or more), compared to one in three white families. "Just a generation ago," Roberts writes, "only 1 in 17 black families" could claim middle-class status; the increase is clearly the result of governmental "prodding." For African Americans, however, it is the best of times and the worst of times. While part of the black community has experienced two decades of unprecedented growth, another part lags dramatically behind. Black America has simultaneously the largest middle class *and* the largest underclass in its history. And the current renaissance of black art and culture—with its inherent schisms and tensions—is unfolding against this conflicted socioeconomic backdrop. Let us pursue this paradox.

Despite their remarkable gains, a certain sense of precariousness haunts the new black middle class and the art that it consumes. Its own economic uplift remains perilously novel. An ambivalent romance with the street and b-boy culture—an intimacy, a freshness, but also a sense that one could go back "there" at any time—haunts much contemporary black literature, film and hip-hop. The partition between the classes, in the minds of many blacks, is as thin as rice paper.

But because the shtetl memory, as it were, is still so very recent, the romanticization of the ghetto is accompanied by its demonization. The movement to censor gangsta rap, for instance, can be seen as part of the black bourgeoisie's anxiety, its deep-seated fear that it, too, is just one or two paychecks away from the fate of the underclass. The black middle class defines itself by consumption, but it is never free from the past and presence of racism. In fact, it often defines itself *against* this very history.

The nature and size of the new black middle class is significant here because of what it implies about patronage and the economics of black art: whereas the Harlem Renaissance writers were almost totally dependent upon the whims of white patrons who marketed their works to a predominately white readership, the sales of some of the most phenomenally successful black authors, such as Terry McMillan, the Delaney sisters, Toni Morrison, and Alice Walker, are being sustained to an unprecedented degree by black consumers. The same is true, if to a lesser extent, in the other arts. Thelma Golden's "Black Male" exhibit, for instance, dramatically lifted annual attendance figures at the Whitney Museum by attracting a large number of new black patrons. The rise of the black middle class is, thus, simultaneous with the rise of black art, especially the black novel. And black novelists—black women novelists in particular—seem to owe a large part of their appeal to their capacity to express the desires and anxieties of this new middle class more freely from the *inside* than any previous generation could possibly have done. (In this way, McMillan's role within black culture is similar to that of Defoe and Richardson in the eighteenth century.) Quite often, too, these black writers have black editors and black agents, and their books are reviewed by other black authors, assigned by black teachers, and sold in black bookstores.

This new presence and authority of blacks in cultural institutions, largely a result of affirmative action programs and the active recruitment of minorities, is unprecedented in American history. And signs of the cultural flowering that define a renaissance are everywhere. On two occasions in the past two years, no fewer than three black authors appeared *simultaneously* on the *New York Times* best-seller list (one author, Toni Morrison, appeared in both the fiction and the nonfiction categories). "All black books these days are trade books," commented Erroll McDonald, a Yale graduate and vice president at Pantheon Books. "The 'one-nigger syndrome' is dead." Black authors have won an unprecedented number of prizes in the last decade, including Pulitzer Prizes, National Book Critics' Circle Awards, National Book Awards, and PEN/Faulkner Awards. The culmination of these achievements, of course, was Toni Morrison's Nobel Prize.

In addition, traditionally white cultural institutions such as the Whitney Museum, the Museum of Modern Art, the Guggenheim Museum, and the Lincoln Center Theater have integrated their boards of directors, and jazz has become a part of the canon of American music as defined by both the Lincoln Center and the Smithsonian Institution. Black Studies departments have never had larger enrollments or a stronger, more solid presence at America's premier research institutions. Public intellectuals representing a wide array of ideologies, such as Gerald Early, Cornel West, Stephen Carter, Derrick Bell, Lani Guinier, Stanley Crouch, Michele Wallace, bell hooks, Trey Ellis, Shelby Steele, Randall Kennedy, and Patricia Williams, publish their opinions regularly in a variety of national journals. George Wolfe's appointment as the director of the New York Public Theater is symptomatic of the growing "crossover" authority that blacks increasingly have come to possess within broader American cultural organizations. And, perhaps most dramatically of all, black filmmakers, following the lead of Spike Lee, have never been more numerous or better funded than they are today.

If we add television shows such as *The Cosby Show*, *A Different World*, *The Fresh Prince of Bel Air*, and *The Oprah Winfrey Show* to the mix, it is clear that the black presence in American society has never been more prevalent and more widely consumed.

One reason for the newest renaissance is that the generation that integrated historically white institutions in the late sixties and early seventies has now, two decades later, returned to those very institutions to occupy positions of power and authority. Never before have so many black creative artists produced so much art, in so many genres, for such a diversified, integrated audience. Case in point: hip-hop, once the marching music of a defiant oppositional culture, is now the music of the white suburbs, the *American Bandstand* of the 1990s, the premier American music.

The current renaissance is characterized by a specific awareness of previous black traditions, which these artists echo, imitate, parody, and revise, self-consciously, in acts of riffing or signifying or sampling. As the jazz and opera composer Anthony Davis puts it, "There are three different strains in the black music revolution today—classical jazz (such as Wynton Marsalis), avant jazz (such as Anthony Braxton), and the fusion of hip-hop and jazz (such as the compositions of Steve Coleman). What each shares, however," he continues, "is a common attempt to rediscover the past." Davis's opera *X, The Life and Times of Malcolm X* (1968) is a prime example. "What this is, is a renaissance of postmodernism, and postmodernism, in America, is quintessentially black," he concludes.

This concern with the black cultural past and the self-conscious grounding of a black postmodernism in a black nationalist tradition are accompanied by a kind of nostalgia for the Black Power cultural politics of the sixties and the blaxploitation films of the early seventies. Unlike the earlier periods, however, the current movement defines itself by a certain openness, a belated glasnost that allows for parodies such as George Wolfe's play *The Colored Museum* (1986); Robert Townsend's *Hollywood Shuffle* (1987); Keenan Ivory Wayan's blaxpoitation parody, *I'm Gonna Git You Sucka* (1988); and, more recently, Rusty Cundieff's *Fear of a Black Hat* (1994), a satire about the hip-hop generation.

The art of this period is also characterized by its deep self-confidence in the range and depth of the black experience as a source for art. Richard Wright once predicted that if "the Negro merges into the mainstream of American life, there might result actually a disappearance of Negro literature—as such." As a Negro, he continued, he was "a rootless man." Few black writers today would agree with Wright on either point. In fact, the opposite seems to have occurred: black writers and artists seem to have become *more* conscious of the specificities of their cultural traditions rather than *less* conscious. Toni Morrison has frequently stated that she is a black writer first, a writer second, effectively reversing decades of attempts by black writers to make their work "universal" by writing about whites. These artists *presume* that black experiences are universal experiences. If, as Wright once put it, "the Negro is America's metaphor," this generation seems to maintain that the experiences of African Americans are metaphors for the entire human condition, with America itself standing as a metaphor for much that has been liberating as well as horrendous in black and human history.

"What defines this renaissance, unlike the others," says the novelist Jamaica Kincaid, "is that people like us are just getting started. Somebody told me recently that literature is dead. But it's not that *literature* is dead; it is that *English literature* is dead. It is as if someone has removed the hands from over our mouths, and you hear this long, piercing scream. There really isn't much that is new to say about being a white person." This art, she continues, is appealing not just because of its content but because of its forms, "its ways of looking at the world, the way the world has forced us to look at it. And what we, as artists, are saying is: 'this is what it looks like.' "

Traditionally, black art has fallen into two large schools of representation. One we might think of as a lyrical, quasi-autobiographical modernism (as found, say, in Zora Neale Hurston's *Their Eyes Were Watching God* or Ralph Ellison's *Invisible Man*), in which a questing protagonist succeeds against oppressive racist odds. The other we can call realism or naturalism (as found, for instance, in Richard Wright's *Native Son* or Ann Petry's *The Street*), in which a protagonist's life choices, and hence fate, are determined by forces, such as racism or capitalism, that are insurmountable—that is, unless the entire system is transformed by violent and dramatic revolution.

In black postmodernist writing, much of the fiction being created by black women in particular consists of coming-of-age tales in which racial politics takes a secondary role to the unfolding of a sensitive, gendered consciousness. Today, a politicized naturalism is more likely to be found in black film, such as John Singleton's *Boyz N the Hood*, and, of course, in gangsta rap, such as the dada vorticism of Public Enemy's *It Takes a Nation of Millions to Hold Us Back*, or in the rap-meets-poetry movement. The most subtle and sophisticated of this art, however, such as Toni Morrison's masterpiece *Beloved*, or Spike Lee's *Do the Right Thing*, brings both tendencies together, creating a new form, which we might think of as a lyrical super-naturalism.

All renaissances are acts of cultural construction, attempting to satisfy larger social and political needs. And the African American postmodern renaissance is no exception. In their openness, their variety, their playfulness with forms, their refusal to follow preordained ideological lines, their sustained engagements with the black artistic past, the artists of this renaissance seem as determined to define their work freely within a black tradition as they are to consolidate a black presence within America's corporate cultural institutions. "There are many neighborhoods in what we might think of as a larger cultural community," Anthony Davis muses. Given the sophistication of so much of this art, and given its demonstrated power to turn a profit, it is highly likely that the achievements of this renaissance will be the deepest, the longest-lasting, and the most appreciated by the larger American society. "Today the white people want to be colored," Jamaica Kincaid asserts. "There is no longer such a thing as an 'American' culture. It's all black culture."

What lessons from the Harlem Renaissance can we draw upon to critique our own?

Many critiques have been made of the Harlem Renaissance's putative faults and purported limitations, which range from overdependence on white patronage to pandering to debased white taste in the form of primitivistic depictions of black sensuality and hedonism in the literature, art, music, and dance of the period. We can debate these claims and even accept some, with enormous qualifications, as true, despite the fact that *all* artists are dependent upon patronage (and all renaissances especially so) and despite the fact that the literature created during the Harlem Renaissance—especially the poetry of James Weldon Johnson, Langston Hughes, and Sterling Brown, and the fictions of Jean Toomer and Zora Neale Hurston—drew upon African American vernacular musical and oral traditions to create *sui generis* African American modernist forms that today, three-quarters of a century later, are judged to be canonical even by the most conservative keepers of the American canon. What's more, the literature created by these fifty-odd brave souls, black inscriptions on a near tabula rasa, proved to be the fertile ground out of which emerged writers such as Richard Wright, Ann Petry, Ralph Ellison, James Baldwin, Gwendolyn Brooks, Amiri Baraka, Alice Walker, and Toni Morrison, to list just a few artists who use the Renaissance writers as their silent second texts.

Harlem as a site of the black cultural sublime was invented by those writers and artists at the turn of the century determined to transform the stereotypical image of Negro Americans as ex-slaves, members of an inherently inferior race—biologically and environmentally unfit for mechanized modernity and its cosmopolitan forms of fluid identity—into an image of a race of culture-bearers. To effect this transformation, the New Negro would need a nation over which to preside. And that nation's capital would be Harlem, that realm north of Central Park, centered between 130th and 145th Streets.

Since the earliest decades of the twentieth century, then, the lure of Harlem has captivated the imagination of writers, artists, intellectuals, and politicians around the world. Stories are legion of African American and African pilgrims progressing to Manhattan, then plunging headlong into the ultimate symbolic black cultural space—the city within a city, the "Mecca of the New Negro" (as Alain Locke put it)—that Harlem became in the first quarter of the twentieth century. Fidel Castro's recent journey uptown, recalling his famous sojourn at the Hotel Teresa thirty-five years ago, is only the most recent of a long line of such pilgrimages into America's very own heart of darkness. The list of pilgrims is long and distinguished, including Max Weber and Carl Jung, Federico García Lorca and Octavio Paz, Zora Neale Hurston and Langston Hughes, Kwame Nkrumah and Wole Soyinka, Marcus Garvey and Malcolm X, Ezekiel Mphaphlele and Nelson Mandela, and so forth. "Harlem was like a great magnet for the Negro intellectual," Hughes wrote, "pulling him from everywhere. Once in New York, he had to live in Harlem." Harlem was not so much a *place* as it was a state of mind, the cultural metaphor for black America itself.

What *does* seem curious to me about the Harlem Renaissance—and relevant to us here—is that its creation occurred precisely as Harlem was turning into the great American slum. The death rate was 42 percent higher than in other parts of the city. The infant mortality rate in 1928 was twice as high as in the rest of New York. Four times as many people died from tuberculosis as in the white population. The unemployment rate, according to Adam Clayton Powell Jr., was 50 percent. There was no way to romanticize these conditions, but Locke and his fellows valiantly attempted to do so. Even James Weldon Johnson, one of the most politically engaged of all the Renaissance writers in his capacity as the first black secretary of the NAACP, wrote *Black Manhattan* to create the fiction of Harlem as a model of civility and black bourgeois respectability, rather than as an example of the most heinous effects of urban economic exploitation and residential segregation. For Johnson, Harlem was "exotic, colorful, sensuous; a place of laughing, singing, and dancing; a place where life wakes up at night." Moreover, he continued, "Harlem is not merely a Negro colony or community, it is a city within a city, the greatest Negro city in the world. It is not a slum or a fringe, it is located in the heart of Manhattan and occupies one of the most beautiful and healthful sections of the city." Locke, always an optimist, whom Charles Johnson called "the press agent of the New Negro," declared Harlem the cultural capital of the black world: "Without pretense to their political significance, Harlem has the same role to play for the New Negro as Dublin had for the New Ireland or Prague for the New Czechoslovakia. Harlem, I grant you, isn't typical—but it is significant, it is prophetic." The "Harlem" of literature and the Harlem of socioeconomic reality were as far apart as Bessie Smith was from Paul Whiteman. The valorization of black rhythm, spontaneity, laughter, sensuality—all keywords of depictions of blacks by blacks at the time—contrasted starkly with Harlem's squalor and the environmental or structural limitations upon individual choices such as those finally depicted in Wright's *Native Son* (1940) in part as a reaction *against* what he felt to be the Renaissance writers' bohemian decadence.

The Renaissance's fascination with primitivism, one could argue, has today found a counterpart in three arenas of representation: the reconstruction of the institution of slavery; the valorization of vernacular cultural forms as a basis for a postmodern art; and the use of a lyrical voice-of-becoming in fictions that depict the emergence of black female protagonists with strong, resonant voices and self-fashioned identities. Subjects heretofore to be avoided—such as slavery and the female tale of the transcendence and emergence of the self—and vernacular linguistic forms have all emerged like the return of the repressed as dominant themes in African American literature. What remains to be explored, however, in the written arts of *this* renaissance, are the lives and times of the grandchildren of the Bigger Thomases and Bessie Mearses of *Native Son,* which by and large have been of interest primarily to young black filmmakers, who far too often seem to be caught in the embrace of a romantic primitivism, navigating us through the inner city more for sexual titillation than for social critique. Given the stark statistics that we all know so well describing the nightmare reality of black inner city life—one in three black men between the ages of twenty and twenty-nine in prison, on probation, or on parole; 46 percent of all black children born at or beneath the poverty line—one is forced to wonder where *this* generation's Bigger Thomas is. Until *this* subject matter finds a voice as eloquent as that voice of the newly emergent and aspiring middle-class black self, today's renaissance runs the risk of suffering the sorts of critique that we level against the Harlem Renaissance seven full decades later. For there are two nations in America, and these two nations, one hopeless, one full of hope, are both black. African Americans live a hyphenated life in America. Morrison's *Beloved* explores what the hyphenation of race costs. It is incumbent upon our artists now to explore what the hyphenation of *class* costs.

Perhaps it is no accident that the most interesting rendering of the tension between the myth of Harlem and its social reality is to be found *not* in a text produced in that period but in Morrison's *Jazz,* which is set in Harlem in 1926. In this novel Morrison succeeds in creating a protagonist whose fate is as shaped by her environment as by her actions, in a curious kind of stasis or equilibrium that seeks to resolve the tension between the naturalism of Richard Wright and Ann Petry on the one hand, and the lyrical modernism of Jean Toomer, Zora Neale Hurston, and Ralph Ellison on the other. "Word was," Morrison's narrator tells us, "that underneath the good times and the easy money something evil ran the streets and nothing was safe—not even the dead." It is in this novel that the Harlem Renaissance finally finds its most sophisticated voice *and* its most pointed critique, the newest renaissance grounding itself in the mirror of the old, bridging that gap between the shadow and the act, the myth and the reality, the fiction and the fact. Morrison's ultimate message would seem to be a warning, a warning that it is only when our artists today speak the city's "loud voice and make that sound human," avoiding "miss[ing] the people altogether," in all their complexity, that *this* renaissance can claim to be the renaissance to end all renaissances. Much depends on whether we get it.

TWO

THE MAKING OF AN ICON

Early Representations of Harlem and the Lower East Side

Catherine Rottenberg

Prominent cultural historians and theorists have already demonstrated that Harlem and the Lower East Side have become sites of intense emotional investment for the African American and Jewish American communities respectively. These scholars have also argued that these two New York City neighborhoods have become exemplary in specific ways over the course of the twentieth century. And yet, no scholarly work comparing these analogous processes of iconization has been carried out. As I suggested in the Introduction, the picture that emerges from such a comparison is one of discrepancy. While the Lower East Side has come to symbolize a relatively unconflicted Jewish American sacred place over the past century, Harlem has come to represent two irreconcilable affective modalities: hope and despair. Therefore, in order to gain further insight into these parallel but divergent processes of iconization, in this chapter I turn to the literature written by authors who lived in and depicted these places during one of the most formative periods in the history of these neighborhoods—the late Progressive Era and the Jazz Age (approximately 1915–1930).

Comparing these early fictional sites of representation reveals that in both literary traditions there is a consistent and profound ambivalence toward these enclaves. In other words, the texts in both the African American and Jewish American canons dramatize the "simultaneous existence of contradictory attitudes, or feelings in the relationship to a single object," namely, a particular swath of city space.[1] The various protagonists' relationships to Harlem and the Lower East Side are, time and again, described as being informed by a complex dynamic of attraction and repulsion (and thus identification and dis-identification). This is already striking, since in contemporary discourse—and in contrast to Harlem—the negative pole of the ambivalence with respect to the Lower East Side is very much in abeyance. In the early depictions of the neighborhoods, however, the theme of ambivalence is very prominent in *both* traditions. However, in each case the source of the ambivalence as well as its manifestations differ significantly. In the African American novels, the ambivalence toward Harlem manifests itself in racialized terms; the fictional depictions of this city space are consistently laced with references to "blackness," which elicits identification *and* dis-identification. In the Jewish American narratives, the ambivalence toward the Lower East Side, especially in its negative manifestation, is much more class-inflected.[2] The repulsion the various protagonists feel toward this space is most often ascribed to its poverty and not to its perceived "Jewishness."

Given their current canonical status and their similar narrative trajectories, the following sections focus on the 1920s fiction of Abraham Cahan, Jessie Fauset, Nella Larsen, and Anzia Yezierska. Indeed, their protagonists are depicted as endeavoring to move from a marginal existence to a more mainstream one while actively attempting to live out some aspect of the American Dream. The novels highlight an intense negotiation between a protagonist's feeling of identification with the Lower East Side or Harlem and his or her desire to escape from the "constraining" neighborhood. These modern and now classic "ethnic" novels, in other words, (re)produce the conflict between minority and dominant culture with particular force, and it is this conflict that brings out both the positive as well as the negative poles of the protagonists' ambivalence toward these urban spaces.

AFRICAN AMERICAN AMBIVALENCE

Helga Crane leaves Harlem and the United States in order to feel that she belongs to herself alone and not merely to the black race. She quickly realizes, however, that even in Denmark she cannot escape the constraints of race, and she begins to yearn desperately for Negroes and for Harlem. Harlem, in Helga's nostalgic longing, represents everything: "Everything was there, vice and goodness, sadness and gayety, ignorance and wisdom, ugliness and beauty, poverty and richness. And it seemed to her that somehow of goodness, gayety, wisdom, and beauty always there was a little more than of vice, sadness, ignorance, and ugliness."[3] Harlem is *the* place to be if only because it contains everything, and everything, in Helga Crane's eyes, is extremely desirable.

The picture Larsen has Helga paint of Harlem, however, can be termed ambivalent in the sense that it is inclusive of both that which attracts and that which repels; the neighborhood concomitantly contains the very desirable and the very undesirable. And after her return to the United States and to "the medley that is Harlem," Helga is described as being swept with a wild surge of gladness when she realizes that "[t]hese terrible, these fascinating; these lovable, dark hordes" once again surround her.[4] Here we notice that the language itself is marked by ambivalence. Larsen's protagonist is simultaneously repulsed by and attracted to the black masses inhabiting these few square miles of city space, and the language captures or articulates the twin poles of her ambivalence.

When Helga arrives in Harlem for the very first time (before leaving for Europe), she is also absolutely enthralled by what she sees: "The continuously gorgeous panorama of Harlem fascinated her, thrilled her." But she is also acutely aware that the neighborhood is an enclave: "The sober mad rush of *white* New York failed entirely to stir her. Of that white world, so distant, so near, she asked only indifference."[5] The text's emphasis even at this point is clearly on the separation and racialization of space, the seemingly strict borders between black Harlem and white Manhattan. Interestingly, just a few lines later Larsen fleshes out her description of this space by bringing in the bodies of the "alluring brown or yellow men" who dance attendance on the beautiful Helga Crane.[6]

This move, from a more positive portrayal to an emphasis on the racialized specialization of Harlem, is a pattern in *Quicksand*. Indeed, whenever Harlem is described specifically as space—as streets, buildings, and people moving in space—the reader senses the hordes, the movement, the congestion. But what the reader most forcefully senses is the "color" of this space. It is not the "teemingness" or the hordes in and of themselves that are stressed over and over again, but rather the "black" people or the "dark-eyed brown folk" inhabiting this space.[7] Thus, even in the pulsating exciting descriptions of the urban enclave, race seems to emerge as paramount, eliding all other considerations, characteristics, and details.

Moreover, once the space has been racialized in this way, a feeling of circumscription and even of being stuck most often follows. Returning to the section where Larsen first dwells on the line of demarcation between black Harlem and the "mad rush of white New York," the reader is also informed that "Helga Crane meant to have a home, and perhaps laughing, appealing dark-eyed children in Harlem. Her existence, now, was *bounded* by Central Park, Fifth Avenue, St. Nicholas Park, and One Hundred and

Forty-fifth Street. . . . Not a narrow life, *as Negroes live it*."[8] As Negroes live it is surely a qualification, and *bounded* carries with it all sorts of undesirable connotations and associations, such a restriction, confinement, and perhaps even slavery. And just a little while later in the narrative, when Helga Crane herself begins to feel restless and "bounded," one gets an even clearer sense of her love-hate relationship toward Harlem: "As the days became hotter and the streets more swarming, a kind of repulsion came upon her. She recoiled in aversion from the sight of the grinning faces and from the sound of the easy laughter of all of these people who strolled, aimlessly now, it seemed, up and down the avenues . . ."[9] Grinning faces, easy laughter, these are all very slightly veiled racialized stereotypes that bring to mind the likes of blackface, Sambo, and minstrelsy. The once muted or latent pole of repulsion has clearly taken over and overwhelmed all else.

Both the attraction as well as the repulsion to Harlem, I suggest, has to do with its being perceived as "black" space. It is, after all, for black Harlem and the "colorful," "dark" humanity that inhabits its streets that Helga yearns while in Europe. Thus, on the one hand, even when Harlem is described as including "everything" and as being a thrilling city unto itself that need not heed white New York, the racialized spatialization emerges and is underscored. On the other hand, Helga Crane's disgust is constantly related to her feeling of "being shut up, boxed up, with hundreds of her race . . . these despised black folk."[10]

In Jessie Fauset's *Plum Bun*, published the same year as *Quicksand*, the protagonist—also a young aspiring middle-class African American woman who moves to New York but who "passes" for white in order to live out the life of freedom she has always dreamed about—describes Harlem in a similarly conflicted way. Like her literary counterpart, the first time Angela Murray lays eyes on this city space, she is "amazed and impressed at this bustling, frolicking, busy, laughing great city within a greater one." Fauset goes on to tell us that Angela "had never seen *colored* life so thick, so varied, so complete."[11] Again, through this description, we get a sense of the pulsating life of teeming, *black* Harlem. Furthermore, this description is qualified in a way we have seen before. The amazement and wonder Angela experiences is later ascribed to the "fact" that these few square miles of city streets included "people of a very high intellectual type, exponents of the realest and most essential refinement living cheek by jowl with coarse or ill-bred or even criminal members of their *race*."[12] Everything exists in this neighborhood: the high and the low, the hope of the race, and what this very genteel protagonist perceives as the shame of the race. A few minutes after Angela's initial thrill at seeing this urban space for the first time, and as she is contemplating more seriously the meaning of this city within a city, she also admits that "[u]nquestionably there was something very fascinating, even *terrible*, about this stream of life."[13] Again, we see the slippage from a depiction that could be called ambivalent in the sense that it paints a picture inclusive of desirable and undesirable components into a language of ambivalence.

What is so striking about the descriptions of Harlem in these two novels is that the language used to portray the people populating these city blocks—fascinating, terrible—is uncannily similar. Also interesting, and I believe important, is that poverty, while certainly mentioned, is not the pivot around which the ambivalent description of space revolves. Considering that both protagonists are struggling to carve out and maintain a respectable middle-class lifestyle, their aversion might have been directed at the dirt, poverty, and meanness of the streets of Harlem. These works, after all, were written and published at a time when Harlem had already become severely poverty-ridden. But race rather than poverty is center-staged, as if poverty were merely a symptom and race the cause of the ills of this urban space.

The particular modes of ambivalence found in the novels need, I believe, to be understood in relation to the process of signification Harlem was undergoing at the time. Harlem is presented in these texts as a segregated enclave with definite borders. African Americans, rich and poor, educated and uneducated, high yellow, blue black, or even those who can pass are all depicted as lumped together. As a desirable place, Harlem signifies race pride and solidarity as well as possibility in the novels. Alain Locke famously wrote that Harlem of the 1920s stood for the possibility of a great race-welding, where, for the first time, "Negro life is seizing upon its first changes for group expression and self-determination," stimulating race consciousness.[14] Nella Larsen has her protagonist express this pride when Helga returns to Harlem after her sojourn in Europe. Speaking about the "hundreds, thousands of dark-eyed brown folk" she is filled with a (albeit fleeing) sense of thankfulness: "*These* were her people . . ."[15] Fauset's protagonist articulates this sentiment more abstractly: Harlem, Angela Murray ruminates, "represents . . . the last word in racial pride, integrity and even self-sacrifice."[16] It is important to remember, after all, that the 1920s—the period in which these texts were written and published—was the time of the Harlem Renaissance and its concomitant hope.

As a site of repulsion, the space of Harlem serves as both a recognition and reminder that the "color line" in all of its various manifestations is that which has circumscribed and limited life for African Americans in the United States. In the novels, the repulsion evinced toward Harlem is consistently linked to the repercussions of forced racial identification and segregation. Helga Crane's feeling of constriction and boundedness is expressed in and through racial terms: "[T]he mere sight of the serene tan and brown faces about her stung her like a personal insult." Life in Harlem "became only a hateful place where one lived in intimacy with people one would not have chosen had one been given choice."[17] Perhaps the repulsion can also be read as gesturing toward the despair of the already betrayed promise of color-blind cultural freedom. After all, when Angela Murray chooses to disavow her "blackness" and pass as white—a dangerous gamble given the one-drop rule, she expresses her great gladness that she had not cast her lot with the dwellers inside Harlem's dark and serried tents.[18] The crucial point for my purposes here, though, is that both the attraction and repulsion are directed much more toward the perceived racialized spatialization of the neighborhood and much less toward its poverty. Fauset emphasizes the dark and the serried—not the dirt and the indigent. While class factors into the ambivalence, it is not, by any means, the represented *source* of aversion.

JEWISH AMERICAN AMBIVALENCE

Appearing in book form in 1917, Abraham Cahan's classic novel *The Rise of David Levinsky* initially describes the Lower East Side with a decided stress on its Jewishness. After debarking at Castle Garden, the protagonist, David Levinsky walks not to the East Side but to the "*Jewish* East Side." The streets are described as swarming with Yiddish-speaking immigrants: "The swing and step of the pedestrians, the voices and manner of the street peddlers, and a hundred and one other things seemed to testify to far more self-confidence and energy, to larger ambitions and wider scopes than did the appearances of the crowds in my birthplace"[19] Like the African American novels described above, Cahan has his protagonist describe this space in quite positive terms in the beginning. Emphasized are the "ethnic" specificity of the space as well as the fact that on these streets Jews are *less* bounded than on the streets in Russia. However, Cahan's stress on the Jewishness of the East Side gives way, relatively quickly, to something else. Almost immediately following his first impression, David Levinsky sums up his introduction to "the Ghetto" in the following terms: "Instead of stumbling upon nuggets of gold, I found signs of poverty. In one place I came across a poor family who—as I learned upon inquiry—had been dispossessed for non-payment of rent."[20] This quote and even the one above, which limns the almost "ethnic" neutral "pedestrians" and street peddlers, serve to background the Jewishness of this space and foreground its indigence. Moreover, throughout the rest of the novel, the descriptions of the Lower East Side focus in on and underscore the penury of the neighborhood.

Cahan's text gestures toward a move that can be seen most profoundly in the Jewish American fiction of the 1920s, and most saliently in Anzia Yezierska's *Arrogant Beggar* and *Salome of the Tenements*.[21] In these novels, there is a striking stress on the economic conditions of the Lower East Side, and it is through the emphasis on the deplorable physical conditions of this space that the negative pole of ambivalence toward the neighborhood is most clearly articulated. "Dirty," "squalid," "Swarming," "verminous"—it is difficult to find a description of the Lower East Side in which these adjectives are not used; they reappear with such frequency that they almost become tropes.

Unlike David Levinsky, who initially describes the "Jewish" East Side in positive terms, Sonya Vrunsky, the protagonist of Anzia Yezierska's 1923 *Salome of the Tenements* has little good to say about her neighborhood. The first description the reader is offered is one that emphasizes its squalor. Sonya, a reporter for a Jewish newspaper, has just completed an interview with a millionaire philanthropist who has opened a settlement house in the Ghetto. She is fascinated by him, and Yezierska portrays their meeting using the Lower East Side as background:

> Oblivious of the squalid humans that swarmed about them, indifferent for the moment to the myriad needs that drove the crowds here and there from pushcarts to shops, from tenements to factories, restaurants and coffee stands, unaware of the raucous orchestra of voices, the metallic bedlam of elevated trains, the pounding of horses and humans scuttling through the middle of the street—this man and this woman stood wholly absorbed in one another.[22]

The emphasis is on the noise, on the bustle, on "humans," and not on the Jewishness—in any of its aspects or however it may be conceived—of the people who inhabit this space. Sonya, who desperately wants to escape the ugliness of the Lower East Side, and who is depicted as "trying to get rid of her poverty" displays sheer disgust at the "the teeming ghetto, the haggling pushcart peddlers, and the dirt and din of screaming hucksters."[23] Her one desire is to find a space that will take her away "from the crowded windows that hung dirty mattresses and bedding—flaunting banners of poverty."[24] And while the "haggling pushcart peddlers" may be a recognizable code word for Jew, the descriptions neither foreground Jewishness nor does the Jewishness of the space become cause for repulsion. The reader, I would argue, most strongly senses the "teemingness" of the ghetto from these negative descriptions and not the "color" or specifically "ethnic" marking of this space.

Similarly, in Yezierska's 1927 novel *Arrogant Beggar*, we find portrayals that emphasize the poverty stricken streets and houses, the noises and the hordes but much less on the particular "ethnic" markings of the bodies inhabiting this space. Like Sonya Vrunsky, the protagonist Adele Lindner is desperate to escape poverty and better her conditions. Initially, she wants nothing more than to live at the Hellman Home for Working Girls, a settlement house, and she first experiences the institution as the antidote to her impoverished existence. Returning to Essex Street after seeing the cleanliness and order of the Home, she is described as being even more conscious of the ugliness and poverty of the Lower East Side: "I saw once again the houses huddled together in neglect, like a poor over-crowded family. On either side of the stoop, rubbish, bags bursting and overflowing, two alley cats pulling the dirt out on the sidewalk. The cracked doors on broken hinges. The cellar windows stuffed with rags. Over this ugliness, my new life beckoned."[25] "The ugliness," "the terrible dirt," and "the gloom" of the Lower East Side are what get reiterated time and again in Yezierska's texts. The negative pole of ambivalence emerges in relation to poverty and not to the protagonists' feeling of "being yoked" to the "despised folk" who also inhabit this neighborhood.

Despite the negative way in which the Lower East Side is portrayed, the Jewish protagonists' relationship to this space is, as I have argued, ambivalent. This means that alongside the repulsion the novels also present a certain attraction to the neighborhood. There are two main modes through which the positive pull of the Lower East Side manifests itself. One finds a certain nostalgia and yearning for the Lower East Side once the protagonists "make it" in the larger "white" world and move uptown. This is perhaps most clearly articulated in Cahan's text. Following David Levinsky's monumental success as a cloak-and-suit manufacturer, he notes: "One day I paused in front of an old East Side restaurant that I had often passed in my days of need and despair. The feeling of desolation and envy with which I used to peek in its windows came back to me. It gave me pangs of self-pity for my past and a thrilling sense of my present power."[26] This is just one of quite a few instances in which he admits that he has "a particular yearning for the days when the doors of that restaurant were closed to [him]."[27]

Yezierska's texts introduce the positive pull of the Lower East Side in a different way. Her female protagonists actually end up returning to the Lower East Side, and this return is depicted as a "choice" of sorts. The problem with this space appears to be, primarily, poverty. Therefore, there is hope of improving it. Adele Lindner, for example, leaves the Home for Working Girls and goes back to her former neighborhood and familiar streets. It is here that she manages to open up a successful café and restaurant. Her goal, the reader is told, is to provide her people with "the most for the least money," and this becomes a way of Adele working out "the hungers" she had suffered.[28] It is interesting to note that while her return is clearly understood to be a return to "her" people and "her" neighborhood, the service she is rendering and the conditions she hopes to improve are articulated in economic terms. Similarly, after Sonya Vrunsky's spectacular success as a fashion designer, she decides to open up a "little shop on Grand Street" to provide "beauty for those that love it, beauty that is not for profit."[29]

Even though the ambivalence in the Jewish American literature is articulated in and through class and economic language, this is not to argue that the divide between Jewishness and mainstream U.S. society disappears in any of these novels. In fact, the yearning in David Levinsky's case and the return of Yezierska's protagonists can be understood as the discomfort or inadequacy these protagonists feel outside the confines of the Lower East Side, perhaps due to anti-Semitism.[30] I am not arguing that the Jewish texts do not include descriptions of Jews or Jewishness; they do. But my objective in this chapter is to understand how these texts depict the *urban space* of the Lower East Side—the kind of language used and the details stressed. Moreover, my assumption is that the representation of this urban space is important because it serves as a crucial site through which the protagonists negotiate their position in social space. Not only are the descriptions suffused with ambivalence but the source of the ambivalence in relation to the "Jewish" neighborhood is less marked in terms of "ethnicity" and is much more class-inflected.

FROM PAST TO PRESENT

I have tried to demonstrate that certain patterns of representation are discernible in the early depictions of Harlem and the Lower East Side. The novels of both groups emphasize a relationship of ambivalence with respect to these two urban enclaves. However, the Jewish ambivalence, at least in its negative manifestation, is not as racially or "ethnically" inflected as it is in the African American literature, where the resentment is usually linked to a sense of being "yoked" to a people not of one's choosing and where one's identity, life chances, and identification are inextricably seen as being tied to race.

Another important difference that emerges from such a comparison is that the Jewish novels, in sharp contrast to their African American counterparts, gesture toward the possibility of leaving the "Jewish" enclave behind, moving up the class ladder, and becoming part of mainstream middle-class America. This possibility is, I believe, intimately related to the fact that the ambivalence toward the Lower East Side is depicted in class and not racial or "ethnic" terms. Two points need to be underscored here. First, these early Jewish Americans texts were meditating on the chances and the possibility of Jews moving into mainstream white and Gentile society. The narratives suggest that for Jews the barriers were being conceived of more in class terms, a view that is both reflected in the novels but also (re)produced by them. Second, unlike gender and race, which have historically been conceived of as biological facts that cannot be altered, in the United States class has not been perceived of as an essence.[31] After all, the American Dream and the notion of pulling oneself up by one's bootstraps are contingent upon a denatured perception of class—otherwise these myths would quite simply be nonsensical. Therefore, if the problem with one's social position is linked to poverty, then one's position can very conceivably be changed. Harlem, by contrast, is represented in racialized terms and as a much more bounded space, both metaphorically and physically. If the problem with one's social position is linked to race, then changing one's position in social space is infinitely less likely to occur. African Americans could carve out a more mainstream middle-class existence, but only within the confines of the black community.

Put somewhat differently, the Jewish novels' relationship to space underscores that the most pressing problem for the Jewish protagonists is perceived to be poverty and not being defined or defining oneself as Jewish. Consequently, the way space is portrayed in the texts can be said to reveal a certain jockeying for a position in U.S. society, a position that would be defined and thus determined much more by one's class status and much less by one's "race." Thus, even though Jewishness was framed within a racial discourse at this time and, as many contemporary scholars have argued, dominant U.S. society was still questioning whether Jews were or could be full-blooded white, the portrayal of space in the novels seems to gesture towards a changing relationship to Jewishness.[32] By emphasizing the obstacles of class rather than of "Jewishness" these texts can be seen as inscribing a less racialized Jewishness, and perhaps even as facilitating the process of "morphing" Jewishness from a racial category into an ethnic one—a process that would only be complete post–World War II.[33] In the African American novels, by contrast, space is conspicuously and consistently racialized. This suggests that the most pressing problem for the protagonists—as refracted through their ambivalence to Harlem—is not poverty but rather race, underscoring, once again, just how intransigent the black-white divide has been in U.S. history and society.

The narrative emphasis on class in the early Jewish American novels therefore points to the very different positionality of Jews in relation to mainstream U.S. society—even during the 1920s when anti-Semitism was on the rise, Jews were a marginalized minority, and Jewishness was still being articulated within a discourse of race. As Cahan's *The Rise of David Levinsky* narrativizes and perhaps even presages, Jews who managed to climb the class hierarchy could and did cross spatial and social boundaries; namely, for Jews, there was not only vertical but horizontal movement as well. For African Americans, on the other hand, climbing the class ladder was not enough to allow for a blurring of spatial and social borders. Thus, while there was some vertical movement, very little horizontal movement was "allowed." The only way blacks could "cross the line" and integrate into mainstream U.S. society was through passing and by denying their "blackness."

However, it is not only that the ambivalence is more class-inflected in the Jewish American novels, but also that the ambivalence manifests itself differently in the language as well as the narrative structure. The picture of the Lower East Side that these novelists depict is not one that includes binary oppositions very often. The negative pole of the ambivalence is actually more pronounced in that the repulsion toward this place is more often represented than the attraction. The Lower East Side is described consistently through its mean streets and tenements, through its smells, its hordes that leave no room to breathe, and, most obsessively in Yezierska's novels, through its ugliness. It is, more often than not, a place from which one wants desperately to escape. Although the Lower East Side figures as a certain site of origins, it is a place from which most of the protagonists want to rise. Therefore, it is not surprising that one does not find the language of ambivalence as often in these novels or even the presentation of the Lower East Side through a yoking of opposites. Rather, there are very clearly marked sections in the novels where one pole or the other of the ambivalence is uppermost.

This, again, is strikingly different from Harlem. Harlem, after all, represents one of the most promising places in which the African American protagonists could attempt to live out the American Dream and make a better life for themselves. This is the place to which the protagonists dream about and come to (or in the case of Angela Murray, where she will probably end up). When these African American protagonists leave Harlem, it is either for Europe where there is hope of less racism or the decision to leave represents the protagonist's demise, self-destruction, or betrayal of race solidarity by passing. When the Jewish protagonists leave the Lower East Side, it is usually to make their fortune. And while the nostalgia and return to the Jewish neighborhood might suggest pressure and desire for "ethnic" solidarity, the departure from this place is coded as extremely desirable.

I would like to conclude this section with some remarks about some possible consequences of these "structural" differences of representation. The fact that the ambivalence toward the Lower East Side is so clearly marked by "sections" can, perhaps, be seen to have helped make easier the future elision of the negative pole of ambivalence. The repulsion toward the Jewish enclave was not only couched in class-inflected language, but it was formulated in such a way that, after Jews did in fact leave the neighborhood and climbed the class hierarchy, this already neatly split representation helped create the conditions of possibility for the almost complete disavowal of the negative pole of ambivalence. By contrast, Harlem's hope and despair are so intimately intertwined or yoked together from the very beginning of the neighborhood's representation that, even had the cultural conditions made such a splitting possible, the total elision of either the negative or the positive pole of ambivalence would have been infinitely more difficult.

CONCLUSION

Looking back at these early representations of Harlem and the Lower East Side can, I believe, help us begin to understand how and why the iconization processes of these two spaces diverged. It is not merely that the ambivalence evinced in the Jewish novels toward the Lower East Side seems to have disappeared in the narratives currently being told about it, but that the poverty of the Lower East Side and the importance of moving up the class ladder—and making it in the larger white and Gentile world—is missing in contemporary representations. It is no longer the poverty but the Jewishness of this city space that is now being emphasized. The comfort (and discomfort) of middle-class existence allows contemporary Jewish Americans to invoke this site as a means of negotiating their ethnic identity at a time when mainstream acceptance has led to *a fear of loss of ethnic and religious particularity*. Therefore, it is perhaps not surprising that what has, since World War II, been stressed in the representation of the Lower East Side is the Jewishness of this city space. The Lower East Side has become the *Jewish* American sacred space.

The "genteel" African American literature of the Harlem Renaissance also helps us understand how and why Harlem emerged as a conflicted metaphor and as a double modality with its Janus-faced legacy. In the fiction from the 1920s, Harlem's dual affective modality—the promise and the despair—was most often related to its spatialized racialization. Race and racialized space continued to play a critical role in the life and life options of African Americans throughout the twentieth century. Thus, unlike the process of iconization vis-à-vis the Lower East Side, one could argue that the negative pole of ambivalence has not been elided with respect to Harlem because the conditions for allowing such an erasure never materialized. Given that the legacy of white supremacy continues to haunt the United States and that race as a category of identity for African Americans has never melted away (or being black has never become as normative as becoming middle-class), it is also not surprising that Harlem as icon still stands for two modalities: promise and despair.

Yet, like the current Jewish American narrative of the Lower East Side, which has been recast and embedded in Jewishness as opposed to class, the representation of Harlem has also been shifting. In chapter 1 Henry Louis Gates urges us to revisit Harlem as metaphor and to uncover the part *class* has played in creating such a sharp division between the African American middle class and the underclass. For Jews today, poverty is no longer perceived to be a problem; losing a sense of uniqueness is. And while for African Americans race and racialization have continued to be a defining feature of life in the United States, the class differential among African Americans has increasingly become both a divisive marker and defining feature. These shifts and changing emphases tell us that these city spaces continue to be crucial not only for the self-representation and self-conception of African Americans and Jewish Americans, but they also continue to be key sites for making sense of the two minority groups' positions in and relationship to mainstream white U.S. society.

NOTES

1. Jean Laplanche and Jean-Betrand Pontalis, *The Language of Psychoanalysis*, trans. Donald Nicholson-Smith (London: Karnac Books, 1973), 26.

2. Today it is axiomatic to say that race, class, and gender interact with and are articulated through one another. While I certainly agree that these categories overlap and interact in complex ways, I am arguing that there is a decided *emphasis* on one category over another in these African and Jewish American texts and that this in and of itself is interesting and in need of explanation.

3. Nella Larsen, *Quicksand and Passing* (New Brunswick: Rutgers University Press), 46. This is my reading of Helga's yearning for Harlem. In the novel, Helga expresses a deep homesickness for "Negroes" (92). Her homesickness, I would argue, emerges out of the desirability described during Helga's initial sojourn in Harlem.

4. Ibid., 95.

5. Ibid., 45; emphasis added.

6. This is an ambiguous section. It is not entirely clear if Larsen is suggesting that Harlem dwellers could and did patronize white New York's shops, theaters, art galleries, restaurants, etc. but "chose" to segregate themselves, or if Harlem dwellers stayed in Harlem without heeding the great monster that is "white" New York. In either instance, I would argue that Larsen is emphasizing the separateness of white and black Harlem and ultimately on a certain kind of segregation between these two worlds. See *Quicksand*, 45.

7. See, for example, ibid., 43, 51.

8. Ibid., 46, emphasis added.

9. Ibid., 48.

10. Ibid., 54–55.

11. Jessie Fauset, *Plum Bun* (1928; reprint, Boston, Beacon Press, 1990), 96; emphasis added.

12. Ibid., 326. This is my interpretation, since the quote I have inserted is from a later section of the novel. But the sentiments that Angela expresses when she first sees Harlem are similar; she is described as being amazed in large part because the colored life in Harlem was so varied and complete: not only do servants and

underlings inhabit this black space, but professionals, glamorous women, and artists (96). The quote taken from a later section seems to articulate the "everything" of Harlem more succinctly.

13. Ibid., 97.

14. Alain Locke, "The New Negro," in *The New Negro*, ed. Alain Locke (1925; reprint, New York: Simon and Schuster, 1992), 7.

15. Larsen, *Quicksand*, 95; italics in original.

16. Fauset, *Plum Bun*, 326.

17. Larsen, *Quicksand*, 53.

18. Ibid., 98.

19. Abraham Cahan, *The Rise of David Levinsky* (1917; reprint, New York: Penguin Books, 1993), 93.

20. Ibid., 95.

21. Another example in which the ambivalence toward the Lower East Side is articulated in class-inflected rather than "ethnically" inflected terms is Samuel Ornitz's 1923 *Haunch, Paunch, and Jowl.*

22. Anzia Yezierska, *Salome of the Tenements* (1923; reprint, Urbana: University of Illinois Press, 1995), 2.

23. Ibid., 3.

24. Ibid., 5.

25. Anzia Yezierska, *Arrogant Beggar* (1927; reprint, Durham: Duke University Press, 1997), 12–13.

26. Cahan, *David Levinsky*, 525.

27. Ibid.

28. Yezierska, *Arrogant Beggar*, 129.

29. Yezierska, *Salome*, 178.

30. Anti-Semitism, though, does not figure prominently in the novels. Interestingly, the discomfort in white space is more pronounced for the Jewish women protagonists. The differential relationship to space according to gender, both in the African American and Jewish American texts, is something that requires further research. For two articles that begin to articulate this gendered difference, see Lori Harrison-Kahan, "Drunk with the Fiery Rhythms of Jazz," *MFS: Modern Fiction Studies* 51, no. 2 (2005): 416–36; and Catherine Rottenberg, "Race and the New Woman," in *Performing Americanness* (Hanover: University Press of New England, 2008).

31. For an in-depth discussion of the way the American Dream helps create a nonessentialist perception of class identity, see Catherine Rottenberg, "*Salome of the Tenements*, American Dream Discourse, and Class Performativity," *American Studies* 45, no. 1 (2004): 5–29.

32. See, for example, Matthew Jacobson, *Whiteness of a Different Color* (Cambridge: Harvard University Press, 1998); and Eric Goldstein. "The Unstable Other: Locating the Jew in Progressive-Era American Racial Discourse," *American Jewish History* 89, no. 4 (2001): 383–409.

33. See, for example, Karen Brodkin's *How Jews Became White Folks and What That Says About Race in America* (New Brunswick: Rutgers University Press, 1998); and Rottenberg, *Performing Americanness.*

THREE

STRANGERS IN THE VILLAGE

Greenwich Village and the Search for Alternative Space in Ethnic Women's Fiction of the 1920s and 1930s

Meredith Goldsmith

INTRODUCTION

Early-twentieth-century narratives of American women reveal a persistent search for identity through space, as female characters migrate between a series of interior and exterior settings: uptown New York mansions, downtown apartments, and rooming houses; cities, countries, and regions.[1] For ethnic women writers of the 1920s and 1930s, what cultural geographer Yi-Fu Tuan has famously described as "topophilia"[2]—the affective bond between individuals and space—is particularly charged: writing as the Lower East Side and Harlem had been established in the literature and culture of the time as privileged sites for ethnic identity formation, the heroines of novels by Nella Larsen, Anzia Yezierska, Jessie Fauset, and Tess Slesinger, among others, maintain ambivalent relationships with such vicinities. Given the primacy of Harlem and the Lower East Side in both the literature of the time and scholarly approaches to the period, alternative spaces for identity formation have received little critical attention. The works I study in this essay, Jessie Fauset's "The Sleeper Wakes" (1920) and *Plum Bun* (1928) and Tess Slesinger's *The Unpossessed* (1934), each demonstrate the efforts of ethnic women writers to articulate a third space, Greenwich Village, as the site for the reconciliation of ethnic and gender imperatives. In these texts, the construction of identity through racial passing and ethnic assimilation is coupled with the New Woman's ambivalent wishes for romantic freedom, on the one hand, and heterosexual union, on the other. For both Fauset, considered a central figure of Harlem Renaissance intellectual life, and Slesinger, typically viewed as the only female member of the first generation of New York intellectuals, Greenwich Village—the paradigmatic social setting for romantic, artistic, and political experimentation of the early twentieth century—offers a temporary solution to their spatial negotiations.

These literary works anticipate those of cultural geographers such as Tuan, reflecting the challenges of articulating individuals' intimate relation to space, which, as Tuan notes, may be a prerogative specific to literature and the other arts.[3] Yet both authors point out that space often reproduces gendered cultural norms. The setting of Greenwich Village serves as a powerful medium through which to negotiate the ambiguous promise of early-twentieth-century femininity. With new access to the public sphere, the heroines of these fictions seek privacy and intimacy as well as professional recognition; with unprecedented sexual freedom, they simultaneously do not reject the traditional goals of the female *Bildungsroman*—love, marriage, and reproduction. Rather than pointing to an alternative space in which problems of class, ethnicity, and gender could be worked out, Slesinger and Fauset demonstrate how ostensibly liberatory urban subcultures, such as the Village, reiterate the norms and problems of the dominant culture.

These two authors' depictions of the Village stand in striking parallel to those produced by Village chronicler Floyd Dell and historian Caroline Ware in the 1920s and 1930s, respectively. In *Love in Greenwich Village*, Dell charted a poignant narrative of flamboyant artists and idealists who migrated to the Village in search of artistic and romantic freedom, soon to be replaced by white-collar workers as the "original" Villagers fled toward middle-class respectability. Ware's feminist ethnography of the Village underscores the changing role of women in the neighborhood and the ethno-cultural conflict between Anglo-American migrants to the neighborhood and Italian American residents. Where Dell at once celebrates and punctures the myth of bohemia, Ware makes clear that the notion of the Village as a "neighborhood," implicitly bound by a common system of values, was a construct,[4] buoyed by cultural discourses of the period (periodical articles, real estate and promotional work, as well as fiction such as Dell's and the poetry of Edna St. Vincent Millay). Her work recasts the Village as a contested site for gender, ethnic, and cultural mores. Fauset and Slesinger, read in tandem with these texts, reveal the implicit whiteness of the Village culture, which remains unexplored in more canonical Village representations of the time, such as those of Millay. Nascent cultural geographers themselves, both authors—despite their differences of race, culture, and class—engage in a common feminist exploration of the opportunities for ethnic women in this alternative space.

As Fauset's and Slesinger's heroines rejected ethnically specific locations, their fiction contradicts spatial archetypes, sometimes archetypes they themselves had helped create. Setting, more than has been previously acknowledged, underpins the ethnic American canon; as works by ethnic women writers roamed beyond ethnically specific communities, they left the critical matrix through which we now evaluate them. New York City itself, apparently homogeneous ethnic communities like Harlem and the Lower East Side, and urban subcultures, such as the Harlem Renaissance, function as conceptual tools that have allowed critics to valorize the work of minority writers. However, such fetishization of place works to the detriment of writers from less stereotypically urban settings. The primacy of the Harlem Renaissance can obscure the African American literature emerging from Washington, Boston, and Chicago during the period, for example; the Wisconsin-born Edna Ferber, immensely popular during her time, is rarely considered in tandem with other Jewish American writers of the period. The class status and ambitions of both Fauset and Slesinger oriented them toward different locales than better-known African American and Jewish American writers of their eras. The unexpected juxtaposition of Fauset and Slesinger reveals their mutual exhaustion with stereotypes of urban ghettos and subcultures coupled with a search for new ethno-spatial paradigms for gendered living.

"HOME AGAIN, HOME AGAIN": JESSIE FAUSET AND THE POSSIBILITIES OF GREENWICH VILLAGE

The heroines of 1920s African American novelist Jessie Fauset's "The Sleeper Wakes" (1920) and *Plum Bun* (1928) flee their working-class backgrounds in the hope of upward mobility in New York, attained, in both texts, through racial passing. In both works, the Village serves as a forum in which passing—at first an exhilarating moment of identity performance—ultimately becomes compulsory. First allowing the heroines of Fauset's and Slesinger's fiction to live free of social convention, the Village binds them to its own set of social and spatial norms.

African Americans constituted a third term in the Anglo-immigrant interactions that had marked Village life since the 1890s, and Fauset's fiction emphasizes the liminality of African Americans in downtown New York. As Lower East Side tenement culture had expanded westward, interactions between Anglo-American artists and bourgeoisie and the Jewish immigrant population had become increasingly common. Villagers came to expect Jewish immigrants to supply a dose of radicalism and exoticism to Village life, and writers such as Hutchins Hapgood, author of *The Spirit of the Ghetto* (1903), moved easily between the Lower East Side and the West Village.[5] The porous boundaries of the neighborhood allowed white Villagers and white immigrants to move back and forth easily. However, such mobility depended on the liminal racial status of Jewish immigrants, for, as Stansell reports, the "Bohemian sensibility in the Village [of the early twentieth century] did not prove so elastic when it came to African Americans."[6] Few African Americans worked or socialized in the Village in the 1910s, and Stansell conjectures that African Americans would not have been served in Greenwich Village restaurants at the time. However, in the late teens *The Crisis* was housed on lower Fifth Avenue, and Claude McKay served on the editorial staff of *The Liberator*. The difference in attitudes between everyday African American workers and visitors and cultural workers such as Fauset, DuBois, and McKay is striking: while Fauset and DuBois are typically considered among the more socially conservative Harlemites, they seem to have worked comfortably in the white Village. Harlem Renaissance fiction evokes a black middle-class skepticism of white bohemia, although more marginalized African Americans seem to have found the Village an alternative to Harlem's occasionally stifling social mores. Consider, for example, Nella Larsen's *Quicksand*, in which Audrey Denney, an "alabaster"[7] African American who lives on West 22nd Street, socializes with whites and blacks indiscriminately to the polite horror of the respectable Anne Grey. In Anne Grey's words, Audrey "hasn't much use for Harlem anymore."[8] To have little use for Harlem implies both miscegenation and sexual license, striking at the heart of the respectability sought by middle-class Harlem dwellers. As Fauset sought that respectability for herself and her heroines, she also cast the Village as a setting in which alternatives to bourgeois conservatism could be initially explored.

The bourgeois conservatism of which Fauset is often accused may have something to do with her literary flight from Harlem; when Robert Bone deems one of Fauset's characters "the first colored woman in New Jersey to wear lounging pajamas,"[9] "New Jersey"—perhaps the classic American symbol of suburban insularity—is intended to elicit a sneer as much as the infamous evening apparel. As Fauset's fellow Harlem Renaissance thinkers and the historiography of the 1960s and 1970s positioned Harlem as the locus of African American identity formation, Fauset's work was exiled to critical suburbia, where it remains, all too frequently, today.[10]

"The Sleeper Wakes" concerns Amy Boldin, a light-skinned orphan determined to profit from her beauty. Enamored of fashion and art, she moves to New York, takes a job as a waitress, passes for white, and marries a white Southerner; when she reveals her racial identity, the couple's marriage dissolves. Returning to New York City as a divorcée, she forges an independent life as a clothing designer, but ultimately leaves the city with the aim of rejoining her black relations. The title signals Amy's awakening to a number of realities: her status as an African American, her objectification as a woman, and her need for productive labor, rather than consumerist pampering, as a source of fulfillment.

Critics have yet to appreciate the Greenwich Village context of this story, which was published in *The Crisis* before the journal moved to Harlem, and which serves as a precursor to the spatial concerns of *Plum Bun*.[11] In Fauset's depiction of the Village, Amy's passing becomes compulsory, as does her need to exploit her good looks. Amy is first employed at a bakery "on the edge of Greenwich Village,"[12] suggesting her doubly marginal position as a middle-class black woman passing as a working-class white woman, working in a doubly marginal location. Ironically enough, Amy works in a setting in which were she a customer, she likely would not have been served; although Amy never intends to reveal her racial identity, it is impossible for her to do so in the white artistic milieu into which she soon assimilates. Characterized by consumerism—epitomized in the "habitués" of the cafe where Amy works—the Village offers little heterogeneity. Once Amy is taken in by a wealthy patron and moves to an apartment building "inhabited only by artists" on Twelfth Street, she learns that the commodification of women is a staple of Village culture as well.[13] A would-be artist and divorcée, Amy's patron Zora Harrison now simply "studies," lives on alimony, and entertains suitors.[14] Zora's salon serves as a forum for the complex web of dating and flirtation that Fauset reveals is necessary to female survival.

If Zora, who advises Amy to "marry wealth,—one can always get a divorce,"[15] appears a refugee from an Edith Wharton novel, counseling divorce as a form of upward mobility, a trace of Wharton's alleged antimodernism also emerges in Fauset's critique of Zora's coterie of "faddist" suitors "crazy not about art or music, but merely about some phase such as cubism or syncopation."[16] But Fauset's ambivalence toward the Village runs deeper than her dislike of trends. Earlier defined through her marginal geographical position, Amy's liminal status as an African American woman in the Village emerges even more clearly as Amy and Zora "stroll" the neighborhood "south of Washington Square":

> The children, the people, all foreign, all dirty, often very artistic, always immensely human, disgusted Zora except for "local color"—she really could reproduce them wonderfully. But she almost hated them for being what they were.

> "Br-r-r, dirty little brats!" she would say to Amy. "Don't let them touch me." She was frequently amazed at her protégée's utter indifference to their appearance, for Amy herself was the pink of daintiness. They were turning from MacDougall into Bleecker Street one day and Amy had patted a child—dirty, but lovely—on the head.
>
> "They are all people just like anybody else, just like you and me, Zora," she said in answer to her friend's protest.
>
> "You *are* the true democrat," Zora returned with a shrug. But Amy did not understand her.[17]

Immigrant children serve whites as a potent source of "'local color,'" objects of aesthetic pleasure kept at a distance. Amy's ambiguous racial and class status, despite her characterization as visually white ("the pink of daintiness"), allows her to mediate between the children and Zora, protecting the white leisure-class woman from contamination and allowing her to displace her act of *noblesse oblige* onto a subordinate. Amy "pats" while Zora paints, nurturing the immigrant children into the democracy that she—as Zora sarcastically but rightfully notes—represents. Through Amy's mediation, Fauset suggests that African Americans, such as Amy, have a place in the Village primarily as assistants, helping to produce the unsullied white femininity of bourgeois women.[18]

By the story's end, Amy pledges to return to the black family that raised her: "She would go home, home—how she loved the word."[19] However, even in her imagination, she knows that her sojourn in Trenton, from which she fled so many years earlier, will not last long: planning to establish herself "in a rich suburb" where she would cater to white women, she simultaneously imagines herself as a "citizen of the world."[20] The rosy conclusion of the story highlights the ambivalence of Fauset's narrators' affective spatial relations. Fauset consistently renders neighborhoods with cartographic precision, reminding her readers of street names, urban layout, and even transit lines. Such nuance suggests not only Fauset's study of realism but a desire to make her characters' experiences of urban space palpable. Such localism would be difficult to reconcile, as *Plum Bun* demonstrates, with a desire for citizenship unhampered by spatial restrictions.

Plum Bun's bifurcated narrative reveals the challenging nature of this search, as its sister-heroines work to establish themselves in Greenwich Village and Harlem, respectively. Juxtapositions of cities, neighborhoods, and urban dwellings structure *Plum Bun* more fully than has been previously appreciated. The novel posits Greenwich Village as a transitional space, in which light-skinned Angela Murray establishes herself as an artist, while her darker sister Virginia develops an identity as a New Negro woman in Harlem. However, through a delicate elaboration of the politics of race, class, gender, and space, Fauset makes clear not only that women's independence in the Village depends on race, but that the freedoms offered Greenwich Village New Women also depend on the reproduction of gendered norms. Ironically enough, Harlem's women enjoy a greater sense of independence than the novel's bohemian white women, reversing stereotypes of racialized women's lives. As Fauset demonstrates, the vaunted sexual freedom of the Village simply exaggerates conventional norms of gendered behavior, rather than reversing them.

From the early pages of *Plum Bun*, Fauset makes her characters' sensitivity to urban geography clear: "Opal Street," the narrator tells us, "is no jewel of the first water."[21] Both "street" and "dwelling" evoke Angela's sense of spatial and racial circumscription—full of identical homes with box-like rooms and "sad, diminutive" yards,[22] the neighborhood harbors neither intimacy nor even physical variety. Angela's sense of suffocation inversely parallels her parents' pride in their success: for them, "the little house on Opal Street represented the *ne plus ultra* of ambition."[23] Home and locale serve as metaphors for achievement, an equation that remains fixed in Angela's mind as she investigates new settings throughout the novel.

After Angela's relocation to New York, she makes a series of journeys to Harlem from her downtown Village residence. Her resistance to and anxieties about Harlem are more complex than initially appear, meriting further exploration. One might easily assume that her discomfort with Harlem is simply a result of internalized racism, and indeed, her feelings toward Harlem evolve in tandem with her acceptance of her blackness. When read as a negotiation of urban space, Angela's feelings emerge as an interaction between herself and the geographic specificities of Harlem. On her first visit, Angela weaves her way through a distinctly bounded area of about ten city blocks (from 135th Street and Seventh to Lenox Avenue, to 147th Street and Seventh Avenue, and finally back down to the "Elevated" which takes her "back to the New York which she knew").[24] Fauset manipulates the mixed readership of the novel as she indicates to readers familiar with Harlem geography both what Angela notices and what she fails to observe (for example, sensitive readers would know that Angela walks past Striver's Row, where Virginia will later establish herself). She guides unfamiliar readers through Harlem and acquaints them with its vibrant street culture as we trace Angela's footsteps through the city. Where Angela's predominant early feelings in the Village are loneliness, as she "browse[s] her chosen thoroughfares," sits in Union Square Park alone, and attends plays at a theatre on Seventh Avenue,[25] in Harlem she is "amazed and impressed at this bustling, frolicking, busy, laughing great city within a greater one."[26] Although Angela's desire for inclusion in white bohemian culture, epitomized in the theatergoers, is clear, the energy of Harlem absorbs her completely. Fourteenth Street, despite its crowds and excitement, leaves Angela fundamentally distant—she "wanders, almost prowls . . . intent upon faces."[27] In contrast, Harlem "seemed to her to run thicker, more turgidly than that safe, sublimated existence in which her new friends had their being. It was deeper, more mightily moving even than the torrent of Fourteenth Street."[28] Her sense of tourism dissolves, as she experiences a momentary sense of merger with the urban masses.

Angela leaves Harlem with both relief and regret, telling herself that "all this was fuller, richer, not finer but richer with the difference in quality that there is between velvet and silk."[29] Although Fauset underscores Angela's class biases, the affective quality of her response is also striking—Harlem envelops, like velvet, in contrast to the smooth surface of silk. Angela's resistance to Harlem also inheres in its size: Angela notes that Harlem was a "city [that] reproduced in microcosm all the important features of any metropolis,"[30] reproducing the features of any other large, dense urban area. For Angela, urban centers are marked by crowds and anonymity: as she glances back at Harlem from the El, she is glad "that she had cast in her lot with the dwellers outside its dark and serried tents"[31] (the word "serried" evokes crowds of soldiers in formation). As Harlem represents the city as modern icon—a "metropolis," a "city within a city,"[32] and finally a "wonderful city"[33]—it also suggests the crowding and alienation of modern urban life that Angela seems unable to tolerate.

If Angela experiences agoraphobia in Harlem, she longs for the intimacy she witnesses among the Village theatergoers, which she views as a function of the environment itself. As Tuan argues, topophilic responses are always produced in contrast to other spaces, and in contrast to the crowds of Harlem, as Tuan might note,[34] the Village evokes a kind of claustrophilia: for example, Angela takes an apartment "so small that almost everything was within arm's reach," and throughout the text, Fauset emphasizes its diminution.[35] A tiny flat in a labyrinthine milieu, Angela's apartment offers the kind of voluntary stasis that theorist of space Gaston Bachelard associates with corners: corners, he writes, are "haven[s] that ensure us one of the things we prize most highly–immobility."[36] In contrast to her youth in Philadelphia, Angela now feels comfortable in a small space without feeling trapped. A sense of willful isolation was reinforced by Village geography: despite the extension of the West Side subway line into the neighborhood in 1917, the neighborhood maintained its reputation for physical detachment from the larger city.[37] In the Village, as Angela begins her artistic career, she finds a space that seems to reflect her own desires for intimacy, diminutive settings, and the protection of corners, instead of the broad avenues of Philadelphia where she roamed with her mother, where she tasted the freedom of racial anonymity while simultaneously risking exposure for racial passing.

The social intimacies Angela seeks are associated with the stereotype of the "bachelor girl," an independent, sexually liberated, New Woman of the 1920s, who often lived alone.[38] As Angela fits into this type, she assumes the "bachelor girl's" typical address and even her customary decor and furnishings. The block on which Angela lives reflects Fauset's appropriation of this stereotype: Angela lives on Jayne Street, alluding not only to the ubiquity of single women in the neighborhood ("Jane Does") but also to Mary Austin's 1920 novel of Greenwich Village feminism, *No. 26 Jayne Street*. For Angela, apartment dwelling offers the freedom and ease of pre-owned, minimal possessions, coupled with built-in neighbors and privacy—a combination she has previously been unable to negotiate. In the realism of Howells and Wharton, as Amy Kaplan asserts, rented apartments "constitute a world filled with things neither known nor valued through well-worn contact, but cluttered instead with mass-produced furnishings and the unknown lives of strangers."[39] Fauset repurposes these images just as Angela and her friends recycle and pass on objects to each other. The dwellings and possessions of others—such as the apartment and phone Angela inherits—facilitate her passing into a category she could not occupy as a woman of color, that of the single, sexually liberated, Village woman.

For Angela, diminutive spaces with minimal possessions epitomize the mix of intimacy and freedom that she seeks. Counterbalancing Angela's developing subjectivity, Fauset's sketches of her friends manipulate details of furniture and decor to comment on their class and sexual status, exploring alternatives to which Angela first aspires, yet ultimately resists. For example, Paulette Lister blends the minimalism of transience, marked by chairs that, as "magazines affirm, may be made out of a large packing box," with "good" mahogany furniture and other elements of a bourgeois background like "fine, dainty china" and good quality art reproductions.[40] Although Angela insists that Paulette's apartment contains "none of the stereotyped things,"[41] a term that in the early twentieth century characterized cheap reprints (originally, it referred to a kind of typeface), Paulette verges on a stereotype herself, that of the Village woman Angela fears becoming as she embarks on an interracial affair. Paulette's air of mobility echoes that of Village migrants of the era: according to Ware's research, multiple moves were taken for granted; secondhand furniture dealers could sell objects back to their original owners at a profit and janitors kept cellars full of cast-off furniture.[42] Despite the appeal of Paulette's "bachelor" flat, such chronic instability threatens Angela's wish for a secure domestic space.

In contrast to Paulette's minimalism, the home of Angela's art-school friend, Martha Burden, offers a possible spatial ideal for Angela. Although Martha appears a signal example of Village unconventionality—"'I don't care what people think,' was her slogan,"[43] Fauset tells us—her display of *accoutrements* bespeaks a rootedness that Paulette lacks. Her home successfully combines her air of individualism with a "simple elegance"[44] that conveys her class origins. Early in the novel, Angela wishes for "a comfortable drawing-room . . . peopled with distinguished men and women who did things, wrote and painted and acted—people with a broad, cultural background behind them."[45] At Martha Burden's home, Angela initially feels as if she has found such an environment: "Their apartment [with her husband, Ladislas Starr] was large and neat and sunny; it bore no trace of palpable wealth, yet nothing conducing to comfort was lacking. Book-cases in the dining-room and living-room spilled over; the *Nation*, the *Mercury*, the *Crisis, a magazine of the darker races*, left on the broad arm of an easy chair, mutely invited; it was late autumn, almost winter, but there were jars of fresh flowers."[46] Martha's decor recalls that of wealthy Villagers during the period: as Ware writes, "[W]ith slight variation on account of income level, they exerted every effort to make their apartments into homes rather than dormitories, with antique furniture, etchings, perhaps some old European brass, and many books . . . .Their magazine reading was confined to the quality journals."[47] Ware's analysis suggests that decor helps the Greenwich Village elite—many of whom were of "cultivated families of old American stock"[48]—stage their position as a deliberate contrast to white and seemingly white migrants to the Village such as Paulette and Angela, respectively. Significantly, the *New Masses* is absent from the display of magazines, emphasizing Martha's elite rather than her proletarian identifications. Angela is initially attracted to this felicitous blend of money, comfort, and intellectual camaraderie, where she finds Paulette Lister's combination of sexual agency and transience threatening.

For both Martha and Paulette, cultural and economic capital, New Woman professionalism, and sexual sophistication combine to form Greenwich Village white femininity. Martha's wealth, her roots among the Long Island elite, and her racial insensitivity suggest white privilege, as do Paulette's crude efforts to flirt with Van Meier. The "Janes" of Jane Street are, with the exception of Angela, almost universally white: even the Jewish Rachel Salting, Angela's upstairs neighbor, enjoys the whiteness that allows her to move through the Village unmolested. Especially once Rachel departs from Angela's apartment building near the end of the novel, Fauset consciously constructs a racialized Village. In contrast to "The Sleeper Wakes," the neighborhood contains no immigrants or African American residents: when Angela recalls strolling the Village with the dark-skinned Miss Powell, the other woman would not foil her racial masquerade because "there were practically no colored people there."[49] Although Angela ponders inviting Virginia and her friends to her Jane Street flat, she never does so, as if aware that a group of young black women would jeopardize her position (when she does socialize with Virginia in public, she does so in the less segregated setting of midtown). *Plum Bun*'s Village sketches reveal the racial and spatial specificity of the sexualized New Woman.

Angela's status as a near-white woman in the Village becomes even more questionable when contrasted with the life of uptown black women. As Angela has an affair, struggles to support herself, and fantasizes that her lover will marry her, Virginia and her friends engage in socially acceptable romantic relationships, enjoy their professional independence, and consume in accordance with their income. *Plum Bun*'s single white females, despite their apparent liberation, are ultimately more susceptible to male predation and economic exploitation than its Harlem bachelor girls: Paulette, even in her lover's eyes, is "a mighty attractive little piece"[50] who only has money once a month; Roger's gifts blind Angela to her waning bank balance. Ware notes that such narratives were common among single Village women in the 1920s: "The story of this girl [the young woman who fell prey to sexual exploitation] could be repeated countless times from the records of the Village, varying in each case according to her luck, her economic security, and her emotional stability."[51] Angela's status as a working white female artist depends upon a fragile gender and economic system; feminist writers such as Ware and Fauset dismantle the myth—propagated by writers like Dell—of the carefree female bohemian.

Ultimately, Fauset refrains from taking Angela's immersion in Greenwich Village bohemianism too far, as she falls in with a wealthier, more sophisticated class of midtown Manhattanites. Experiencing a renewed sense of spatial circumscription, she becomes more critical of Greenwich Village culture: "The slight bohemianism which she had there encountered was here replaced by a somewhat bourgeois but satisfying sophistication. These people saw the 'Village' for what it was, a network of badly laid off streets with, for the most part, uncomfortable, not to say inconvenient dwellings inhabited by a handful of artists in the midst of a thousand *poseurs*."[52] Angela's criticism echoes changes in urban demography, as middle-class tenants assumed the places of artists driven out by rent increases. Fauset's diction suggests that "streets" and "dwellings" do not a neighborhood make; the legendary charm of the Village is revealed as an element of false consciousness. Significantly, though, Angela can now function as a guide to the neighborhood for her midtown friends: the "luncheons to which she treated [one friend] Elizabeth in the Village tea-rooms and the department stores brought as great satisfaction as the more elaborate meals at the Algonquin."[53] Angela now occupies an opposite position to that of Amy Boldin, treating guests in Village tea-rooms rather than serving in them. However, her position as tour guide depends upon her continued passing—she would neither have been served nor been able to serve were her racial identity known.

Angela's feelings of entrapment lead her to Paris, where she implicitly continues to pass, rather than to the bustling streets of Harlem. As urban ethnic communities are flawed by gender conservatism and bohemian enclaves are marred by racial exclusion, Fauset provides a bleak resolution to the problem of home for her characters. Perhaps unsurprisingly, then, her final two novels would cast New York as a dystopian space, a site where her black middle-class characters were treated with disrespect (*The Chinaberry Tree* [1931]) and otherwise admirable people violated sexual taboos (*Comedy: American Style* [1934]). *The Chinaberry Tree* offers a utopian conclusion in the New Jersey suburbs; *Comedy: American Style* offers a tentative model for a renewed African American family in Depression-era Philadelphia and explicitly rejects expatriation for African Americans. Throughout her career, Fauset continued to elucidate her characters' spatial negotiations, emphasizing the ongoing nature of the process; as *Plum Bun* and "The Sleeper Wakes" make clear, the interaction between subject and locale would continue to resist simplistic conclusions.

"GO ANYWHERE OUT OF OUR GODDAMNED CITY": TESS SLESINGER AND THE WANING OF VILLAGE SUBCULTURE

Where *Plum Bun* underscores Angela's final realization that the Village would not provide a haven for her as a working-class woman artist or as a black woman no matter what her economic or professional status, Tess Slesinger debunks the myth of free love among downtown bohemians in her underappreciated novel *The Unpossessed* (1934), published six years after *Plum Bun*. In this novel, typically viewed as an exploration of 1930s fellow-travelers and their failure to live up to their leftist ideals, Slesinger also shows how the economic challenges of the Depression mesh uncomfortably with the New Woman's desire for equality. Where we see in *Plum Bun* that New Women in the Village enjoy a precarious freedom, the women of *The Unpossessed* long for an end to an ostensibly limitless liberation—as one, Elizabeth Leonard, suggests, they long to get off the "twentieth century sex-express."[54] While Elizabeth's metaphor is temporal, the mores Slesinger describes are enforced spatially as well. Where *Plum Bun* ponders the costs of bohemian female liberation, *The Unpossessed* mourns both the loss of stability and the failure of bohemian ideals of equality.

Slesinger's novel underscores the ambiguous status of 1920s and 1930s Greenwich Village New Women with respect to gender roles: as Ware argues, young women who had migrated to the Village "found themselves often in an *impasse*"[55] between their commitment to progressive ideals and their desires for love and marriage. *The Unpossessed*, even more explicitly than *Plum Bun*, critiques the ideal of the Village as a utopian setting for the resolution of gender and ethnic conflict. Although Slesinger's characters—even those marked as Jewish—enjoy the mobility of whiteness and class privilege, they evince an increasing sense of pessimism about migration to the Village from rural climes or even from urban middle-class neighborhoods as a means to settle unsettled questions of gender, ethnicity, and identity.

The Unpossessed comments on the failure of the Village to provide what one character calls an "armistice"[56] between a number of competing constituencies—men and women, Jews and Gentiles, native-born and immigrants, and varying brands of progressive intellectuals. Much of Slesinger's discussion of the architecture and demographics of the Village echoes Ware's demographic observations: groups who migrated to the neighborhood in the early twentieth century (immigrants, artists, and factory workers) were replaced in the 1920s by an increasingly demoralized avant-garde and bourgeois professionals. Coupling the narrative of heroine Margaret Banner's faltering relationship, ending with her abortion, with the failed efforts of the novel's intellectual group to establish a magazine, *The Unpossessed* portrays a bohemia shorn of its vibrancy. Significantly, Margaret, in contrast to some of the other members of the novel's intellectual class, is cast as ethnically neutral despite a seemingly privileged upbringing in early-twentieth-century New York. Slesinger makes Margaret's religious, ethnic, and class identity all slightly unclear, in contrast to her intellectual characters who hail from rural areas (Miles Flinders and Norah Blake), the Chicago Jewish bourgeoisie (Bruno and Elizabeth Leonard), and working-class New Yorkers such as Comrade Ruthie Fisher, the novel's one avowed communist and Bruno's students, the ironically named "Black Sheep." Margaret's deliberately ambiguous identity, I would suggest, allows Slesinger to explore the complex relationship of middle-class, assimilated urban Jews to urban space, ethnicity, and reproduction.

The novel is framed by images of Greenwich Village that underscore its characters' negotiations with urban space. Significantly, Slesinger's characters rarely acknowledge more ethnically specific urban locales; while its Jewish characters never venture to the Lower East Side, those who teach and study at City College fail to acknowledge its Harlem location. We see how class, combined with the transitional whiteness of American Jews, insulates these characters from ethnically defined spaces; arguably, white privilege allows the City College professor Bruno Leonard and his cohort of young radicals to deny their geographic link to Harlem. While physically located in Greenwich Village, the amorphous intellectual class lacks a center. Slesinger marks a transitional moment in the identification of ethnicity with urban space: while her middle-class, Depression-era intellectuals would be alienated from the working-class, first-generation immigrant valences of the Lower East Side, they simultaneously reject the explicitly racial otherness of

Harlem in the 1930s. The Village becomes a liminal state, as Jews remain ambivalently poised between uptown and downtown, white Jewishness and racialized Jewishness.

In contrast to Fauset, who emphasizes the coziness of tiny flats and crooked streets, Slesinger depicts the Village as a site of undirected movement leading toward entrapment. As Margaret thinks to herself as she walks home from work early in the novel: "This year on Charles street, last year on Tenth; surely these were locations on some route?"[57] For Margaret, as we see, the fabled mobility of Village dwellers represents not freedom, but confinement. Margaret's lack of trajectory reflects her discomfort with the ostensible social progress that the Village represented for white women: a child-free woman in a common-law marriage, she nonetheless plays the role of the traditional housewife, cooking, cleaning, and remaining sexually available. Such a paradigm was common among the Villagers Ware surveyed: most Village partnered women worked, and typically, white Villagers eschewed reproduction, contributing to a sharp drop in the local birth rate in the 1920s.[58] Children of bohemia were excluded from archetypal Village discourse: Floyd Dell's narrator, in "The Fall of Greenwich Village," is shocked to encounter his adult friends' children, who force him to recast his fellow bohemians as "grown-up people, and not the most delightful and irresponsible artist-children in the world."[59] Margaret and Miles's ostensible unconventionality in fact represents a local, prescriptive notion of normalcy, as the novel's women attain a qualified freedom under the guise of sexual liberation. As Margaret wonders whether "the room on the fourth floor is too small," or whether "Charles street" itself "is too narrow,"[60] she indicates her shrinking horizons: the spatial intimacies of the Village no longer produce the privacy necessary for identity formation, but instead generate their own constricting homogeneity—of apartments, of conversations, and of personal lives.

Where Fauset hints at the frequency of Village Anglo-immigrant interactions in "The Sleeper Wakes," Slesinger charts more explicit contact between the immigrant locals and the waning bohemian class. While the immigrant population was in decline by the early 1930s, the Village still afforded contact between white progressives and Italian Americans, whose religious practices, politics, and wishes were often very different from those of their middle-class neighbors. If the Village requires whiteness and aids in gendered exploitation, as we see in Fauset, it also reinforces the racial singularity of the progressives, who essentialize immigrant otherness, failing to see the links between white and ethnic women.

Minor immigrant characters offer alternatives to Margaret's brand of New Womanhood. German immigrant men such as the local greengrocer who resembles a "gynecologist"[61] and the taxi driver who "kn[ows] how to carry a woman home from a maternity hospital"[62] offer prescriptions for normative femininity. The musician Arturo Teresca (Americanized through the name "Art Terry") offers a similarly traditional notion of gender roles, with a "dark and healthy beauty" of a wife and three strapping boys.[63] Most significant, though, is the Flinders' Italian female neighbor, Mrs. Salvemini, who offers a template of ethnic, reproductive, traditional femininity against which Margaret defines her white, middle-class nonreproductive womanhood. Ostensibly simply a local busybody, Mrs. Salvemini guesses Margaret's pregnancy: "It didn't take a doctor, Mrs. Salvemini said, to tell *her*; she knew it; had the feeling; a heaviness in the eyes, a lightness in the heart—it was she who told the doctor. And I always ask God, said Mrs. Salvemini, I always ask God."[64] Devout where Margaret is secular, a source of instinctive versus medically rational knowledge, the older woman (nominally cast as Margaret's "savior"), appears a figure of essential maternity. These immigrant characters, while apparently part of Village local color, function as reproductive rebukes to white middle-class bohemia.

Margaret's decision to terminate her pregnancy thus functions not only as a defense against maternity, but as a defense against an earlier, more obviously ethnic identity as opposed to the fluid Jewishness that marks so many of Slesinger's bourgeois intellectuals. Italian American reproductivity, evoked through Mrs. Salvemini, poses a threat to whiteness: during Miles's brief acceptance of Margaret's pregnancy, Flinders wonders whether Margaret is "taking up with the Salveminis" and whether Margaret will "look like Mrs. Salvemini . . . when . . ."[65] If the birth of one child might induce a reproductive cascade, maternity might render white women akin to immigrants. Margaret's abortion thus prevents her from becoming one of the mothers whose children litter the Village streets, like those in "The Sleeper Wakes." Fauset's depiction of the Village in *Plum Bun* is also conspicuously child-free; even happy couples such as Martha and Ladislas do not have children, and Paulette's bathroom features men's shaving gear rather than contraception. In *Plum Bun*, only the visibly black middle-class women, such as Virginia and her roommates, aim for marriage and children. In Walter Benn Michaels's well-known formulation about high modernism, incest saves the family from marriage, and thus metaphorical miscegenation; in these novels of Greenwich Village, "free love"—free of children as well as commitment—cordons off white bohemian femininity from its immigrant female neighbors.[66]

The repression and displacement of Jewish American ethnic markers form a possible third term in the construction of white middle-class, bohemian femininity in relation to immigrant working-class femininity. Slesinger's Italian Americans arguably contain the residue of immigrant Jewishness in the process of erasure. For example, in her religious devotion; excessively feminine, reproductive body; and rootedness in the home and neighborhood, Mrs. Salvemini evokes the "East Side mothers with heroic bosoms"[67] of Michael Gold's *Jews Without Money*, published just four years before *The Unpossessed.* Such a reading also illuminates the Americanized immigrant artist Art Terry, whose Americanized renaming echoes the transformation of the immigrant artist Jake Rabinowitz into Jack Robin in *The Jazz Singer* (1927). Michael Rogin, in his influential reading of that film, has shown how blackface offers a vehicle for Jewish artists' transition into whiteness.[68] Here, the fluid ethnicity of middle-class Jews is offset by an ethnicity that is bodily, nominally, and culturally inscribed. And despite the efforts of Jewish intellectuals to escape their ethnic identifications, the urban landscape of *The Unpossessed* remains haunted by their presence.

If Margaret's pregnancy illuminates the novel's class, ethnic, and spatial politics of reproduction, such issues emerge with further clarity in the novel's final chapter, "Missis Flinders," which charts Margaret and Miles's journey back to their Village apartment after her abortion.[69] Told solely through Margaret's point of view as the couple ride in a cab throughout Manhattan, the chapter documents both Margaret's growing despair over her relationship to Miles and her exclusion from the hospital's normative models of maternity.[70] The cab ride emphasizes the intellectuals' alienation from urban geography: as they leave the hospital, they go first "past a park; past a museum, past elevated pillars" and then

> past Harlem now; past fire-escapes loaded with flower-pots and flapping clothes; dingy windows opening to the soot-laden air blown in by the elevated roaring down its tracks. Past Harlem and through 125th street: stores and wise-cracks, Painless Dentists, cheap florists; Eighth Avenue, boarded and plastered, concealing the subway that was reaching its laborious birth beneath. But Eighth Avenue was too jouncy for Mr. Strite's precious burden of womanhood (who was reaching passionately for a cigarette); he cut through the park, and they drove past quiet walks on which the sun had brought out babies as the fall rains give birth to worms.[71]

The couple's hasty movement through Harlem—mediated by an ethnic cab driver who might himself wish to escape the derelict connotations of the neighborhood—suggests the alienation of downtown intellectuals from the extreme poverty of Depression-era Harlem. As the couple pass farther downtown into Central Park, they are confronted with reproductive realities that the narrator casts as natural, products of sun and warmth. Occluded from both the world of new mothers and the material world of the working poor, Margaret appears increasingly placeless.[72] As a woman struggling to maintain her middle-class position through the Depression, Margaret recoils from the unvarnished image of urban poverty she encounters in Harlem; similarly, as a representative of childfree bohemia, she is alienated from the mothers and carriages of prosperous central Manhattan.

While Harlem evokes a side of the class struggle from which white leftists are ironically excluded, the couple's return to downtown Manhattan immerses the couple in a world of working-class aspirations and uncontrolled reproduction:

> Down Fourteenth Street they would go, past the stores unlike any stores in the world: packed to the windows with imitation gold and imitation embroidery, with imitation men and women coming to stand in the doorways and beckon with imitation smiles; while in the sidewalks streamed the people unlike any other people in the world, drawn from every country, from every stratum, carrying babies (the real things, with pinched anemic faces) and parcels (imitation finery priced low in the glittering stores). There goes a woman, with a flat fat face, will produce five others just like herself, to dine off one-fifth the inadequate quantity her Mister earns today. These are the people not afraid to perpetuate themselves (forbidden to stop, indeed) and they will go on and on until the bottom of the world is filled with them; and suddenly there will be enough of them to combine their wild-eyed notions and take over the world to suit themselves.[73]

As in *Plum Bun,* Fourteenth Street becomes the author's vision of a working-class, mobile New York that is vibrantly, even frighteningly, alive. Here, Margaret experiences a threatening vision of untrammeled working-class reproduction, a fantasy of immigrant fertility that harbors the possibility of bohemian race suicide, echoed in Ware's discussion of the decline of the white birth rate in the 1920s Village. In contrast to the novel's stifled progressive movement, the real revolution may arrive—as Margaret suggests—with the propagation of working-class white ethnics whose "wild-eyed notions" will push past the intellectuals' stasis. For Slesinger, Fourteenth Street, rather than the Lower East Side, becomes the novel's figure for mass immigration, a Depression-era melting pot whose result is mass consumption ("imitation men and women" with cheap "imitation finery") rather than Americanization. A consolidated class identity, rather than a specifically Jewish ethnic identity, becomes the novel's predominant vehicle for social change.

By the novel's end, Slesinger makes clear that the Village's symbolic power as a haven for the like-minded is fleeting. As Miles and Margaret return to their neighborhood, Margaret imagines her apartment as "a group of rooms unalive as rooms with 'For Rent' still pasted on the windows."[74] As in

Plum Bun, the Village's transiency overwhelms its opportunities for intimacy. Homogeneity is soon to replace the aura produced by the juxtaposition of working-class and middle-class life: as they enter the neighborhood, "they rolled softly past No. 14; on past the tenement which would eventually be razed to give place to modern three-room apartments with In-a-Dor beds; and then slowly, so slowly . . . drew up and slid to a full stop before No. 60, where two people named Mister and Missis Flinders rented themselves a place to hide from life."[75] Both Ware and Dell noted the demolition of Village tenements to make way for high-rise apartment buildings; Slesinger signals the march of gentrification as middle-class anonymity and Jewishness, epitomized in the urban high-rise, would soon replace the odd mix of immigrant traditionalism and bohemian experimentation that had previously characterized Village life.

CONCLUSION

During his climactic speech, Bruno Leonard tells the Black Sheep to "go west, young men, go south, go north—go anywhere out of our God damned city. New York is the precocious head of the adolescent body of America."[76] Bruno invokes the classic American rhetoric of migration as self-renewal, even as he underscores the stagnation of the New York intellectual class. By the conclusion of both *Plum Bun* and *The Unpossessed*, Fauset and Slesinger would also move their characters away from New York's precocity, replacing the youthful enthusiasm both heroines had brought with them to Greenwich Village with a tempered cynicism. Exploring alternate settings for the development of ethnic female subjectivity, they would finally suggest that even the potentially emancipatory setting of utopian spaces such as the Village would enforce their own normative demands. No setting could serve as a panacea for national—even global—problems of class conflict, ethnic and racial subordination, and culturally imposed limitations on women.

Plum Bun and *The Unpossessed* direct our attention to cultural spaces that receive relatively little attention in the canonical fiction of the period. In the works of Abraham Cahan, Anzia Yezierska, Langston Hughes, and Nella Larsen, for example, the Lower East Side and Harlem became paradigmatic sites in which ethnic and racial identities could be forged. As scholars built the field of ethnic literature in the 1960s and 1970s, these spaces would become tropes, carrying their own embedded set of assumptions. Typically, these assumptions were classed as well as gendered, privileging the theme and representation of urban poverty and casting working-class men, from Abraham Cahan's Jake to Richard Wright's Bigger, as the exemplary heroes of ethnic American literature. Writers like Fauset and Slesinger—feminist critics of place and culture, subtle analysts of classed behavior and mores, and literary artists—identified new spaces, new class positions, and new artistic and intellectual affiliations for the ethnic heroine.

Just as Fauset's ambivalence about Harlem and Slesinger's indifference to the Lower East Side helped occlude them from the canon, spatial marginality can push texts off the critical map. In the mid-twentieth century, as the Jewish immigrant diaspora spread across the United States and Harlem struggled to move past the Depression and wartime poverty, ethnic women writers would continue to demarcate new spaces for identity formation. For example, although Ann Petry is best-known today for her bestselling novel of Harlem life, *The Street* (1946), her powerful final novel *The Narrows* (1953) is set in a small Connecticut city reminiscent of Bridgeport; *Wasteland* (1946), by Jewish American writer Jo Sinclair, charts a Jewish family's diaspora beginning in the Pale of Settlement, continuing through New York and Argentina, and coming to an endpoint in Cleveland, Ohio. The spatial metaphors of both titles are telling: Petry widens her perspective in her capacious last novel, showing how problems of race, class, gender, ethnicity, and immigration in exurbs and suburbs can be dismissed by critics with their own limitations of perspective; the "wasteland" of Sinclair's title is not a culturally arid Midwest but a stifled household that has never made good on the promise of American ideals. These second or third cities of ethnic American fiction remind us that ethnic identities are forged in settings far beyond those viewed as paradigmatic by scholars; just as Fauset and Slesinger destabilize the archetypes of ethnic identity in New York, Petry and Sinclair expand our horizons to the North and West. Such relatively understudied works offer excellent opportunities for critics interested in suburbanization, ethnicity, race, gender, and sexuality in the postwar period, but both works have remained exiled to critical suburbia. Readers of ethnic fiction should question the tendency to celebrate any space, whether city, countryside, or suburb, for as the fiction of Fauset and Slesinger reminds us, productive settings for self-exploration emerge in places surprisingly far from "home."

NOTES

1. See for example, Theodore Dreiser, *Sister Carrie* (New York: Library of America, 1987); Edith Wharton, *The House of Mirth* (New York: Scribners, 1905) and *The Custom of the Country* (New York: Scribners, 1913); and Nella Larsen, *Quicksand* (New York: Knopf, 1928).

2. Yi-Fu Tuan, *Topophilia: A Study of Environmental Perception, Attitudes, and Values* (Englewood Cliffs, NJ: Prentice-Hall, 1974), 6.

3. Yi-Fu Tuan, *Space and Place: The Perspective of Experience* (Minneapolis: University of Minnesota Press, 1977), 6.

4. Caroline Ware, *Greenwich Village, 1920–1930: A Commentary on American Culture in the Post-War Years* (Boston: Houghton and Mifflin, 1935), 81.

5. Christine Stansell, *American Moderns: Bohemian New York and the Creation of a New Century* (New York: Henry Holt, 2000), 16, 22–25.

6. Ibid., 25.

7. Larsen, *Quicksand* (New Brunswick: Rutgers University Press, 1986), 60.

8. Ibid.

9. Robert Bone, *The Negro Novel in America* (New Haven: Yale University Press, 1965), 120.

10. Addison Gayle's reading of *Plum Bun* is thus striking. Gayle argues that Fauset's heroine moves to Harlem and "surrenders her identity as a white woman," ignoring the conclusion of the novel (Addison Gayle, *The Way of the World: The Black Novel in America* [New York: Doubleday, 1975], 121). Gayle's omission recasts the novel as a celebration of Harlem rather than an exploration of its potential.

11. See Harrison-Kahan and Ammons, who read this work as part of Fauset's critique of whiteness. Lori Harrison-Kahan, "No Slaves to Fashion: Designing Women in the Fiction of Jessie Fauset and Anzia Yezierska," in *Styling Texts: Dress in Fashion and Literature*, ed. Cynthia Kuhn and Cindy Carlson (Youngstown, OH: Cambria Press [2007]); Elizabeth Ammons, "Black Anxiety about Immigration and Jessie Fauset's *The Sleeper Wakes*," *African American Review* 42 (2008): 461–476.

12. Jessie Fauset, "The Sleeper Wakes," in *The Sleeper Wakes: Harlem Renaissance Stories by Women*, ed. Marcy Knopf (New Brunswick: Rutgers University Press, 1993), 9.

13. Ibid., 6.

14. Although the echo of "Zora Neale Hurston" is intriguing, Hurston did not arrive in New York until 1925.

15. Fauset, "The Sleeper Wakes," 6.

16. Ibid., 8.

17. Ibid., 7–8.

18. However, Fauset did not fully eschew the possibilities for genuine progressivism in the Village. In *There Is Confusion*, Fauset locates African American working-class childhood in the heart of Greenwich Village, racializing the immigrant-Anglo encounter of "The Sleeper Wakes." Jessie Fauset, *There Is Confusion* (reprint, Boston: Northeastern University Press, 1989).

19. Fauset, "The Sleeper Wakes," 24.

20. Ibid., 24–25.

21. Jessie Fauset, *Plum Bun* (reprint, Boston: Beacon Press, 1990), 11.

22. Ibid.

23. Ibid., 12.

24. Ibid., 96.

25. Ibid., 90–92.

26. Ibid., 96.

27. Ibid., 97.

28. Ibid.

29. Ibid., 98.

30. Ibid., 96.

31. Ibid., 98.

32. Ibid.

33. Ibid., 326.

34. Tuan, *Topophilia*, 275.

35. Fauset, *Plum Bun*, 120.

36. Bachélard, *The Poetics of Space*, trans. Maria Jolas (New York: Beacon Press, 1994), 137.

37. Floyd Dell, *Love in Greenwich Village* (New York: George H. Doran, 1926), 15; Nina Miller, *Making Love Modern: The Intimate Public Worlds of New York's Literary Women* (New York: Oxford University Press, 1999), 19.

38. For a lively history of this type, see Betsy Israel, *Bachelor Girl: The Secret History of Single Women in the Twentieth Century* (New York: William Morrow, 2002).

39. Fauset, *Plum Bun*, 12.

40. Ibid., 103–104.

41. Ibid.

42. Ware, *Greenwich Village*, 33.

43. Fauset, *Plum Bun*, 112.

44. Ibid., 113.

45. Ibid., 67.

46. Ibid., 113.

47. Ware, *Greenwich Village*, 247.

48. Ibid., 245.

49. Fauset, *Plum Bun*, 156.

50. Ibid., 220.

51. Ware, *Greenwich Village*, 259.

52. Fauset, *Plum Bun*, 268.

53. Ibid., 270.

54. Tess Slesinger, *The Unpossessed*, ed. Janet Sharistanian (New York: Feminist Press, 1984), 127.

55. Ware, *Greenwich Village*, 256.

56. Slesinger, *The Unpossessed*, 38.

57. Ibid., 6.

58. Ware, *Greenwich Village*, 38.

59. Dell, *Love in Greenwich Village* (New York: George H. Doran, 1926), 305.

60. Slesinger, *The Unpossessed*, 8.

61. Ibid., 4.

62. Ibid., 343.

63. Ibid., 273.

64. Ibid., 172.

65. Ibid., 176.

66. Margaret fails to see the similarities between Italian and white women in the areas of both romance and reproduction. The young Italian American women Ware studied were affected by the rise of consumer culture and the decline of the patriarchal family, expressing their desires for self-determined relationships. The larger cultural drive toward smaller families affected Italian American Villagers as it did whites; despite religious prohibitions and the denial of male responsibility for pregnancy, Italian women reported secretly acquiring contraception from Italian midwives, some of whom also performed abortions (Ware, *Greenwich Village*, 278).

67. Michael Gold, *Jews Without Money* (New York: Carroll and Graff, 2004), 14.

68. Michael Rogin, *Blackface/White Noise: Jewish Immigrants in the Hollywood Melting Pot* (Berkeley: University of California Press, 1996).

69. "Missis Flinders" was first published independently in *Story Magazine*, after, as the editors of the magazine reported, it had been "rejected all over America" (Slesinger, *The Unpossessed*, "Afterword," 385).

70. Although one character has a stillbirth, Margaret nonetheless marks even her doomed maternity as a sacrificial ideal: as the other mothers think to themselves, "wasn't Missis Butter their symbol and their pride, the one who had given up their baby that they might have theirs . . ." (Ibid., 344).

71. Ibid., 346.

72. For comparison, see Viña Delmar's bestseller *Bad Girl* (New York: Harcourt Brace, 1928), whose white protagonist also gives birth in a maternity hospital on the edge of Harlem. Delmar links blackness to sexuality and reproduction, as the blues waft through the window during the heroine's labor.

73. Slesinger, *The Unpossessed*, 354.

74. Ibid., 355.

75. Ibid.

76. Ibid., 330.

FOUR

CITY PLACE/COUNTRY PLACE

Negotiating Class Geographies in Ann Petry's Writing

Cherene Sherrard-Johnson

Ann Petry (1908–1997) is most often thought of as a "neighborhood novelist":[1] however, the Harlem personified in her most famous novel, *The Street* (1946), is a far cry from her insular New England hometown of Old Saybrook, Connecticut. In fact, Petry actively cultivates urban/rural dichotomies as a defining tension in her writing by linking seemingly oppositional settings. In particular, I focus on how Petry's fiction maps Harlem through the mirror of New England. Essentially, Petry imports New England, rendered as a set of class-based, gender-qualified racial ideals, into Harlem. Regionally specific understandings of respectability, ladyhood, and aesthetics profoundly inform how she shapes intimate and public space in *The Street*. As a result, it is impossible to comprehend the Harlem inhabited by Lutie Johnson, the protagonist of *The Street*, without some recognition of its putative opposite: the New England "country place," depicted in her relatively understudied novel *Country Place* (1947). I argue that the conversations and juxtapositions that occur between her presumably oppositional representations of black womanhood as "street women" and "parlor ladies" in their respective environments subvert the seemingly deterministic plot trajectory of Petry's narratives. Identifying these specific ruptures in Petry's literary universe through intertextual readings can point us toward alternative, less binary conceptualizations of black womanhood. In Petry's oeuvre, black womanhood and female subjectivity are not only profoundly shaped but also intricately fractured by spatial crossovers that occur within and without Harlem's iconic cityscape.

Taking a spatially informed, ethnographic approach to her fiction allows Petry to transgress that fine line between what her interviewer Mark Wilson calls "the prim and the primitive."[2] Her flexibility with regard to genre is one manifestation of her ability to challenge this dichotomy. Petry is as comfortable crafting literary fiction that incorporates the ethnographic novel of manners as she is writing pulp fiction. The markers of urban and rural geography often coexist in her fiction regardless of setting, and the ease with which she slipped into multiple narrative forms allowed her to defy the constraints of genre and fictional categories over the course of her writing career. Her spatially sensitive understanding of class stratification and how race complicates African Americans' ability to cross and/or maintain middle- or upper-class status is partially a result of her New England upbringing.

Petry's father was a pharmacist who ran Lane's Pharmacy in Old Saybrook, Connecticut, with her aunt.[3] Her New England background and writing interests mirror those of Dorothy West, whose novel *The Living is Easy* (1948), published two years after *The Street*, also takes on the intersections of class, race, and gender in a way that foregrounds space, specifically Boston and South Carolina, as informative locales. I read Petry's *The Street*, *Country Place*, and select Harlem stories intertextually and interspatially to show how location informs multiple aspects of identity construction across and along the color line. The oppositional pairings of people and locations that appear in Petry's fiction partially derive from her own movement from Connecticut to Harlem: an individual migratory act amplified by the paths taken by various constituencies of African Americans to New York during the Great Migration.

NEITHER HILL NOR HOLLOW

Significantly, Ann Petry's first introduction to Harlem print culture marks her journey from Connecticut to Harlem in an 1936 article appearing in the *Amsterdam News* entitled "Connecticut Druggist Likes Shows, So She Comes Here."[4] The headline underscores Petry's regional origin, her occupational and educational status as a pharmacist, and most importantly: her desire for, and the necessity to travel to access, Harlem's unique cultural benefits. A lovely, glamorous photograph of Petry's profile establishes her as a provisional Harlemite and documents her interest in the neighborhood's performance culture. In 1938, her marriage to George Petry led her move to New York where the newlyweds settled into an apartment on 125th Street in Harlem. There she encountered many people whom she used as models for her fictional characters. Wilson, in his interview with the author, inquired, "Do you think your writing career would have developed in the same way if you had stayed in Saybrook?" to which Petry replied, "The kind of experience I had in New York in terms of work I never could have had here in Saybrook."[5] She would use her experiences in Harlem to write her best-selling and critically acclaimed novel *The Street*, and the geography of her childhood would animate her short fiction and later novels.

In 1949, Ann Petry wrote a lengthy photo essay entitled "Harlem" for *Holiday* magazine. "Harlem" was one of the many neighborhood portraits in the April issue devoted to the city of New York. It appears alongside treatments of the "Bowery" and the "Upper West Side." Petry's contribution is a study in visual and textual dualism. In this nonfiction photo essay of Harlem she demonstrates a narrative technique she would deploy successfully and continually in her novels and short stories such as "Mother Africa." Her portrait of Harlem is essentially a tale of two Harlems. For those unfamiliar with the cultural geography, she seeks to overturn misconceptions of Harlem as a ghetto without sugar-coating the real challenges of its working-class and impoverished residents. Her first images present the affluent side of Harlem: those well-to-do residents whose "lives refute the picture of Harlem as a poverty stricken community."[6] She includes photos of a sweet sixteen party, of a society lady being helped into a fur coat by her husband, fashion show templates, and shots of famous residents such as Adam Clayton Powell Jr. and his wife Hazel Scott to emphasize that while "there is no inherited wealth on the Hill," "[t]he leisure class is composed of the wives of successful doctors, lawyers, dentists, real-estate operators and businessmen." Juxtaposed against such images of respectability and leisure are graphic photographs of a mother holding a child who has been attacked by a rat in a public housing apartment and a police snapshot of a murder victim.

Throughout the essay, the dual nature of Harlem life is expressed through her opposing observations: "Not all Harlemites spend their time carving each other with knife and razor. Sometimes they carve out a financial empire instead"; or "But Harlem is not all Hill and wealth and empire. It is also the ugly elements and the scarred, evil-smelling rooms in the Hollow."[7] Constant shifts between prosperity and destitution mark the journey through Harlem. Poetry from Langston Hughes, strategically placed inside the text of the article, amplifies the dualistic structure of the piece: his poem "College Formal" depicts the high life sought by a young, fashionable, educated couple on a "magic" "melody night in Harlem town," while his "Ballad of the Landlord" presents a doomed protest against the deleterious practices of slumlords. "Ballad" provides a bluesy echo of Petry's critique of the overcrowded, "vermin-ridden" rooms in the dilapidated brownstones of the Hollow. As the study in opposition draws to a close, Petry attempts a synthesis by offering a cosmopolitan glimpse of the City Market as a place "under the bridge" where Harlem transforms into Spain, the Caribbean, and Italy, where residents whose ethnic and cultural locations put them at odds trade insults and commodities that reflect the global marketplace. Out of this hodge-podge, Petry introduces George Jackson, a man who is neither Hill nor Hollow, but a combination of both. He has an apartment, but takes in roomers: he attends church and his dissatisfaction with his environs motivate him to become "one of Manhattan's most sophisticated voters, crossing and re-crossing party lines, voting for issues and men, ignoring party labels."[8] In Petry's Harlem, the relationship between class position and political desire can be murky. Jackson embodies Petry's expansive understanding of the black community as one that is in constant flux and cannot be defined by clear class divisions. In fact, her representation of Jackson reflects her novelistic characterizations of men and women caught in between opposing forces and competing values.

The same narrative techniques of contrast and the subsequent destabilization of fixed notions of the black community as a stable coherent entity that Petry deploys in her nonfiction analysis of "Harlem" manifest in her fiction. Like Petry's nonfictional portrait of George Jackson, *The Street*'s protagonist Lutie Johnson is also "neither hill nor hollow," but her class aspirations cause her to invest in a Franklinian narrative of success that is instrumental in her downfall. Petry's personification of Harlem in her article recalls the agency she ascribes to the Harlem streets in the novel. The slippery, dual nature of the Harlem to which Lutie relocates following her estrangement from her husband is deceptive. She is drawn to the apartment by an advertisement that promises "respectable tenants" and "reasonable" rent. Lutie rightly observes: "Reasonable—now that could mean almost anything. On eighth it meant tenements—ghastly places not fit for humans. On St. Nicholas Avenue it meant high rents for small apartments; and on Seventh Avenue it meant great big apartments where you had to take in roomers in order to pay the rent. On this street it could mean almost anything."[9] How is one supposed to negotiate the geography of class in an environment that so easily shifts from the inhuman to the tolerable? "Reasonable," the "it" whose various meanings Lutie contemplates, includes the myriad possibilities contained within Harlem. Petry identifies potential outcomes and situations commensurate with the "thousand varied faces" of Harlem in her photo essay when she writes: "The truth is Harlem is as varied and as full of ambivalences as Manhattan itself."[10]

LOCATING DOMESTIC SPACE IN *THE STREET*

In *The Street,* Petry skillfully personifies 116th until it becomes a living, breathing entity that seems to lead its denizens into deterministic downfalls.

The plot follows the destruction of Lutie Johnson, a single mother whose travails result from her ill-fated decision to rent an apartment on 116th Street in Harlem after the dissolution of her marriage. The tragic outcome of the novel seems preordained from the moment the "cold fingers of the wind" blowing down the street "touched the back of [Lutie's] neck."[11] In addition to its stark realism, *The Street* is also informed by Gothic images that invoke a sinister mood of inevitability to which the lovely protagonist and her son seem oblivious.[12] From its publication, Petry's incorporation of realist and naturalist elements in *The Street* prompted comparisons with Richard Wright's *Native Son* (1940). Although Petry would write several more novels, most scholars have disproportionately examined *The Street*, overlooking her forays into pulp fiction, the historical novel, and children's literature.

Recent critics, however, have questioned analyses that privilege Petry's unqualified determinism by suggesting that Lutie is more than a cornered victim of socioeconomic factors beyond her control; instead, Lutie asserts her own agency by making a series of bad decisions that readers often overlook. For Candice Jenkins, Lutie's single-minded adherence to a flawed notion of respectability fuels what Jenkins terms a "salvific wish" that results in "Lutie's deliberate endangerment of herself and her son."[13] Jenkins suggests that Lutie's class aspirations motivate her irrational decision to leave her father's seven-room apartment, which she perceives as an illicit space because it was "full of Lil" her father's girlfriend, whose unrestrained, unmediated sexuality threatens Lutie. Her "literal and figurative proximity to Lil" fuels her desperate decision to find a separate living space where the supposed distinctions between their positions in the social and racial hierarchy of the novel can be more firmly demarcated. In other words, Lutie's desperate investment in the kind of respectability valued in the "country place"—one that her race makes inaccessible—and the nineteenth-century concept of constrained, idealized black womanhood that has long inhabited the discourse around respectability work together to facilitate her downfall.

An advertisement Lutie sees on a train of a young blond girl posing in a kitchen both triggers and frames the flashback scenes of her experiences working in a Connecticut country house:

> It was, she thought, a miracle of a kitchen. Completely different from the kitchen of the 116th Street apartment she had moved into just two weeks ago. But almost exactly like the one she worked in in Connecticut.

At the end of her extended reverie she reflects: "That kitchen in Connecticut had changed her whole life."[14] This flashback is one of many examples where Petry smuggles in "New England" through a fracture in the cityscape. In this case, Lutie interprets an image designed to provoke desire within consumers as an inaccessible ideal: "a miracle" that is the opposite of the domestic space she now occupies. Yet, the image is also a simulacrum, in that it is "exactly like" the kitchen in which she labored in Connecticut. That Lutie positions an intimate, interracial domestic space as the site of the cataclysmic implosion of her personal life, rather than the presumably overwhelming force of the Harlem ghetto, emphasizes the impact of those train rides to and from Connecticut. The decision to "work out" of the home, mother another woman's child, and leave her own husband to fend for himself and their two-year-old has disastrous results. Moreover, Lutie's uncritical internalization of the class-based white privilege demonstrated in the Connecticut country home compounds her already fragile domestic situation.

If the advertisement is the mnemonic trigger that allows the narrative intercourse between the city place and the country place in *The Street,* the train upon which Lutie views the image is the literal mode of transportation from Harlem to Connecticut. Later in the novel, a train provides her escape route out of Harlem after she has killed Boots in self-defense. In African American literature and culture, the train has multiple significations. It represents literal and metaphorical mobility, serving alternatively as a conduit out of the South with its legacies of racial violence and economic depression and providing an ambivalent economic opportunity for class advancement by employing black men as Pullman porters.[15] In *The Street,* all of these various iterations are at play when Lutie boards the train to Connecticut that precipitates the end of her marriage. She also returns to the train at the close of the novel when she buys a one-way ticket to Chicago, thinking pessimistically: "I've had one since the day I was born." As the train "roared into the darkness," Lutie wonders "by what twists and turns of fate she had landed on this train."[16] Yet, even though Petry posits the personified urban geography—the street and the train—as the causative agents for Lutie's demise, her own judgment, informed by false notions of respectability and her misunderstanding of how deeply capitalism is welded to white privilege, also affects the novel's outcomes, which perhaps are not as inevitable as the environmentally deterministic setting suggests.

In *The Street,* the pastoral geography of Lyme, Connecticut, jars violently with the tight three rooms that comprise Lutie's apartment in Harlem. The "kitchen that changed her life" haunts her even after she has left it. Working for the Chandlers afforded her a glimpse "through a hole in a wall at some enchanted garden." As she travels from her train to the house in Connecticut for her interview Lutie wonders "if the Chandlers lived in a forest." Although her employers' abode is figured as a natural, magical, insulated retreat light years away from the concrete jungle of Harlem, Lutie quickly detects that the expansive rooms and sparkling décor hide an internal rot. Yet the discovery that Mrs. Chandler is a poor mother and Mr. Chandler is an alcoholic does not destroy the façade of privilege that whiteness and wealth can provide:

> After Mr. Chandler's brother killed himself in the living room, she didn't lose her belief in the desirability of having money, though she saw that mere possession of it wouldn't necessarily guarantee happiness. What was more important, she learned that when one had money there were certain unpleasant things one could avoid—even things like a suicide in the family.

Lutie is not impressed by the family's detached response to the suicide, but she does observe how quietly they hushed up what they saw as a shameful act until it became an "accident with a gun."[17] Rather than an instructive moment about the inability to ensure happiness through material acquisition, Lutie reads this incident as an example of the power of economics to shape the truth, even though she knows the Chandler home is a dysfunctional space.

New England sensibilities imbibed from her experience working in Lyme cause Lutie to misjudge the situation in her father's house. As a result, she reads Lil, her father's girlfriend, the way her employers view her: outside the accepted parameters of respectability. She bases her judgment on the same spurious, racial stereotyping that Mrs. Chandler's friends apply to Lutie. Despite the fact that her father's girlfriend is "home all day" and therefore available to look after Lutie's son Bub after school, she fears the "education he will get from her father's blowsy girlfriend" apparently more than she fears the possibility of her unsupervised son engaging in criminal activity (19). Candice Jenkins's analysis, which makes a similar argument about Lutie's faulty decision-making processes, also points to literary critics' avoidance of Lil as a critical factor that forces Lutie to flee out of the proverbial frying pan. Critics, according to Jenkins, do not question Lil's disreputability due to their own class bias. However, I believe that it is Petry's careful transposition of the values of the country place into the city place that submerges and even subtly disguises, the complex reasoning that prompts her decision to take the 116th apartment.[18]

Ironically, moving into the 116th street apartment also places Lutie in comparison to another woman with questionable status: Min, the Super's girlfriend. In the Super's lustful mind, the "swish-swish" of Min's house shoes competes with the clicking of "Lutie's high-heeled shoes."[19] Petry draws on imagery integral to Claude McKay's famous 1922 poem "Harlem

Shadows" to heighten the contrast; this incorporation is in concert with her willingness to integrate Langston Hughes's poetry within her *Holiday* essay on Harlem. The most resonant image of McKay's poem—the title poem of his collection and its haunting invocation of Harlem as a threatening place for women—is of feet, specifically "slippered feet." Lutie's high heels convey her ultra-femininity, her value of fashion over comfort, and her visibility as an object of appeal on the public streets of Harlem; by contrast, Min's slippers circumscribe her wholly within the confines of apartment building. Like the Super, the narrator of "Harlem Shadows" is haunted by:

> the halting footsteps of a lass
> In Negro Harlem when the night lets fall
> Its veil. I see the shapes of girls who pass
> Eager to heed desire's insistent call:
> Ah, little dark girls, who in slippered feet
> Go prowling through the night from street to street.

The symbolic language of McKay's refrain, the "wandering" "weary feet" of "dusky half-clad girls," finds its way into Petry's juxtaposition of Lutie and Min and her exploration of how women negotiate the shadowy streets of Harlem.[20] More than simply overdetermining Lutie's victim status, Petry's explicit and implicit references to the two most famous poets of the Harlem Renaissance in her fictional and nonfiction portraits of Harlem productively invoke the friction between the glittering world of New Negro Renaissance that was and the sobering reality of Harlem in the aftermath of the Depression.

One of the striking qualities of the novel is Petry's ability to show that despite the promotion of Harlem as a cosmopolitan black mecca in the preceding decades, it is really a neighborhood with small town sensibilities. The characters that live on 116th street engage in petty power plays of rumor and conjecture. As such, they scrutinize every aspect of Lutie's life, creating a claustrophobic atmosphere that is present indoors and outdoors. The small town attributes of Harlem, while promoting its coherency as a distinct space, foreclose its potential as cosmopolitan or self-actualizing space. Lutie's class anxieties reflect concerns about residential segregation that forced middle-class blacks to live in close proximity to impoverished families. From a geographical perspective, Petry's depiction of interiors and exteriors, private and public spaces, maps the world her characters inhabit and influence, though it does not entirely circumscribe, their actions. Harlem, as "neither hill nor hollow," remains an ambiguous space, where the possibility of cultural cosmopolitanism and the economic advancement Lutie hopes for vies with geographic constriction and fragile distinctions between a tight-knit community and socioeconomic prison.

FRACTURING CLASS BOUNDARIES IN *COUNTRY PLACE*

At the same moment Petry was writing *The Street*, she was also experimenting with a new genre, crafting another novel in which the spatial dimensions of class and color are, on the surface, dramatically different from the Harlem milieu. *Country Place* incorporates elements drawn from popular, mass market fiction to create a compelling novel that draws its readers along Main Street, geographically miles away from 116th, but conceptually just on the other side of the mirror. Despite its title, *Country Place* also unfolds in a harsh landscape; much of the story takes place during a hurricane, which actually swept through New England in 1938 leaving a devastated community in its wake. In "Pulping Country Place" Paula Rabinowitz writes that Petry "marr[ies] "the environmental destruction of the weather to the social and psychological upheavals of WWII."[21] Ironically, at one point the narrator comments disdainfully on romance novels and detective stories even as he tells a story about a love triangle of betrayal, sex and violence. *Country Place* centers on the story of a World War II vet's homecoming to his unfaithful wife from the perspective of the village druggist; several subplots reveal historic class divisions and how they have circumscribed the inhabitants of the suffocating town. It is part World War II homecoming narrative, part film noir.[22]

To my mind what makes *Country Place* a compelling novel to juxtapose with *The Street* is not its distance from Harlem or putative racelessness. Instead, it is useful to consider how race operates in the presumably oppositional locales represented by the shorthand of "country" and "city or "rural" and "urban." Until recently, critics privileged *The Street* as a naturalist masterpiece based primarily on comparisons to Richard Wright and incorrectly positioned *Country Place* as a failed experiment at so-called "raceless" writing. [23] The inside flap of the first edition of *Country Place* promotes the idea that it is a colorblind novel: "Country Place is as profoundly moving and disturbing as *The Street*, although the tragic problems of race and colour have no place in it, and its outwardly peaceful setting is seemingly far removed from the violence and cruelty of Harlem."[24] My reconsideration is part of a concerted effort to rectify *Country Place* and Petry's other "truant" novels' excision from the African American canon by showing that, as Emily Bernard argues, "race does move meaningfully in [*Country Place*]."[25] Rather than an experiment in raceless writing, Petry consciously attempts, not always successfully, to write against the presumed universality of white-authored fiction. Petry slyly imbues the ostensibly white town of Lennox with ethnic markers that disrupt both its putative racelessness and stereotypical New England liberality. Moreover, as in *The Street*, female pairings in *Country Place* draw attention to the subtleties of class division in a community that is regionally, but not ethnically, secluded.

Though the novel is devoid of an actualized African American community what Toni Morrison calls the Africanist presence is present throughout the narrative.[26] In order to establish a falsely universalist (presumably white male) perspective, Petry tells her reader that the narrator is "a bachelor" with "a prejudice against women" who is "medium tall, medium fat, medium old [65] . . . and medium bald."[27] She does not offer a description of skin color, but lets the reader determine this on the basis on his or her presumptions of narrative authority. Petry uses the popular genre of World War II veterans' homecoming stories and a fascinatingly unreliable narrator to challenge race-based categorization of fiction, anticipating Toni Morrison's experimental attempts to expose and free up "racially inflected language" in works such as "Recitatif" and *Paradise*.[28]

In *Country Place*, the most sympathetic characters are those who belong to minority groups: Jewish, Irish, and Portuguese immigrants and a lone African American woman. Petry modeled these characters after the friends and neighbors she knew growing up in Old Saybrook. She acutely perceived the liminal, incompatibility of her position as "black yankee." Despite their class status as highly educated business owners "the Lanes of Old Saybrook" were the friends of "servants . . . not of the aristocrats themselves"[29] Over the course of her life, Petry became more skeptical of the idea that the African American New Englander was somehow separate or particular. She was convinced that whites could not see past the visible markers of racial difference to understand class affinities. As such, in *Country Place*, she portrays white New England culture as either decaying and isolationist, like Mrs. Gramby, who is trapped in her house with an infertile daughter-in-law, or, like the unchivalrous "Weasel," as having degenerated as a result of the loose morals and violent behavior of the working-class whites. By exposing unsavory secrets hidden beneath the veneer of New England respectability, she reiterates the dangers of imbibing the values of the white upper class.

In *Country Place*'s fictional town of Lennox (which accurately maps Petry's hometown) the everyday pettiness and class battles seem to conjure the unnatural storm that uproots everything in its path. Similarly, the inexorable pull of *The Street* is able to work its mischief on Lutie because she has absorbed the wrong values from her time in New England. My comparative close reading of Lutie's experiences in "that kitchen in Connecticut" with Neola's experience working as a domestic in a grand house in Lennox works against deterministic readings that presume urban black space is always already inherently destructive (and that country place is a viable escape) while acknowledging Petry's use of traditionally naturalist representations of the influence of environment on one's fate. Petry's New England sense of small town culture informs how she portrays Harlem as an intraracial microcosm in *The Street*. Conversely, her urban experiences in Harlem enable her to imagine a town rife with adultery, betrayal, petty gossip, and an ossified understanding of class beneath the picturesque New England facade.

Considering these two novels, which Petry most likely wrote simultaneously—as some sections of *Country Place* actually precede *The Street*'s publication—as mirrored texts reveals how the idea of a "country house" as an escape from the perils of urban life is a false ideal that haunts Lutie and informs her ill-fated decision to rent an apartment on 116th Street in the hopes of having a private place of her own.[30] Petry amplifies the mirroring effect of her novels through her homonymic pairing of character names and places. For instance, *Country Place* takes place in Lennox, Connecticut, which invokes Lenox Avenue in Harlem. Both novels also feature sexually compromised, promiscuous characters named "Lil." Over the course of *The Street*, the supposedly disreputable Lil appears less threatening, more nurturing, and more personally fulfilled than Lutie. On the other hand, the behavior of the white "Lil" of *Country Place* replicates racialized pathology normally ascribed to black women. Both representations disrupt conventional, racialized understandings of respectability. While there are multiple pairings in each novel, I am particularly intrigued by how each portrays the figure of the black domestic worker and an intimate, domestic space—the kitchen—within the broader spatial dynamics of the novel. Their participation in, or disruption of, rituals of respectability call into question the claims of power and prestige such rituals are meant to enforce. In African American women's writing black domestic workers often provide implicit critiques of their white female employers by enacting a "genteel performance" that establishes them as the true barometer against which ladyhood should be evaluated.[31]

Petry uses a similar strategy of comparison when she portrays Neola in *Country Place* and Lutie Johnson in *The Street* as ideal domestics deeply invested in appropriate behavior almost to the exclusion of their own safety. Just as the nineteenth-century African American modiste Elizabeth Keckley was vilified for having the cheek to presume to air the First Lady's dirty laundry, Lutie is not rewarded for her exemplary performance. Despite her attempts to present herself as a legitimate wife and mother with "a husband of her own," the friends and family of the Chandlers consistently label her with the pathology of promiscuity and sexual availability they attribute to all black women. Lutie reflects:

> Here she was highly respectable, married, mother of a small boy, and, in spite of all that, knowing all that, these people took one look at her and immediately got that now-I-wonder look. Apparently, it was

> an automatic reaction of white people—if a girl was colored and fairly young, why, it stood to reason she had to be a prostitute.[32]

Lutie is part of the structure that upholds their intimate family life, yet her labor is largely invisible, even if her body, which they view as sexually available, remains highly visible. In this way, Petry anticipates arguments about the invisibility of domestic labor in works such as Barbara Ehrenreich's *Nickel and Dimed* (2001).[33]

In *Country Place* the reader understands Neola's place in the household through the racialized perspectives of the white characters to whom she serves tea. Despite *Country Place*'s promotion and critical reception as a raceless novel, Petry forces readers to consistently view Neola, the Irish cook, and a gardener named Portulucca, who is referred to in the novel as "the Portegee," through a racialized telescope. Glory, the protagonist's wife, remarks: "If Neola was white and didn't have that dead-pan expression on her face, she wouldn't be bad-looking."[34] Mrs. Gramby's dependence on Neola extends beyond the mundane tasks she performs. She literally and figuratively illuminates the dark rooms of the house. Mrs. Gramby observes that the "room is empty without her," and sadly reflects that the one thing Neola cannot get her is "peace of mind and a quiet heart." Although race and class markers are used to distinguish the servants from the white inhabitants of the Gramby house, the servants' response (or lack of response) to Lillian (Mrs. Gramby's daughter-in-law) and her daughter Glory also mark them as interlopers who do not belong. Indeed, Glory views Neola's presence in the house "as inhibiting as Mrs. Gramby's." Although Neola is a minor character, I claim that Petry positions her as a moral compass against which the other women in the novel are judged; two critical scenes indicate that Neola contains a complex interiority that belies her position at the margins of the story. First, the act of serving tea illustrates Neola's moral elevation in the intersecting hierarchies of Lennox society even as the reader views her from the racialized perspectives of the white women she serves. Later, Petry's treatment of Neola's romance with the gardener Portulucca goes against the grain of domestic fiction that marginalizes black female characters as asexual foils for white heroines.

Like Lutie, Neola bears assaults on her character in silence; however, in contrast to Lutie, through the performance of the genteel ritual of tea pouring, Neola is able to both take on the authority of her employer and convey her contempt for Glory and her mother with the practiced discipline required by the genteel performance:

> Neola said, "Mrs. Gramby ordered tea for you." Her voice was matter-of-fact, her face expressionless. She put the tray down on a low table in front of the fireplace.

> Lil said, "Neola's getting a divorce." Her voice was smooth, silky.
>
> "Really, Neola?" Glory said. This led somewhere, but she didn't know exactly where.
>
> "That's right," Neola said. She was going out of the room. She was ignoring them.
>
> "Who ever heard of a nigger divorce?" her mother said softly.
>
> Neola stopped in the doorway, turned around slowly and stared at Lil, at Glory. Her face was expressionless, but her eyes blazed with contempt. She went out of the room without saying anything.[35]

This scene demonstrates a persistent tension in Petry's work: the conflict between the symbolic value of good manners, epitomized by the act and ritualization of tea pouring, and the acknowledgment that such class-based performances often hide deep antipathy. In a later scene, Mrs. Gramby models good manners for Neola: "When Neola brought the tea, Mrs. Gramby poured a cup for Lillian, and one for herself. She sipped the tea, thinking, This is proof of the great advance of our civilization, this pouring tea for a woman I despise, a woman I hate, when what I want to do is turn her out of the house."[36] Yet Petry also shows that adhering blindly to this kind of genteel behavior can be dangerous. Lillian is a gold digger who desires Mrs. Gramby's death; she will later use Mrs. Gramby's ritual love for sweets to send her into a diabetic coma.

Petry places a high value on afternoon tea as a ritual of gendered gentility; the accoutrements featured in *Country Place* also materialize in her autobiographical short fiction. The china set that appears in "Has Anybody Seen Miss Dora Dean?" symbolizes the importance that Petry ascribes to the accoutrements of the genteel performance. In "Dora Dean," a chocolate set that "could easily have belonged to one of the kings of France" is bequeathed to the narrator by a family friend: "It was of the very old, soft-paste type of porcelain. It had been made in the Sevres factory and it was exquisitely decorated in the lovely color known as rose pompadour."[37] This aristocratic artifact belonged to a woman who, like several of Petry's characters, straddled respectability and recklessness. The narrator repeatedly describes Sarah Trumbull as resembling a chorine from "The Creole Show" with a love for ragtime, dancing, and gaiety that "scandalized the religious black folk of Bridgeport." In fact, the title of the story references "Dora Dean"—a song and performer from one of the first African American burlesque shows featuring "a chorus of sixteen beautiful brown girls."[38] *Miss Muriel and Other Stories* includes several short stories that make use of Petry's favorite settings: Harlem and her hometown of Old Saybrook. Many of the characters in the stories are modeled on her family members. The incorporation of afternoon tea has a particular resonance as Petry has a passion for the ritual:

> She took tea every afternoon between three and four o'clock, and [Petry's daughter] joined her whenever [she] was at the house. Unless we had company we just drank tea and ate crackers and cheese, but regardless of who was present she served the tea in delicate porcelain, selecting the pattern according to her mood. One of my friends was afraid to touch the china and exclaimed after a visit, "I could see through the cup!"

Petry's daughter, Elisabeth, not only remembers the Sevres' chocolate cups—"I know those cups, the saucers"—she inherits them from Stella Hicks, on whom Sarah Forbes from the story is based. Moreover, she believes that "[m]aintaining appearances and acquiring the trappings of the upper class did not allow my mother to feel any more a part of the culture when she was growing up, or later when she returned to Saybrook."[39] Tea, its paraphernalia, and its dual function as a meal and ceremony comes to embody the tension Petry experienced as a famous, black writer who lived inside and outside New England's middle and upper classes.

A similar tension underscores Neola's status in Mrs. Gramby's house. In *Country Place*, after Mrs. Gramby has taken ill, Neola surmises that "[s]he would use the best silver, the Meissen china, and one of the old thin goblets; and perhaps Mrs. Gramby might show some interest in food when she saw the tray." This private act of caretaking, which is distinct from the public ceremony performed for Lillian and Glory, nevertheless illustrates Neola's faith in objects that symbolize class status without seeing that the emptiness that accompanies the single-minded pursuit of capital tarnishes such items.

Working within and against genre constraints, Petry fuses her intimate, familial knowledge of New England with her journalistic, ethnographic experience of Harlem so that these two disparate spaces create and reflect the feelings of incompatibility and alienation experienced by her characters in both *The Street* and *Country Place*. In *The Street*, Lutie feels trapped on 116th Street and longs for the black and white linoleum kitchen in the midst of the enchanted woods of Connecticut. In *Country Place*, one of the protagonists, Johnnie, a war veteran, imagines that New York is the right place for him to start over with his wife and pursue his desire to be a painter. Both characters wish to be elsewhere, and yet both are entangled in their respective locales. Johnnie's excessively romantic love for his wife entraps him: even her shining hair, which he adores, is likened to a net. Conversely, Lutie single-mindedly adheres to a Franklinian individualism combined with an intense desire to combat the pathology of black female sexuality. Not surprisingly, the effort of these tensions leads each character to violence. Even before Lutie commits murder in self-defense, twice in *The Street* she strikes her son hard enough to "make him deaf."[40] And Johnnie rapes and almost strangles his wife when she refuses his advances upon his return:

> It took a few minutes for him to realize what it meant. And he thought, This is what rape is like—to hold a woman close to you, and force your body on hers, ignoring her protests. For she had protested, by pulling away from him, by the final shrinking submission, by this silent withdrawal. He was so hellbent on having what he wanted that he had turned a deaf ear, a sightless and unheeding eye.[41]

Though far from colorblind, Petry's characters, regardless of ethnicity, are often oblivious, as Johnnie is, to what truly imperils them and those they love.

By choosing a white narrator and relegating her characters of color to the margins in *Country Place*, Petry is able to freely explore issues of female sexuality without replicating pathological representations of black women as "Jezebels." And by giving Neola a love interest of her own she is able to complicate, while also deploying, Hollywood's cinematic pairing of the sexualized white starlet with the asexual, unattractive black maid. The white female characters in *Country Place* inhabit and explore a sexual terrain that ranges from the fairly perfunctory to the deviant and abusive. In *The Street*, Lutie has to present herself as sexually unavailable to distinguish herself from her father's girlfriend who shares his "wide bed" and parades around the house in "housecoats that didn't quite meet across her lush, loose bosom."[42] There is no room for a fulfilling romantic or sexual relationship and despite her worship of propriety she is continually beset with unwanted sexual advances. There seems to be no space for an agentive black female sexuality or successful protective mothering.

In *Country Place* the white relationships are marked by obsession, adultery, or manipulation whereas Neola's sweet interracial romance serves as a counterbalance to the dysfunctional relationships in the text. Chapter 16 stands out as an intimate interlude from the main narrative. It begins with Neola and Portulucca sitting by the fire. The narrator paints a scene vivid with domestic delights: "Two people in the kitchen" "with a coal fire burning in a mountain of a stove, the coals showing red here and there through the lids, sending out waves of warmth; and the candles on the kitchen table with the copper of the candlesticks glowing." While a storm rages outside destroying everything alive, inside Portulucca ponders how best to propose to Neola. Through his eyes, floral imagery transforms and aestheticizes her uniform—the static symbol of her position as a domestic:

> He could see that blue uniform she wore, blue the color of the delphiniums, with the white apron so white, like a white peony—if she would sit there he would be able to dwell on the uniform. If he could keep his mind on the uniform, nothing else, just the delphinium blue and the peony white of it, why, when she came

> back into the room he would propose to the uniform. That way he wouldn't get confused, he would be able to say the words easily: protect and cherish and worship and water well and feed with the rich, life-giving—Godalmighty! no, he had plants and Neola completely mixed up.[43]

Petry has invested this scene with some pulp humor; the metaphors are worthy of the dime store romances Mrs. Gramby (and Petry) favor. But more importantly, this rare portrait of ideal domesticity, in which even a maid's uniform, the emblem of domestic labor and conformity, is transformed into something natural and sublime, directly opposes the vulgar and violating acts connected to Johnnie's homecoming.

In *Country Place* the figure of the black domestic functions as an exemplar whose behavior and manners rip away the facade of Anglo gentility. Though she fulfills her role as a loyal servant, Neola is always aware "there is so much hate in [the Gramby] house." In fact, it is Lillian's bigoted response to Neola and the racial others of the novel during the reading of Mrs. Gramby's will that reveals her true motives for marrying into the family:

> "I won't have niggers living here—this is my house—that fat old bastard with the diamond—that slob of a woman with the pearls—that nasty cripple—pigpen Irish—everyone in the will but me . . ."

Lillian's shocking, public outburst stands out in a novel where race is understated, and presumably—at least according to the inside flap and its reception—nonexistent.

In *Country Place*, Petry rewards Neola and Portulacca with the house that Mrs. Gramby's son acknowledges that they love. While Lutie cannot inherit her workplace and ultimately has to leave once it destroys her home life, Neola's faithful service is rewarded. And, yet neither *The Street* nor *Country Place* provides a satisfactory, alternative model of black or white womanhood. Emily Bernard argues that: "*Country Place* represents Petry's ambition to imagine a new society in which traditional, small town American culture would join forces with changing racial and ethnic demographics in order to combat the ideologies of the shameless pursuit of materialism and white supremacy."[44] But the persistence of ethnic stereotyping and Neola's ultimate lack of agency seems to undermine, or at least draw a question mark around the idealized domesticity of a working-class interracial romance that is, after all, only part of a subplot subordinate to the white characters' melodrama.

By way of conclusion, I wish to turn briefly to Petry's "Mother Africa," another work of fiction that vacillates between New England's rural landscape and Harlem's cityscape. Next to *The Street*, "Mother Africa" is Petry's most famous "Harlem" story. In "Mother Africa," Petry mines her profile of George Jackson to shape the unforgettable character of Emanuel "Man" Turner, also known as "Junk," a man who has to confront the complex relationship between Afrocentric and Eurocentric ideas of beauty. Junk receives a mammoth bronze statue of a naked woman from a white woman in Long Island for whom the artifact has become distasteful. Over the course of the story, the larger-than-life statue, which horrifies the junkman's female customers and becomes the object of lewd gesticulations for the men, is worshipped by Junk:

> He brushed the dust off the metal woman and he washed her and then he rinsed her off. When he was finished he stared up at her, entranced. The dark naked figure glowed . . . .He felt something stir within him, an emotion that he could not put a name to. It was like seeing something dark and beautiful beyond description for the first time and yet recognizing it, because in the deepest part of your mind you had always known that that kind of dark glowing beauty existed. Mother Africa, he thought. That's what she really is: Mother Africa.[45]

As it turns out, the personified statue worshipped by Junk is actually the statue of a white woman. Junk inscribes his desire for a black beauty that is permanent, that he can own and cherish—unlike his wife whom he loses in childbirth—upon this inanimate bronze statue only to find that the facial features, in contrast to the fecund curves of the body, are European. He makes this discovery when he climbs the statue to remove the "red bandana" and "gaudy print" dress vandals have tied around the statue. The costume suggests the image of the black woman as a mammy figure and recalls a time when "Africans were ashamed of their good strong black bodies." When Junk finds himself face to face with the statue, he is shocked: "It had never occurred to him that this alive-looking statue was of a white woman." The discovery causes him to crash to the ground and suffer a severe injury. He then calls Harlem Metalworks and in a reversal of sorts, sells "her for scrap."[46]

"Mother Africa" parodies a stereotypical black nationalist's desire to affirm the superiority of Afrocentric beauty. It is also a complex portrait of an often-misunderstood urban fixture: the Harlem junkman. Junk, as he is called by the narrator, is an enigmatic figure who refuses to conform to mainstream values (such as shaving or keeping oneself clean) but still participates in the capitalist economy by buying, selling, and recycling discarded and unwanted items. The feelings of protectiveness and worship stirred in him by the statue evoke the desire to conform visually to society's expectation of manhood. At the same time, his desire to own and exhibit the statue reifies objectified notions of womanhood. Junk is a character with a racial perspective shaped by the Mississippi of his youth, despite his urban existence. His migration from South to North does not alter his persistent belief in white duplicity: Junk "truly believed that if they hadn't been black and lived in Harlem, that Mary Lou and the baby might have survived."[47] Moreover, he won't accept the statue as a gift without a signed statement affirming it belongs to him. The original owner's name is "Mrs. Charles Edward Treadway" another intertextual, homonymic reference; the name refers to the powerful white family in Petry's *The Narrows*. The heiress to the "Treadway Munitions fortune," Camilo Treadway Sheffield, wrought disaster for the black inhabitants of the Narrows through her interracial affair with Link Williams. When Camilo falsely accuses Link of rape, they murder him. The statue of "Mother Africa" travels from the "Treadways" of Long Island and Connecticut to a Harlem where it becomes the official property of Junk. Once again, Petry smuggles New England into Harlem and similar to Lutie's idealized kitchen, the statue—a virtual embodiment of Eurocentric values—does pernicious work within the community as a result of Junk's misreading and misnaming.

Petry further interrogates how notions of respectability are shaped by space and inextricable from gender, racial, and class norms in "Mother Africa" through the neighborhood women's response to the statue's nakedness. The nakedness of the metal figure outrages the women: "They vented their feelings in a heavy-handed assault on the children. They cuffed their offspring about the head, the back, slapped them smartly across the legs, shouting, 'You take that and that! You laughin' at that nekkid huzzy!' "[48] The women, like Lutie, misplace their rage, and in an effort to uphold their warped notions of respectability they abuse their children. In light of the revelation regarding "Mother Africa's features," are the mothers trying to work against the dominant cultural reification of Eurocentric beauty? Perhaps Ginny the Baptist's attack on the metal statue—she beats her "with the rusted fender of a car"—becomes more sympathetic in light of Junk's discovery of the statue's "real" racial identity? In hindsight, the women may be protesting the outrage of a black man enshrining an icon of white femininity in the heart of a black urban community. In its compactness "Mother Africa" seems to narrow Petry's exploration of black womanhood to the parameters of the junkyard; however, the title and the provenance of the statue, which moves from New England to Harlem, offers a succinct commentary on the underlying thematics in *Country Place* and *The Street*: the narrative techniques of contrast, which manifest themselves in spatial terms, between oppressive Eurocentric values and ideology and essentialized Afrocentric notions about the black community—a contrast that leads, in

Petry's oeuvre, to the subsequent destabilization of fixed notions of female subjectivity.

Placing Petry's "black" novel in conversation with her "white novel" should explode simplified, racialized categorizations of Petry's writing. The innovative character pairings and setting juxtapositions—where Harlem meets New England—in her early fiction anticipates *The Narrows* (1952),[49] a novel that seeks to answer "what are the costs of striving for social and domestic perfection, of diehard efforts to 'uplift the race'?."[50] In 1948, Petry and husband returned to their "country place" in Old Saybrook, but the social and spatial dynamics of Harlem viewed from New England would continue to animate and inspire her later fiction: innovative explorations of race, class, sexuality, and gender that result from the deft manipulations of genre and geography begun in early sketches such as "Harlem" and her first two novels.

NOTES

1. Hilary Holladay, *Ann Petry* (New York: Macmillan, 1996). Holladay quotes Arna Bontemps who declared Petry a "neighborhood novelist," a storyteller who "elects the neighborhood as her unit," 1.

2. Mark Wilson, "Interview: Ann Petry. The New England Connection," *MELUS* 15, no. 2 (1988): 82.

3. Although no longer owned by the family, Lane's is still a working soda fountain.

4. *Amsterdam News*, "Connecticut Druggist Likes Shows, So She Comes Here," 1936.

5. Mark Wilson, "Interview: Ann Petry": 77–84.

6. Ann Petry, "Harlem," *Holiday* (1949), 112.

7. Ibid., 110, 116.

8. Ibid., 164, 165, 166.

9. Ann Petry, *The Street*, 4.

10. Petry, "Harlem," 164.

11. Petry, *The Street*, 2.

12. Evie Shockley's analysis of *The Street*'s gothicism treats Lutie as Petry's doppelganger. I do not contest this rather apt characterization but my emphasis considers the books, rather than Petry and her characters, as mirrored texts. For the purposes of my argument, *Country Place* is the doppelganger of *The Street*.

13. According to Candice Jenkins, the salvific wish, which has its roots in the late-nineteenth-century discourse of racial uplift, "attempts to repress and discipline black intimate conduct in the hopes of limited that conduct to patterns of 'respectability'—thereby shattering, through force of will, the distortions and myths surround black eroticism and domesticity—is thus a sociopolitical response to the discursive and ideological dilemma." Jenkins, *Private Lives, Proper Relations Regulating Black Intimacy* (Minneapolis: University of Minnesota Press, 2007), 44.

14. Petry, *The Street*, 28, 56.

15. The Pullman porter was a respected occupation that allowed black families access to the middle class. Unfortunately, the economic mobility of the Pullman porter came at a high cost as the position often entailed an erasure of individual identity—passengers indiscriminately referred to all porters by the name "George"—and compulsory subservience. For women, the train motif, especially in the blues tradition, can signify a "mournful signal of imminent desertion and future loneliness." Hazel Carby, qtd. in Farrah Griffin, "*'Who set you flowin'?": The African-American Migration Narrative* (New York: Oxford University Press, 1995), 19.

16. Petry, *The Street*, 434, 436.

17. Ibid., 36, 49.

18. I am in agreement with Candice Jenkins who argues that "[o]bsessed with creating a 'respectable' home for herself, away from Lil's generally harmless, if 'improper,' behavior, Lutie walks directly into the demoralizing fate that awaits her on " 'the street' " (57). Unlike the reviews that cast Petry as a "Native Daughter," Jenkins's reading of Petry's naturalism pinpoints Lutie's flawed decisions and naïveté.

19. Petry, *The Street*, 10, 95.

20. Claude McKay. "Harlem Shadows," in *Harlem Shadows* (New York: Harcourt, Brace, 1922).

21. Paula Rabinowitz, "Pulping Ann Petry: The Case of Country Place," in *Revising the Blueprint: Ann Petry and the Literary Left*, ed. Alex Lubin (University of Mississippi: Jackson, 2007), 32.

22. Rabinowitz considers Petry's novels to be pulp fiction; she describes Petry's writing process as a retranslation of "cinematic trash—already a translation of literary pulp—into narrative form" (64). While the popularity of film noir may have informed Petry's subject matter and narrative style, I see *Country Place* as a novel that experiments with multiple literary and cinematic genres.

23. I'm thinking here of Gene Jarrett's understanding of certain figures within the African American canon who push against the boundaries of genre and expectation of black fiction as "truant." See Gene Jarrett, *Deans and Truants: Race and Realism in African American Literature* (Philadelphia: University of Pennsylvania, 2007).

24. As quoted in Emily Bernard, " 'Raceless,' Writing and Difference: Ann Petry's 'Country Place' and the African-American Literary Canon," *Studies in American Fiction* 33, no. 1 (2005): 98, 88–117.

25. Ibid., 89.

26. Toni Morrison's term describes how a fabricated, nonwhite persona was constructed and imaginatively deployed in American literature. *Playing in the Dark: Whiteness and the Literary Imagination* (New York: Random House, 1993).

27. Ann Petry, *Country Place* (Boston: Houghton Mifflin, 1947), 1.

28. Toni Morrison, *Playing in the Dark*, 13.

29. Elisabeth Petry, *At Home Inside: A Daughter's Tribute to Ann Petry* (Jackson: University of Mississippi Press, 2009), 52.

30. Rabinowitz argues that outlines of the novel suggest that "parts of *Country Place* preceded her first novel," "Pulping Country Place," 55.

31. I'm thinking here of Karen Halttunnen's definition of the "genteel performance" in conjunction with ideologies of middle-class true womanhood as "a

system of polite conduct that demanded a flawless self-discipline, practiced with an apparently easy, natural and sincere manner" (28). Carolyn Sorisio, "Unmasking the Genteel Performer: Elizabeth Keckley's Behind the Scenes and the Politics of Public Wrath," *African American Review* 34, no. 1 (2000): 19–38.

32. Petry, *The Street*, 45.

33. Ehrenreich, an undercover journalist who took several low-paying jobs and then wrote about her experiences in *Nickel and Dimed: On (Not) Getting By in America* (New York: Holt, 2001). In addition to the expected revelation of how low-wage earners are exploited within capitalist economies, she offers the astute recognition that "[t]o be a member of the working poor is to be an anonymous donor, a nameless benefactor, to everyone" (221).

34. Petry, *Country Place*, 149, 61.

35. Ibid., 61.

36. Ibid., 157.

37. Petry, "Has Anybody Seen Miss Dora Dean?" in *Miss Muriel and Other Stories* (Boston: Houghton Mifflin, 1971), 111.

38. Petry, "Dora Dean," 96. John Isham's *The Creole Show* was one of the nation's first burlesque shows to feature African American women. "Dora Dean" starred in the 1890 debut and later performed on the international circuit where she was known as the "Black Venus." A voluptuous performer, Dean was known for her luxurious costumes and her innovations to the cakewalk. For more on African American chorines and stage performers see Jayna Brown, *Babylon Girls: Black Women Performers and the Shaping of the Modern* (Durham: Duke University Press, 2008).

39. Elizabeth Petry noted that her "mother wrote in detail about the sources of some of her fiction but hid the origins of others." Petry, *At Home Inside*, 76, 51, 52.

40. Petry, *The Street*, 11.

41. Petry, *Country Place*, 30.

42. Petry, *The Street*, 10.

43. Petry, *Country Place*, 172.

44. Ibid., 108.

45. Ann Petry, "Mother Africa," in *Miss Muriel and Other Stories*, 139.

46. Ibid., 160, 162.

47. Ibid., 154.

48. Ibid., 140.

49. Petry's novel, aptly named *The Narrows*, introduces Abbie Crunch, a black female character who manages to self-critically reflect on the incompatibility of certain tenets of New England values with the realities of African American urban life.

50. Joyce Pettis, "Reading Ann Petry's *The Narrows* into Black Literary Tradition," in *Recovered Writers/Recovered Texts: Race, Class, and Gender in Black Women's Literature*, ed. Dolan Hubbard (Knoxville: University of Tennessee Press, 1997), 120.

FIVE

SEPARATED AT BIRTH?

Henry Roth's Call It Sleep *and James Baldwin's* Go Tell It on the Mountain

Cheryl Greenberg

A boy from a family outside mainstream U.S. culture grows up in an ethnically iconic, poor ghetto in New York. His father, prone to terrifying rages, beats him. His mother, who adores him, harbors a secret about her romantic past that keeps her tied to this violent man. And this man, in turn, believes the boy is not his, despite having embraced him as a son since the boy's earliest years. The growing boy struggles with his identity as an outsider in American life, an increasingly sexually aware being, and as a member of a religion both alluring and difficult to embrace. The novel builds to its inevitable dramatic climax as the father, mother, and well-meaning but intrusive aunt confront one another about the romantic secret and the domestic violence, and the boy escapes through a religious epiphany full of pain and light.

If this plot line sounds familiar, it is because Henry Roth's *Call It Sleep* is a classic of Jewish American literature. Or it is because James Baldwin's *Go Tell It on the Mountain* is a classic of African American literature. Two novels, two communities, two time periods, two different ghettos. Same dramatic story arc. The parallels go further. Beyond the similarities of plot, both authors vividly invoke their characters' otherness as rooted in their geography. Roth's David and Baldwin's John (both Biblical heroes of their respective religions) live lives deeply enmeshed in their own communities but set apart from others both physically and psychologically. Both the sense of identity and the heightened sense of difference are made vivid by their locations, the Lower East Side in David's case, and Harlem for John. In the public imagination these neighborhoods are poor but ultimately a place of safety, ethnic intimacy, and cultural expression. In their vivid depictions of domestic violence, however, both novels turn this romanticized image on its head. Intimacy and ethnic expression lead to danger and emotional turmoil.

At the same time, the two locations are also distinct, quintessentially and uniquely understood as Jewish or African American. Indeed, neither novel could be evoked as powerfully nor embedded so integrally into its ethnic or racial canon if it had not been set in its own particular—and iconic—neighborhood. By means of their distinct geographies, then, David's Jewishness and John's blackness become a unifying thread between them.

The historical connections between the black and Jewish communities in the United States have been well documented. These connections have not always been positive—or even actual. Some, such as the identification of enslaved African Americans with the Biblical children of Israel, have occurred primarily in imagination, as so many slave songs like "Go Down Moses" and "Didn't My Lord Deliver Daniel?" reveal. Both African Americans and Jews see themselves—with some accuracy—as persecuted; both have understood their identity as shaped by their marginalization. Black and Jewish traditions also share an element of timelessness. Both view the present overlaid by an imagined past and understand contemporary commitments as universal and transcendent truths. That is, both traditions place the sufferings of their people at the center of their understanding of the moral universe. Modern Jews cite the Passover liturgy, "Because we were slaves in the land of Egypt," as the force driving their broader human rights activism, and link more contemporary tyrants such as Hitler to Biblical and Talmudic foes who sought to annihilate the Jewish people. Similarly, slavery and racism are broadly understood in the African American community as perpetual human evils that link them to oppressed people everywhere.

In what follows, I argue that juxtaposing Henry Roth's *Call It Sleep* and James Baldwin's *Go Tell It on the Mountain* reveals much about the particularity of each group at the same time that it highlights the novels' linkages to the broader narrative of black-Jewish relations, or what Adam Newton has called blackjewishrelations.[1] The settings of these stories within these iconic neighborhoods allow these distinct yet linked identities to emerge and interact.

CRITICAL RECEPTION

Call It Sleep has often been discussed as a reflection or invocation of modernism in its embodiment of the uncertainties, terrors, and dislocations of industrialization and global movement.[2] Other scholars have looked at Roth in relation to other Jewish writers, suggesting that Roth's novel evokes a Jewish world both familiar and jarring. Ezra Cappell, for example, combines both points, observing that Roth's depiction of Judaism, as compared to those of other Jewish writers, is both negative and modern; by mocking Jewish texts and interrupting ritual continuity, Roth reveals modernism's discontinuity and disregard for tradition.[3] David's search for meaning thus reveals the sterility of older religious practice and community norms in the face of new challenges. Both of these interpretations are critical in understanding the power of the novel as well as its location in time and space; importantly, they also dovetail with commentary on Baldwin's work.

Baldwin's canonical *Go Tell It on the Mountain* is recognized by critics for its evocation of the potency—and constraints—of black religious tradition as well as the dysfunctionality of black families struggling against devastating poverty, degrading bigotry, and the crippling effects of racial discrimination. While critics differ on whether Baldwin is rejecting religion or drawing a distinction between the rigid practice of black Christianity and its liberating spiritual potential,[4] all acknowledge the inability of the traditional black church in this novel to offer meaning to John.[5]

All of these approaches to understanding the novels are indispensable in helping set each book into its multiple contexts. Less studied, however, are the startling overlaps between these two novels in particular, and the ways in which they reflect or even help clarify the much more commonly examined relationship between African Americans and Jewish Americans. For example, Leslie Fiedler compares the protagonist's epiphany in *Call It Sleep* to *Ulysses* and *The Waste Land* in its symbolism of modern life as futile and anarchic. Yet, no one has compared *Call It Sleep* to Baldwin's protagonist's remarkably similar epiphany whose response to modern life is to resist its anarchy through a return to traditional links to the divine. Similarly, Michael Lynch compared Baldwin to Richard Wright and Dostoevsky in his depiction of existential suffering, but not to Roth.[6] By juxtaposing these two similar yet uniquely personal texts we may gain greater insights into the ways in which black and Jewish experience in America have intersected with and reflected each other. At the same time, the dangers of too closely equating the two communities' histories or interests also become increasingly clear. Both the parallels and the divergences help clarify the complex history and politics of black-Jewish relationships in America.

THE WORLD OF DAVID SCHEARL

David Schearl arrives with his mother from Austria to join his father Albert in Brownsville, a poor immigrant neighborhood in Brooklyn inhabited largely by Jews: "A row of frame houses . . . a pitted gutter, a yawning ashcan, flotsam on the shore, his street."[7] We soon discover, however, that it is not, in fact, "his street"; it offers him neither comfort nor sanctuary. Outside his apartment young David finds himself bullied by neighborhood children and pressed into unwanted sexual exploration. Each interaction with a shopkeeper brings humiliation. He loses his money. The street is frightening, the buildings dirty. The dark cellar door lurks menacingly. Here is a typical immigrant setting, and, so far, David is a typical, if timid, immigrant child.

This world is also radically proscribed. David's mother Genya comments, "I know there is a church on a certain street to my left, the vegetable market is to my right, behind me are the railroad tracks and the broken rocks, and before me, a few blocks away is a certain store window that has a kind of white-wash on it—and faces in the white-wash, the kind children draw. Within this pale is my America and if I ventured further I should be lost. In fact," she laughed, "were they even to wash that window, I might never find my way home again."[8] The immigrant world is constrained, a bit messy, and in the process of construction. Exits exist, in this case a railroad, but they are few. And while this narrow "Pale" may feel homogenous and therefore comforting, in fact we learn immediately that this presumed neighborhood of Jews also contains enough Christians to warrant a church. This touch of multicultural life reflects historical reality, certainly. No immigrant community was ever fully separated from the rest of the world. But it also reflects emotional reality as well, in contradictory ways. First, the Jewish world is not even safe in its insularity, because even here can be found the potentially dangerous *goyim*. Second, and conversely, Genya's lack of any meaningful interactions with the non-Jews who obviously share her space suggests the Jews' almost existential social isolation. Non-Jews are physically present but functionally absent. The proscription of the Jew's world is as much psychological as actual.

Within a year or so the family moves to the much more crowded but more iconically inscribed Jewish Lower East Side. Although nostalgia, exemplified by the popularity of photo books such as Irving Howe's *World of Our Fathers*, today evokes images of warmth, entrepreneurship, and community,[9] to David it was a "new and violent world." Roth, like Yezierska before him, challenges the comforting and retroactive stereotypes of first generation Jewish immigrant communities by invoking David's internal disquiet. On Ninth Street, where they lived, one encountered

> [a]n avalanche of sound. There were countless children, there were countless baby carriages, there were countless mothers. And to the screams, rebukes and bickerings of these, a seemingly endless file of hucksters joined their howling cries. On Avenue D horse-cars clattered and banged. Avenue D was thronged with beer wagons, garbage carts and coal trucks. There were many automobiles, some blunt and rangey, some with high straw poops, honking. Beyond Avenue D, at the end of a stunted, ruined block that began with shacks and smithies and seltzer bottling works and ended in a junk heap, was the East River on which many boat horns sounded. On 10th Street, the 8th Street Crosstown car ground its way toward the switch.[10]

All is foreign. And that feeling of alienation, of difference, is internalized. David's father observes, "I think when you come out of a house and step on the bare earth among the fields you're the same man you were when you were inside the house. But when you step out on pavements, you're someone else. You can feel your face change."[11]

This sense of discomfort, of being out of place, is equally true inside, off the streets. The toilets are in the hall and the family bathes in a washtub. The linoleum is worn and the stair treads black and hollowed with use. The onslaught of sound in the streets is replaced inside the apartment by the ominous silence of his father's presence. When the family takes in a boarder—a common practice in overcrowded and impoverished immigrant communities—he becomes increasingly sexually aggressive toward David's mother, who is caught between his pressure and her husband's great affection for the man. Roth invokes both neighborhood and home in such a way as to suggest degradation, threat, and alienation, places to escape from rather than to find comfort in. Jews, Roth seems to be suggesting, are fully safe and comfortable nowhere. Certainly this is the case for David.

David's father Albert is dangerously angry and mean-spirited from the start, but nonetheless supports the family through his labor. His temper frequently gets the better of him at work and he changes jobs often, moving from one ill-paid menial task to another. Albert is caught in a spiral of his own making—he is angry at his inability to rise economically and his sense that he is better than the job he holds. He is convinced his employers are anti-Semites, bigots, or greedy. This may well be true. Yet it is his violent temper as much as his unskilled, outsider status that keeps him trapped at the bottom of the economic ladder. The lack of safety and the sense of being trapped in an evil and dangerous world that Roth invokes in this novel is not merely a product of external forces of poverty or discrimination, but also internal. The Lower East Side might be the physical location for the novel but its characters have brought to that place past experiences from other places that have made them what they are.

Albert's behavior is little better at home, and readers are hard-pressed to understand why his wife Genya remains with him. Through a conversation between Genya and her sister, readers finally learn that back in Austria Genya had fallen in love with a non-Jewish boy who rejected her. Her humiliated parents had hushed the affair up and married her off as best they could. The traditional Jewish community, its norms and values, are here revealed to be additional forces that keep Jews trapped. Jews seem to be safe nowhere, not even within their own world.

Albert and Genya's son, David, is both fearful and precocious, inducted into a world of violence and sex well before he is ready to face either. He has overheard his mother's tale, and although he does not fully understand it, he absorbs its drama and its threat. He is afraid of the dark cellar and terrified of his perpetually angry father. Although the myth of the Lower East Side embraced by so many contemporary Jews asserts residents' deep connection to Judaism, David's sense of Jewishness seems limited to mechanical observance of religious rituals, victimization, Hebrew letters, and the promise of transcendence. His knowledge of Judaism as either a full religion or a culture is limited. For their own reasons, neither of his parents believes in any traditional Jewish truths. Rather, they practice because it is custom and to avoid the opprobrium of their neighbors. One Friday afternoon finds Genya waiting by the window with the laundry. She will not hang the clothes out to dry until after dark, so the neighbors don't see that she's violating the Sabbath. Yet she describes God (separating it from her own beliefs by identifying the information as coming from a pious old woman from her youth): "She said that He was brighter than the day is brighter than the night. . . . Brighter than day."[12] It is in the lacunae between ritual and meaning that David finds the promise of relief from his terrors. Within the Jewish world of the Lower East Side religion has changed from the transcendent link between practice and meaning into a series of empty behaviors performed only to conform to community norms or superstition. Far from a place of pious devotion, the Lower East Side appears in *Call It Sleep* as one more constraint on meaningful Jewish life. Yet the sense that only transcendence offers an escape from his struggles leads David to seek the divine light his mother describes through his limited religious understanding.

The link between God and bright light is reinforced at his otherwise violent and rote learning–based religious school, where David hears the story of the angel who helps man see God by means of a hot and glowing coal. Later in the novel he meets a Catholic boy, Leo, who tells David about Jesus, who died dramatically to take away humans' sins. Intrigued, David asks for a crucifix, which he obtains after helping his friend kiss and fondle

David's cousin. Finally, after all the stories come together and his aunt, his religious school teacher, and his mother and father confront one another about sex and violence in the present and in both Albert's and Genya's past, David plunges a metal bar onto the live third rail of the subway—one of the few physical exits from his world—and has his long-sought moment of religious ecstasy bathed in blinding light.

> He screamed, descended. Down! Down into darkness, darkness that tunneled the heart of darkness, darkness fathomless. Each step he took, he . . . shed the husks of being, and himself tapering away always downward in the funnel of the night. . . . But out of the darkness, one ember . . . flowered. . . . And it was brighter than the pith of lightning and milder than pearl. . . . Horror and the night fell away. Exalted, he lifted his head and screamed.[13]

David's world is strange to him, not only as a boy but as an immigrant whose non-Jewish encounters almost uniformly terrify him. Whenever he leaves his block (or later, his small neighborhood), he becomes lost and disoriented. The streets look different, the people speak differently. He cannot make himself understood and he cannot find his way back to the comfort of home. He asks a stranger for help but his address, "a hunder 'n' twenny six Boddeh Stritt" makes no sense to the man.[14] A police officer finally figures it out. "Boddeh? . . . Say, I know where he lives! Barhdee Street! Sure, Barhdee! . . . Be-gob, he'll be havin' me talk like a Jew. Sure!"[15] Nor is this sense of marginality simply an interpretation of the fearful David. As Fiedler, Wirth-Nesher, and other scholars have observed,[16] Roth shows the alien nature of this outside world not only in its physical description but also in its language. When Genya speaks to David she speaks in almost poetic prose, full of imagery and passion. After giving him a glass of water she reminds him, "It is summer . . . the weather grows warm. Whom will you refresh with the icy lips the water lent you?"[17] Yet when she speaks to non-Jews outside, we see her broken English, her inability to communicate. She stutters, searches for words, speaks in ungrammatical and mispronounced phrases. "T-tanks so—so viel!" she thanks a police officer. "Er— . . . Herr—Mister. Ve—er—ve go?"[18] At home, she is an elegant Yiddish speaker, at home in her world and in her mind. Outside, she is clearly marked as the inferior other. Indeed, all of the immigrants in the novel speak with clearly marked accents since "[i]n the street David spoke English."[19] Because English is a foreign tongue, immigrants ironically reveal their marginality at the very moments they struggle most to fit into America.

In other words, this inability to speak proper English serves as another iconic shorthand for foreignness. "Dey's two goils in my class, an' anudder kid a goy [non-Jew]," Yonk tells Moish and David. And in case the division these boys felt between themselves and others is not clear enough, Yonk concludes, "Goys is dumb."[20] Yet, as Roth reminds the reader, New Yorkers are all foreigners. "Hot ain' id?" asks an evidently non-Jewish man named Hennessey trying to strike up a conversation before helping himself to milk from David's father's wagon.[21] Yet each immigrant community's version of butchered English is different. "You no tella me waddaduh push! I cleanuh dis street," warns an Italian street cleaner. The butcher's wife fears that he, like all Italians, carries a knife. "'Go on with ye! None o' yer guff!'" one Irish cop says to another. Then, reassuringly to David, "'Don't mind him, me lad!"[22] David himself understands the importance of language in the ascription of identity. Fearing anti-Semitic hostility from two men he encounters on the piers, he denies he is Jewish when asked. He explains that he is Hungarian, a janitor's son living on an otherwise all-Jewish street. When challenged for proof he replies by pretending to speak Hungarian. "'Abashishishabababyo tomama wawa. Like dot."[23] The only people in the novel who speak grammatically correct English are those from the upper class, presumably native-born, at home in America. None of them live in or near the Lower East Side.

Ironically, perhaps, David's experiences with non-Jews is in fact not as dangerous as he has imagined them. As Kremena Todorova has observed, linguistic differences do not in fact prevent effective communication or aid;[24] Tomas Ferraro argues this multiplicity of cultures and tongues actually reflects a uniquely American form of melting pot "syncretism."[25] The policeman who finds him when he is lost is quite kind and Leo, while manipulative and casually anti-Semitic, is not vicious and bullying like his Jewish playmates. It is in David's mind that the outside world, alien as it is, is inhospitable. Ultimately, Roth seems to be suggesting, we are trapped not merely by external forces but also by our perception of them. If Jews are safe nowhere, it may have less to do with being Jewish or even being trapped by a place, than it does with the burdensome experiences and assumptions of the past, both communal and personal, that Jews drag with them. Indeed, the history of Jewish acculturation into American life, which began just as Roth wrote the novel, would seem to prove this point: so much of that process has been bound up in the Jewish imagination with the long history of Jewish suffering and persecution.

When David and Aunt Bertha venture out into the world beyond the Lower East Side, they choose as their destination the unmistakable mark of Americanness, the Metropolitan Museum of Art. On the way they pass grand Third Avenue buildings. David feels "uneasy" and out of place, but his aunt is much more critical. "Who would want to live in these houses?" she asked, linking their wealthy owners with the evil Baron Kobelien of her youth. At the museum they are so fearful of its capaciousness that they subordinate looking at the artwork to following close on the heels of an American couple so as not to get lost. Aunt Bertha vows never to return. "A raw jade like yourself ought to learn a little more before she butts into America," advises Albert.[26]

Yet if the outside world is foreign and frightening, Roth also paints an ambivalent portrait of David's own community. It is a place that offers no decent employment to facilitate moving up and out. It is not only Albert who has miserable and dead-end jobs. His Aunt Bertha anguishes, "Why did I ever set foot on this stinking land? Why did I ever come here? Ten hours a day in a smothering shop—paper flowers! Rag flowers! Ten long hours, afraid to peek too often because the foreman might think I was shirking."[27]

The Lower East Side is filled with terrors for David as well. Beyond bullies, and dirt, the neighborhood is an extension of the terror and anxiety he feels in his home, the usual site of his father's rages. When with his father on the street, everything familiar in David's world turned sinister. "The stable lineaments of the mask of the world had overlapped, shifted configuration as secretly and minutely as clock hands, as sudden as the wink of an eye. It was strange. It had happened before. A vague, diffuse aching filled his breast."[28] No wonder David seeks ever more extreme solutions to his anguish, finally finding his own glowing coal via the electrified third rail.

Much of the novel's power today comes from these iconoclastic challenges to rosy-hued Jewish collective memory of their immigrant experience in neighborhoods like the Lower East Side. For Jews, whose self-understanding relies on the retelling of Jewish history, memories are particularly significant, and prone to shift toward nostalgia. In contrast to the mythic image of the Lower East Side as a center of religious community, David's religious teacher strikes any children who make a mistake in their reading. The religious school itself is dark and dank. The children exhibit no knowledge of either Hebrew or Judaism, understanding only that breaking the laws of the Sabbath or the Passover are sins. Ezra Cappell makes a similar point in *American Talmud*, calling the novel anti-Jewish and even "self-loathing."[29] I would argue instead that Roth is contrasting the emptiness of Jewish ritual with the transcendent possibilities of a religion that gives life meaning. In either case, however, Roth's iconoclasm is startling here.

Nor are Brownsville or the Lower East Side entirely Jewish enclaves in the novel (or in historical fact). There is at least one "goy" in David's public school class; Polish Catholic Leo lives on Eleventh Street, and at least one Hungarian family lives on David's own block. On the Lower East Side in particular, however, the diversity seems more ominous because the reality contradicts the iconic illusion of a unified and uniquely Jewish space peopled only by Yiddish writers and performers, socialist Jewish workers' collectives, Jewish peddlers, Orthodox rabbis, and Yezerskia's and Cahan's families, businesses, and institutions. Had Roth placed David elsewhere, difference might not seem so threatening. The contrast between real and imagined experience extends also to the Jewish community of these quintessentially Jewish neighborhoods; far from havens of loving family life, they host Albert's rages, the constant bickering of David's aunt's family, the cursing of children by parents, the squabbling and betrayals of siblings. David's alienation—perhaps that of all immigrant Jews—is highlighted by the alienation felt by most modern Jews from the reliable and comforting neighborhood of an imagined Jewish past.

Roth's Jewish community, then, is hardly communal at all. The neighborhood, ordinarily associated in contemporary Jewish imagination with safety, opportunity, and cohesion, is revealed to be a place of uncertainty, constraint, and danger. Some of these dangers are real, imposed by the hatred of others or the alienation of the modern industrial city. Others are imagined, rooted in Jews' collective memory. Still others are passed on from one generation to the next by parents whose own faults or failures have been redefined as reactions to Jewish victimization. The fact that these dramas play out in the very location most Jews today revere as the nurturing birthplace of American Jewish life makes them that much more potent. David's burdens are his own, but in this novel they become the burdens of all Jews.

THE WORLD OF JOHN GRAVES

John Graves is the oldest son of Gabriel, a black Baptist minister who moved from the South into Harlem many years earlier, after abandoning a woman carrying his child. Despite his self-professed rebirth in Jesus, John's father has not given up on all his previously evil ways. He remains angry, bitter, and violent, and holds only contempt for John. Like Albert, Gabriel blames racism and bad luck for his failure to prosper. While indeed racism and bad luck do play a role, Gabriel's temper and general misbehavior seem to account for more of his failure. Both fathers seem incapable of self-reflection, instead relying on a historically legitimate sense of victimization to place blame anywhere else but on themselves. Even in the way they tie their own faults to their people's broader narrative, African Americans and Jews can be linked to each other. And both fathers' religious commitments are rendered suspect from the start.

John's mother, like David's, also has a romantic secret. Elizabeth too had an illicit love; her shame was an out-of-wedlock pregnancy. Unlike Albert, then, Gabriel is correct in believing that John is not his true son. Yet Elizabeth had married him not out of shame but hope: he had promised Elizabeth when he married her that he would look upon John as his own, and never hold her past against either of them. "'And I'll love your son, your little boy,' he said at last, 'just like he was my own.' . . . And she had wept, in her great joy that the hand of God had changed her life, had lifted her up and set her on the solid rock, alone."[30] The betrayal of that promise is as painful as the beatings by his hand.

John is precocious as well, aware of his father's hatred but not of the reason for it, desiring salvation in the Holy Spirit but unable to suspend the awareness of his own sinfulness long enough to allow salvation to enter him. He seeks his redemption through religion, as David does, struggling to come to terms with the church's harsh strictures and impossible expectations. The church provides his only hope of psychic survival, and yet it seems unattainable.

John's family's church, a small storefront, is a staple of Depression-era Harlem where large, established congregations like the Abyssinian Baptist Church competed for parishioners with the usually smaller and more emotive Holiness and Pentecostal churches and with more esoteric religious communities such as those of Father Divine, Daddy Grace, or Mother Horn. Religion, one of Harlem's two most powerful images—the other being a compelling and colorful social scene—is on full display in this novel. Baldwin does not need to spend a great deal of time on description since his father's church is so well embedded into the actual and the mythic Harlem landscape. And yet religious fervor here is not without its negatives. His father has never risen farther than head deacon in this church, has never led his own congregation, despite the promise of his powerful preaching performances in Southern revivals. And John's way to faith is blocked by his father's harsh, uncharitable form of religious practice.

Like David, John explores the world outside of his own ghetto, traveling through white residential neighborhoods around Central Park, astonished at the elegance and wealth he sees there. Here people live in such freedom and comfort as he can only dream of. Mixed with that awe, however, comes both anger and sadness that he can never become a part of this ideal world, thanks to his poverty and his color:

> Niggers did not live on these streets where John now walked; it was forbidden . . . did he dare enter this shop . . . this apartment . . . ? John knew he did not dare, not today, and he heard his father's laugh: "No, nor tomorrow neither!" For him there was the back door, and the dark stairs, and the kitchen or the basement. This world was not for him.[31]

John wears his marginality on his skin; he has no need of an accent to mark it.

On the brink of sexual awakening, he decides to enter a movie theater in midtown featuring a "wicked woman, half undressed . . . apparently quarreling with a blond man who stared wretchedly into the street. The legend above their heads was: 'There's a fool like him in every family–and a woman next door to take him over!'"[32] Both horrified and fascinated at the brazenness of the heroine, he finds himself longing to "be like her, only more powerful, more thorough, and more cruel; to make those around him, all who hurt him, suffer as she made the student suffer, and laugh in their faces when they asked pity for their pain."[33] Yet he wrestles with himself, recognizing that this is the path of pain and damnation.

This white, wealthy world is clearly set out as foreign and unfriendly, filled with people "whose eyes held no love for him."[34] His focus is as much on religion as it is race and class: "It was the roar of the damned that filled Broadway," John thinks, a place hurtling toward perdition.[35] Csaba Csapo suggests that Baldwin is here equating New York and sin.[36] Yet whether faith or race divides the two worlds, John's feelings of exclusion and rejection are, like David's, overstated in this case. John's specific interactions with white people, from an old man in Central Park who smiles at him to the ticket taker at the movie theater, are only pleasant or matter-of-fact. He remembers with gratitude a white teacher who took an interest in him. In the end, however, these actual interchanges do not alter his conviction that he is inevitably and irrevocably barred from entry into the greater promise of American life. Instead, he is trapped in the same degraded world he already lives in. His membership in his community promises him only "humiliation forever; there awaited him, one day, a house like his father's house, and a church like his father's and a job like his father's, where he would grow old and black with hunger and toil."[37] Yet in this conviction lies the profound distinction between his and David's fear of poor treatment at the hands of outsiders. While non-Jewish whites in this novel by and large behave fairly toward both David and John, John's fears are rooted in the inescapable historical reality of American racism that constrains every part of his life. David and others like him will be able to move out of his ghetto; John and others like him will not.

Neither does home provide refuge. Like Roth's Lower East Side, Baldwin's Harlem also inverts nostalgic images of the neighborhood during the Jazz Age as a place of community and safety; for John, Harlem provides no sanctuary, no haven from the heartless and godless white world outside. Unlike Manhattan's white neighborhoods, "where his people walked . . . the houses . . . huddled flat, ignoble, close to the filthy ground, where the streets and the hallways and the rooms were dark, and where the unconquerable odor was of dust, and sweat, and urine, and homemade gin."[38] His brother, swallowed by the streets, is shot while committing a crime.

Even his own apartment is irredeemable. The rug in the front room stands here for the whole; when John sweeps it,

> he felt that should he sweep it forever, the clouds of dust would not diminish, the rug would not be clean. . . . [F]or each dustpan he so laboriously filled at the doorsill demons added to the rug twenty more; he saw in the expanse behind him the dust that he had raised settling again into the carpet; and he gritted his teeth, already on edge because of the dust that filled his mouth, and nearly wept to think that so much labor brought so little reward.[39]

John's life, internally and externally, is a sinkhole of filth from which he can never hope to escape. Yet while this Harlem violates one iconic image, it validates another, more powerful one. If iconic Harlem is a world of jazz and sociability, stereotypical Harlem is a synonym for urban degradation. John fulfills Harlem's dark promise of poverty, crime, and dirt, bounded by racism and hopelessness. Set elsewhere, the deep, almost existential grit and misery of John's life might not have had such resonance.

Yet he does not stop trying to escape, through increasingly intense religious experiences. He spends a great deal of time at his father's church and speaking to his own religious mentor, a young man appropriately named Brother Elisha. He struggles with his thoughts, his urges, his anger and his despair. And finally, the secrets and the violence within his family—the forbidden love of his mother, the beastly cruelty of his father—come to a head, provoked by his aunt (this time his father's sister) and by his father's beating of his brother Roy. John falls down, so deep into darkness that he cannot imagine rising. His father's eyes "thrust him out" of the community of the saints and an "ironic voice" reminds him that he is cursed because he comes from a cursed people: "All niggers had been cursed."[40] Again, John's fate is tied explicitly into that of his people and embodied by his community, the so-called "Negro capital of the world." Yet in his case the curse comes directly from his father: "Then his father stood just above him, looking down. Then John knew that a curse was renewed from moment to moment, from father to son."[41] Racial inheritance is not simply external and inevitable, Baldwin is suggesting. It is actively transmitted and perpetuated by a people so dragged down that they cannot save others from the same fate. Csapo suggests that in Baldwin's novel love is shown to be impossible, first in the individual sense, and then in the communal—both the black person and black people are rejected, oppressed.[42] While his discussion centers specifically on sexuality and lack of autonomy, it can stand equally well for the relationship between individual and group failings. In this sense, Baldwin's reference to the endlessly renewing curse overlaps with Roth's. In both communities, the past weighs down the present through both family dynamics and traditional community practices. And in both novels, the father blames his own inadequacies on those of his community. Albert sees anti-Semitism in his frequent firings, and in his lack of opportunity just as John's father blames racism and discrimination for his own failures. Both are partially correct, but both also pass off their own responsibility for their actions onto the larger world. Thus is a people's curse renewed.

And yet John's pain "cracks him open" until, at last, "he saw before him the fire, red and gold, and waiting for him—yellow, and red, and gold, and burning in a night eternal, and waiting for him. He must go through the fire, and into this night."[43] Go through it he does. "Then John saw the Lord—for a moment only; and the darkness, for a moment only, was filled with a light he could not bear. Then, in a moment, he was set free."[44] When he awakens, he sees around him the "saints" of the congregation, his aunt, mother, and Brother Elisha. Although his father refuses to embrace his newly saved son, Harlem itself has been altered. "Now the storm was over. And the avenue, like any landscape that has endured a storm, lay changed under Heaven, exhausted and clean, and new."[45] His religious epiphany has transformed his filthy and constrained world into one of beauty and possibility. While he understands that this happy state will not last, he nevertheless clings to the fact that he has attained it. He touches Elisha's arm. "'Elisha,' he said, 'no matter what happens to me, where I go, what folks say about me, no matter what anybody says, you remember—please remember—I was saved. I was there.'"[46]

THE POWER OF PLACE

David and John, Brooklyn and Harlem, Judaism and Christianity. David is quintessentially a Jewish immigrant—he cannot be otherwise for his story to work its power. Anti-Semitism, Yiddish, potato pancakes, and Torah shape who he is and how he interprets what happens to him. His neighborhood is defined by both Jewishness and poverty, from the decrepit religious school to the kosher butcher, from the smells in the hallways to the exoticism of the non-Jewish police. John, for his part, is a black Baptist living in Harlem with Southern-born parents. His father's church, his understanding of what it means to be good, the family's poverty, the activity of the Harlem streets, the criminality of his brother, his fear of white people, shape John, his concerns, and his worldview. Once again, the central character's characteristics and geography mark him as a representative of his own people. These two stories, these two identities, could not be more divergent. Jew, Christian; white, black; immigrant, native. Yet while different in fundamental ways, they are nonetheless tied to one another by pain, violence, sexual awakening, and forbidden love, by poverty, migration, and hardship, by dysfunctional families shaped by the intersection of internal, individual personality traits and external, collective oppression, by the desperate need to find redemption through a religious interpretation of the world and of the past, by the fear of the outside, the sense of marginality, and membership in a despised group. Both are explorations of identity in a world that does not welcome them.

Too, they are tied to one another by the iconic neighborhoods they inhabit, simultaneously actual and mythic. Both Harlem and the Lower East Side are, and are understood as, concentrated ethnic communities, rife with poverty and populated by strivers eager to achieve what they believe the outside world already has. They are crucibles for distinctive cultural identities. They are also both oppressive and parochial neighborhoods; their residents' options are restricted by both external discrimination and internal community dynamics. They are two-faced symbols, embodying despair and community, cultural richness and relentless poverty. The constraints and the opportunities of these neighborhoods shaped the authors and their narratives in significant and in many cases similar ways.

At the same time, because Jewish American and African American experiences differed, so too do their neighborhoods differ. Harlem, for example, and Baldwin's portrayal of it, has more crime and police repression, but at the same time a deeper sense of shared community. The demons Harlemites must exorcize are not only internal but also vividly external, embodied in color as well as in geography. Jewish demons are portrayed in this novel as located largely within the community. The outside world seems more absent than threatening. These distinctions reflected reality. Historically, race has been a far starker dividing line than religion or ethnicity in the United States. Jews may not have been perceived as, or considered themselves as, fully white, but to the outside world, their skin color made all the difference. Jews were permitted entry into that forbidden yet alluring outside world far earlier and more extensively than were African Americans. When David grows up, educated and light-skinned, his challenge will largely be the psychological burden of his experience. John, on the other hand, will confront both his personal experience and the reality of racial discrimination.

The two locations, then, reveal the sharp differences between black and Jewish experience, between David and John, as well as similarities. If, as Diner has suggested, the Lower East Side has come to signify an unconflicted Jewish sacred space, Harlem has continued to signify a double-edged legacy of hope and despair, possibility and imprisonment. Even their iconic geographic centers reveal the divergences as well as the parallels in black and Jewish perceptions of themselves and the world.

David's Jewishness and John's blackness, David's Lower East Side and John's Harlem, both different and the same, nonetheless serve a similar purpose. They define the physical and emotional parameters within which these characters' stories can unfold. And they represent the imagined locations of a black American and a Jewish American past. Sometimes the novels confirm the expected truths of these locations; other times they challenge them. But because Jewish and African American identity is so bound up in memory, in converting history into a progressive, even transcendent narrative, historically significant places such as Harlem and the Lower East Side grow to almost mythic proportions. They become metaphors for blackness, for Jewishness. It is in these places that the characters come alive most vividly; it is because of these places that the books have the power that they do.

Despite the stark differences of race and opportunity between African Americans and Jewish Americans, however, Harlem and the Lower East Side also speak to similar sensibilities of the two groups that have been so visible in twentieth-century urban America. Both understand their experience as one of relentless persecution on one hand, and persistent struggle on the other. Both perceive their own community's narrative in grand, Biblical terms. And both see themselves as quintessential Americans, at home only here, yet with their own cultural and historic identity. They cannot return anywhere if life in America fails, as other ethnic and racial immigrants can. Their fight for their future is here. Both the sense of grand and timeless narrative, and the appreciation that America offers their best hope, have led both blacks and Jews to understand their suffering and their struggle in transcendent, universal terms.

These two communities, more than most others, have understood that the infringement of anyone's rights or opportunities threatened their own tenuous position, and have, more quickly and reliably than most, reached out to others who have been threatened. This understanding has shaped an identity that has, at its best, recognized kinship, both real and imagined, with all who struggle. For all these reasons, from their understanding of their marginality to their response to it, blacks and Jews have often made common cause in American politics. More than that, these two communities have engaged with one another more frequently and more intensely than they have with any other group. Not without struggle—any deeply felt relationship is also deeply fraught, and the stark differences in power and opportunity between the two groups have created their own tensions. But that engagement pervades both communities. Baldwin himself spoke many times about Jews, about what we now call black-Jewish relations, and about his own relationships with Jewish people.[47]

None of this is to negate the significance of black and Jewish differences, not the least of which is a general blindness in the American Jewish community of the privileges and benefits they have gained by their whiteness. Both groups may understand themselves as victims, but in America only black people have endured the structural and institutionalized discrimination of society and the state. Roth's people succeeded in ways that Baldwin's could not, aided by conditions not of their own making. This different experience of American opportunity, which has in turn led to a power differential far more evident to black people than to Jews, has shaped blacks' and Jews' worldviews in ways that remain radically divergent, despite the shared sense that their identity is bound up in their engagement with the world. And it is revealed in these two novels as well; David's fears and the threats to his well-being are entirely internal to his community and his family while John's are rooted in both his own world and the larger white world that constrained him as it constrained all black people.

Whether Baldwin consciously modeled his novel after Roth's is in some sense beside the point. His worldview and Roth's, the ways each understood the problems of their people, took similar forms. The fact that in so many aspects these characters' experiences ran parallel, that such different life stories have such similar resonances, reinforces the fundamental parallels between black and Jewish self-understanding. At the same time, the fundamental American dividing line of race meant the dramatically different outcomes to the black and Jewish communities. So it is no surprise that Roth's and Baldwin's settings, the sacred and mythic spaces of their community, were employed as the physical embodiment of their narrators' experience. John is part and parcel of Harlem; his story could not have been as personally powerful and yet as quintessentially black, had it been set elsewhere. David, Roth's essential Jew, is reflected in the Lower East Side he inhabits and embodies. The very specificity of geography and sensibility that marks *Call It Sleep* as an American Jewish novel and *Go Tell It on the Mountain* as an African American one is what ties the two together as particularist versions of a universalist sense of communal self-understanding.

NOTES

1. Adam Newton, *Facing Black and Jew* (Cambridge: Cambridge University Press, 1999), 10.

2. See, for example, Karen Lawrence's "Roth's *Call It Sleep*: Modernism on the Lower East Side" and Leslie Fiedler's "The Many Myths of Henry Roth," both in *New Essays on* Call It Sleep, ed. Hana Wirth-Nesher (Cambridge: Cambridge University Press, 1996).

3. Ezra Cappell, *American Talmud: The Cultural Work of Jewish American Fiction* (Albany, State University of New York Press, 2007), 29.

4. For the claim that Baldwin is rejecting religion, see Csaba Csapo, "Race, Religion, and Sexuality," in *James Baldwin's* Go Tell It on the Mountain: *Historical*

and Critical Essays, ed. Carol Henderson (New York: Peter Lang, 2006); for the opposite claim, see Michael Lynch, "A Glimpse of the Hidden God" and Brian Norman, "Duplicity, Purity and Politicized Morality," both in Henderson's *James Baldwin*.

5. Both novels also, of course, contain autobiographical elements that make them singular and personal expressions of the authors' worldviews. Baldwin was himself a young preacher in Harlem; Roth grew up in Bronxville and the Lower East Side. Indeed, many of the specific events in these novels mirrored those in the lives of their authors, and the richness of their emotional tone suggests the authors' close identification with the situations described. Not surprisingly, then, virtually every literary critic of either Baldwin or Roth has also explored how their separate histories informed their work.

6. See Lynch, "Glimpse," 38.

7. Henry Roth, *Call It Sleep*, 20.

8. Ibid., 33.

9. See, for example, Hasia Diner, *Lower East Side Memories* (Princeton: Princeton University Press, 2000) and Irving Howe, *World of Our Fathers* (New York: New York University Press, 1976).

10. Roth, *Call It Sleep*, 143.

11. Ibid., 31–32.

12. Ibid., 241.

13. Ibid., 431.

14. Ibid., 97.

15. Ibid., 101.

16. See Fiedler, "Many Myths," 21; Hana Wirth-Nesher, *Call It English* (Princeton: Princeton University Press, 2006), chap. 4; and Werner Sollors, "'A World Somewhere, Somewhere Else'" in *New Essays*.

17. Roth, *Call It Sleep*, 18.

18. Ibid., 106.

19. Ibid., 21.

20. Ibid., 219.

21. Ibid., 276.

22. Ibid., 104.

23. Ibid., 250.

24. Kremena Todorova, "'Oy, a good men!' Urban Voices and Democracy in Henry Roth's *Call It Sleep*," *Texas Studies in Literature and Language* 48, no. 3 (2006): 250–72.

25. Thomas Ferraro, *Ethnic Passages: Literary Immigrants in Twentieth-Century America* (Chicago: University of Chicago Press, 1998), chap. 3.

26. Roth, *Call It Sleep*, 147–51.

27. Ibid., 158.

28. Ibid., 274.

29. Cappell, *American Talmud*, 27.

30. James Baldwin, *Go Tell It on the Mountain*, 188.

31. Ibid., 36.

32. Ibid., 37.

33. Ibid., 39.

34. Ibid., 33.
35. Ibid., 34.
36. Csapo, "Race, Religion, and Sexuality," 62.
37. Baldwin, *Go Tell It*, 4.
38. Ibid., 34.
39. Ibid., 26–27.
40. Ibid., 196, 197.
41. Ibid., 197.
42. Csapo, "Race, Religion, and Sexuality," 63.
43. Baldwin, *Go Tell It*, 202.
44. Ibid., 204.
45. Ibid., 215.
46. Ibid., 220.
47. See, for example, James Baldwin, "The Harlem Ghetto: Winter, 1948," *Commentary* 5, no. 2 (February 1948): 170; W. E. B. DuBois Department of Afro-American Studies, *James Baldwin on Blacks and Jews*, Pamphlet, University of Massachusetts, 1988.

SIX

"THE GESTURE WAS NEVER ENOUGH"

Harlem as a Problematic Proving Ground for Jewish Reformers in the Post–World War II Period

Adam Meyer

The post–World War II years were a transitional period in the history of Harlem, but then so had been every other period in the area's history up to that point. From a small Dutch village founded in the eighteenth century to a bustling neighborhood in the 1920s and, shortly thereafter, the heart of African American culture, Harlem had already gone through many changes. Nevertheless, the changes that occurred after World War II were largely responsible for creating the image of Harlem as a metonym for the urban slum or ghetto—conceived of as an overcrowded, economically deprived, and largely black environment—that dominated the public perception for the next half-century at least. Although Jews had lived in significant numbers in Harlem since the 1880s, one of the first out-migrations from the Lower East Side, by the end of World War II only two significant categories of Jews remained in Harlem: mercantile concerns, those who had established their stores to cater to Harlem's Jews and had stayed behind to serve Harlem's blacks,[1] and a certain breed of idealistic liberal reformers who had not grown up in Harlem but who saw value in trying to improve the situation in America's best-known racialized urban slum. Having escaped their own ghetto on the Lower East Side, in some cases literally and in others figuratively, they would now try to help these other others to do the same.

Although little remarked on by scholars, the tradition of Jewish reformism in Harlem dates back to roughly the turn of the twentieth century and the Settlement Movement spearheaded by Lillian D. Wald,[2] but it became especially pronounced in the postwar period (roughly 1945 to 1975). A new generation of Jewish reformers arose who wanted to put the ideals of antifascism into practice in America by destroying entrenched racism and prejudice in the largest of her black ghettos,[3] turning Harlem into a testing ground for the validity of their claims. These postwar reformers, like their predecessors, were an example of the larger historical connection of Jews to liberal causes that has become a commonplace in American political life.[4] While there is some controversy about why American Jews have for so long been and continue to identify as liberals, even when being so might be against their own self-interest, there can be no doubt that a feeling of solidarity with the stranger has been construed by many American Jews as a central tenet of Jewish social life.

The "'traditional Jewish values' of social justice,"[5] which scholars such as Marc Dollinger and Michael E. Staub date back to the days of the Hebrew prophets,[6] are understood to encourage empathy and identification with the downtrodden and the underdogs. Whether as a result of their interpretation of the Jewish tradition as requiring solidarity with the stranger or not, American Jews have consistently been at the forefront of promoting strong and positive race relations, as many scholars have shown.[7] In their important study *Beyond the Melting Pot*, Nathan Glazer and Daniel Patrick Moynihan pointed out, for example, that "the Jewish community in New York is the one most actively committed to the principles of racial integration and group tolerance."[8] As with the Settlement Movement, the "new generation of Jewish professionals" that emerged after World War II "led the American Jewish Committee, the Anti-Defamation League, and the American Jewish Congress into the vanguard of the emerging intergroup relations movement."[9] Such organizations, embracing the "unitary concept of prejudice,"[10] the idea that anti-Semitism, racism, and all other forms of bigotry are essentially the same, encouraged young Jews to go into and work in places like Harlem as a way of effecting true change, and many answered this call.

These reformers no doubt viewed their actions as being magnanimous and helpful, as dispensers of aid almost always do, but those who received their assistance were often affected by it in a different way. The very positioning of these liberal Jews, as outsiders coming to offer assistance to the underprivileged, sometimes made it difficult for them to carry out their own agendas. It is not a coincidence that these reformers were frequently referred to with the somewhat derisive epithet of "do-gooders." Just as relations between Jewish merchants and black customers in Harlem became an increasingly tense flashpoint of antagonism in the postwar period,[11] so did those between these Jewish do-gooders and their clients, and partly because these roles indicated something about how Jews were moving into the mainstream during this period while the blacks living in Harlem were seen to be stagnating. Despite their deeply rooted historical identification with these other outsiders, the realities of their present situation resulted in feelings of dis-identification as well. The results of these Jewish reformers' attempts at amelioration, therefore, often did not live up to their expectations, for reasons that they frequently contributed to but could not see. In several novels of the period by Jewish American writers, such do-gooders appeared as policemen, as in Benjamin Appel's *The Dark Stain* (1943) or Ed Lacy's *In Black and Whitey* (1967), or as doctors, as in Gerald Green's *The Last Angry Man* (1956), or as social workers, as in Sol Yurick's *The Bag* (1968). While these novels thematize the popular conception of Harlem as a black slum in need of redemption, they also serve to emphasize the ways in which the harsh realities of life in the ghetto for its African American residents prove to be more resistant to change than the protagonists expected, leading to feelings of frustration and futility that cause them to question the very basis of their enterprise.

Even more often than as social workers, however, whose presence in postwar studies of the Harlem ghetto is commonplace,[12] Jewish reformers in Harlem came to be found in connection with the educational system, particularly the public schools. Among "Jews [who] made efforts to assist blacks in various ways," Murray Friedman points out, "most notabl[e were] Jewish teachers who chose to go into Harlem."[13] Not surprisingly, then, two novels by Jewish American writers that are particularly significant in terms of revealing the problematic position of Jewish reformers in Harlem are ones that depict Jewish teachers at work in Harlem public schools, Irwin Stark's *The Invisible Island* (1948) and Sheila Solomon Klass's *Come Back on Monday* (1960). Both Stark and Klass had experience teaching in Harlem and wrote their novels with a kind of reformer's zeal, hoping to correct what they saw as serious flaws and abuses in the system. Their protagonists, Matthew Stafford and Deborah Lieb respectively, represent precisely the kinds of progressive, idealistic liberal Jews who gravitated into the teaching profession in general and into "difficult" instructional situations in particular. Because the texts are presented from the points of view of the Jewish teachers, they largely attempt to portray the positive aspects of Jewish do-gooderism's encounter with Harlem's blacks. The reader is certainly intended to empathize with the Jewish teacher and hope for the success of his or her educational project. At the same time, however, and perhaps unwittingly, the texts also show the problematic nature of that encounter, particularly when it is seen from the perspective of the black students. The do-gooderism that Matthew Stafford and Deborah Lieb embody can also be seen, by the reader if not by the characters themselves, to be self-serving and paternalistic, on the one hand, and of no real practical help on the other.

This view is even more pronounced in a novel that serves as an interesting counter to Stark's and Klass's texts, the African American writer Alice Childress's young adult novel *A Hero Ain't Nothin' but a Sandwich* (1973). Here a Jewish teacher in Harlem, Bernard Cohen, is part of a group of concerned adults who attempt to help a boy who has started using heroin; while one chapter of the narrative is told from Cohen's point of view, we also see a good deal of the Jewish teacher from the black student's perspective, as well as that of a fellow black teacher, again raising questions about the position of the Jewish do-gooder in Harlem. Taken together, these three novels seem to indicate the difficulty of truly building bridges between the two communities, at least through the actions of Jewish reformers.

IRWIN STARK'S *THE INVISIBLE ISLAND*

This very image of the bridge is the quite literal conceit with which Irwin Stark both begins and ends *The Invisible Island*; in fact, when an earlier and much shorter version of the novel had been published to some acclaim in *The Antioch Review*, it had been titled "The Bridge." The thematic significance of the bridge, as we shall see, refers not only to the separation between the white and black sections of New York but also provides a symbol of Matthew's crossing over from his comfortable life to his activist one. This thematic concern is undergirded, if you will, by the structural significance of the bridge, since the novel is built on the axis of two intertwining halves. On the one hand, there are chapters entitled "The School," which take place from March to June of 1943 in a Harlem high school; on the other hand, interspersed with these, there are chapters entitled "Matthew Stratton," which tell us of the protagonist's life from the time he is a small boy until March 1943, when he makes his decision to seek work as a teacher in Harlem. The two sections meet up at the end, such that the last scene in the penultimate chapter—Matthew standing in the Bronx and looking across a bridge at the new environment he will be entering—takes place only a few seconds before the first scene in the first chapter—as Matthew crosses the bridge; the novel's closing chapter is a "Finale." The notion of crossing the bridge clearly shows Matthew's desire to reach those on the other side, but also implies the potential difficulties involved in doing so.

In the biographical chapters, we learn of the factors that ultimately led to Matthew's decision. One of these factors, although he can't entirely explain how, is clearly his Jewishness. Three of Matthew's grandparents had been Jewish, and his father had grown up on the Lower East Side,[14] but he himself does not feel particularly attached to this religion. Being a member of the post–Lower East Side generation, Matthew is closer to being a completely assimilated American than he is to his Jewish roots. Even as war murmurings begin in Europe, Matthew's position is that "anti-Semitism was something he felt no more keenly than his own Jewishness" (128), that is to say, very little. Nevertheless, when he takes one of the first significant actions of his life, one that will have significant implications for later events—coming to the aid of a man who is being beaten for having heckled a pro-Nazi speech and getting severely beaten himself as a result—he can't help but wonder "why he had sailed into [the mob]? Was it because he was a Jew somewhere still in the dark chambers of his unconscious?" (249). Whatever the cause, Matthew understands that this action, "the first time he had clearly and dispassionately willed an act for himself" (249), marks a turning point in his life, one that will eventually take him to Harlem. It is the sense of Jewish outsiderism that he experiences at the speech that eventually creates the connection in his mind between a desire to help others and the idea of Harlem as a place in need of help. His empathy for the stranger who is being mistreated is clearly on display here, arising from an unacknowledged Jewishness and leading to political liberalism.

For a long time prior to this event, Matthew had described himself as "not [being] interested in politics" (91), even referring to himself at one point as "a natural born fence-sitter" (136). Although he roughly aligns himself with the liberals—his girlfriend and her brother both use this term in referring to him (184, 135)—he is much less committed than are most of his college friends, several of whom, including this brother and sister, are quite radical. Nonetheless, the growing political consciousness that causes him to aid the heckler becomes another factor that draws him to Harlem. After being beaten, Matthew can no longer be "the spineless creature . . . who had stood on the edge of the crowd" (251); once he recovers, therefore, he looks for a way to bring this new resolve into practical action. The logical thing for him to do, given the novel's time frame, would be to go off and fight in World War II, but the beating has left him deaf in one ear and therefore 4F. Feeling that "all his previous life had been an escape" (336), he bemoans the irony that the one moment when he did act has led to the "travesty" (336) that makes him now unable to do so again. It is this desire to make a stand that leads Matthew, "well-intentioned liberal and potential reformer," according to Alain Locke in his review of the novel,[15] to undertake his mission of outreach. Here, again, his identification with those who are getting the short end of the stick drives him to make a decisive step.

Another significant factor that plays into Matthew's monumental decision is his friendship with the African American Ben Dawson, a minor Harlem Renaissance poet whom Matthew, a radio scriptwriter and would-be novelist, meets when they are both working at the post office. Ben leaves the post office for a job teaching in the public schools and Matthew follows him, although, unlike Ben's position at the all-male Emerson High School in "the Blackbelt," Stark's name for Harlem in the novel,[16] Matthew gets a job in an all-white school on Long Island, Grant High. He enjoys teaching at Grant, but even more he admires the way in which Ben has been "accepting [of] his classes in the Blackbelt, accepting [of] what he could do to push out the horizons of his pupils" (220). Growing up, Matthew had seen Harlem as "the forbidden neighborhood of the black people" (26), and even in the novel's opening scene referred to above he calls it "a dark jungle" (1), but Ben, explaining what teaching at Emerson has given him, eventually convinces Matthew to face the "challenge" (351) as well. His decision to enter the Blackbelt therefore marks a dramatic "moment . . . of inner change" (17) in his life. Because Harlem represents the place of ultimate degradation, it also represents the place of ultimate challenge, a place that calls for one to put one's political idealism to the test, as Matthew is now poised to do.

The final event that pushes Matthew into his new career path is the death of his best friend, Howard Whitman, member of a pacifist family but volunteer for the war, killed fighting in Africa. This is what he tries to explain to Philip Johnson, the African American assistant principal at Emerson, in the novel's opening chapter. The assistant principal is curious about Matthew's motivation in requesting a reassignment from Grant to Emerson as a full-time substitute for the last few months of the term. Although Matthew has been thinking about this question for quite some time, he doesn't have a very good explanation; finally he comes up with "[t]he guilt of safety," the idea that he "could be more useful" at Emerson, which, being "the toughest spot in the [school] system" (2), "is a bit closer to the front than Grant" (3). He cannot avenge Howard's death on the battlefield, so he decides to make this Harlem school his personal war zone.[17] Matthew's idealistic zeal is obvious to everyone who comes into contact with him. Johnson, for example, prefaces an offer of advice with the following awkward comment: "There's one serious mistake a man like you is bound to make. A—a white man. Not all white men, of course, but men like you, men who are motivated by a deep sense of uh . . . idealism" (14). Ben Dawson is also aware that Matthew has "his own ideals" (52) and uses this knowledge to his advantage in recruiting Matthew to Emerson. Even Wilber MacIntosh, the principal at Grant, offers him a warning against being too enthusiastic about what teaching in Harlem will mean: "'Don't exaggerate the hope of what you can do at Emerson,' he said. 'Don't lose perspective and think you can remake the world by yourself. . . . The world can't be remade by a gesture'" (356). Nevertheless, there is no doubt that Matthew enters into his job at Emerson in much the same spirit that St. George had when he went off to slay the dragon.[18]

Once he actually steps into the fray, however, Matthew finds there to be a number of obstacles that need to be overcome before he can bring his idealistic vision to fruition.[19] First of all, there are his colleagues and superiors within the school. Many of his fellow teachers have fallen victim to the fatigue that is inherent in the job of teaching in an inner-city high school. Martin Coates, upon first meeting Matthew, tells him that "[s]ome of us came here with the same idea [that you have.] You don't know what you're up against yet, that's all. It doesn't work out your way, and after a while you learn to sit back and forget the ideals. For your own good" (53). Matthew feels generally positive about Johnson, at least at first, but he immediately dislikes the black police officer who is assigned to the school, Tom Mallory, and wishes that Johnson would stand up and speak out against his bullying tactics. He is also dismayed by the principal himself, Charlie Connors, a racist and anti-Semitic Irishman who hides himself away eating bon-bons whenever anything serious is taking place. Secondly, there are Matthew's students themselves, who have also been beaten down by the system for years and are naturally wary of this new and somewhat green teacher. When he first meets them, he immediately senses "undertones of fear and resentment, the indelible suspicion which dulled their eyes and turned their speech always into sullenness and defiance" (12). He gets himself off to a bad start, furthermore, by embarrassing one of the students, encouraging him to take off his coat but regretting it when the boy reveals that all he has on beneath it is a tattered undershirt; often "his advances toward genuine friendship with the young Negroes are checked by perversities of circumstance,"[20] namely the ingrained hostility of these black students to any white authority figure. Matthew may identify with them philosophically, but his immediate actions and reactions are ones of dis-identification.

Matthew himself must thus be seen as part of the problem as well, although he doesn't recognize himself in that role. His outward demeanor toward the students is an attempt to deny the obvious differences between him and them, his position as outsider in terms of class and background as well as race, not to mention his power advantage, but they see through to the truth anyway, as in the awkwardness of the situation with the boy who wanted to wear his jacket.[21] The students spend a long time "trying to get used to him, still puzzled, always distrusting the color of his skin, resenting his sympathy perhaps" (166). Here Stark indicates something to the reader that the black students realize but Matthew does not: that the very fact of his position vis-à-vis his students makes it quite difficult for him to carry out his bridge-building desires. Because he cannot see this, the more Matthew works at Emerson, the more the shine is rubbed off of his idealism and the more frustrated he becomes; as Locke notes, he gets inside Harlem, but only "at the price of embarrassment and disillusionment."[22] When he "faced the rows of black faces, the laughing, mocking, sullen, hurt, and fearful faces in which defiance was the sum of all they felt, he had nothing for them except words. . . . And they weren't enough. They could not be understood. They could not be trusted" (316). He acknowledges his shortcomings here, but not quite his own complicity in creating them. He does not realize that his liberal, idealistic plan about rescuing Harlem youth is, at the same time, also geared toward making himself feel good about his own bravery and magnanimity, a motivational doubling that, while perhaps endemic to all liberal reformers, nevertheless seems an unhealthy mix for all concerned. Here Stark seems to be making a larger point about liberalism in general, or at least about the idea of social uplift: that it reinforces a white, middle-class ideal. Matthew does not fully recognize the structural inequalities involved in his Harlem teaching, and the fact that he thinks he can do good through education and caring demonstrates a certain blindness to the complexity of the interrelations of race and class inequalities in the United States. He wants to identify with his black students, but he doesn't take into account the way in which his privileged position as a white liberal reformer makes it almost impossible for his students to identify with him.

During the course of the novel, Matthew's entire project comes to be symbolized by his relationship with one of his students in particular, Johnny Boston. Arriving late to class the first day, Boston exudes an air of defiance, but Matthew "knew at once that this one was somehow different from the rest" (10). And he is different, if for no other reason than Matthew's thinking that he is; Matthew makes rescuing Johnny Boston his personal mission. Later in the novel Matthew comes to Johnny's defense when, after having been framed as a crap game participant, the youth is roughed up by Mallory. He complains to Johnson and Connors, but to no avail; he can express his disgust and bewilderment that "teachers [are] on the other side" (329), but he can't do anything to change the system and save Johnny Boston.[23] Nevertheless, he persists in his mission, still hoping to find some way to "speak to" Johnny, to tell him "that he had found at least one ally here, that the issue had been joined, that they were together in this against Mallory and Johnson and the school" (330). Having come to distrust words, Matthew decides that the way to show Boston his camaraderie is to buy him a symbolic gift, "something that would have to be bigger than any words he could say to Johnny" (330). By the time Johnny returns to school a week later, however, he offers no response when Matthew gives him the present. Matthew further attempts to express his message to the boy when, in a scene reminiscent of his coming to the aid of the Nazi denouncer, he refuses to allow Mallory to conduct an inspection of the students during his instructional time.[24] The policeman is shocked by what the teacher has done, as is the rest of the class, but Matthew feels only that he has waited so long to take such a stand that doing so no longer has any effect on Johnny, whose face presents "nothing to show that this had meant anything to him, nothing to disturb the numb and paranoiac silence" (334). It seems clear to Matthew at this point that he has failed in the task that has become the primary symbol of his mission, the rescuing of Johnny Boston. His idealistic liberalism has proven to be no match for Harlem's harsh reality.

Matthew's failure with Johnny Boston is particularly disappointing to him because he had gone so far out of his way to try to communicate with Johnny but it had not worked. What Matthew fails to see is that the very method by which he had gone about trying to reach the youth provides an explanation of why the attempt failed. First of all, the present that Matthew picks for Johnny, a blue polka-dotted necktie, is ridiculous; not only is it insufficient as a receptacle of so many of Matthew's hopes, but it is completely impractical for Johnny. Secondly, the fact that Matthew tries to give Johnny something to make up for what has happened to him only reinforces Johnny's view that he has no control over his own life but always has to accept what others give him. Here the necktie may have some symbolic value for Johnny as a kind of yoke, but that is certainly not Matthew's intent. Finally, that intent itself, particularly the intensity of it, the way in which Matthew describes the moment when he hands Johnny the package—"The silence was pressing in on them. It was a substance, a white protoplasmic jelly moving out from every corner to engulf them" (331)[25]—puts far too much pressure on Johnny Boston, who now finds himself in the position of having to save the teacher rather than of being saved by him. It is no surprise that he refuses Matthew's outreach, or that he turns and leaves without even opening the package. Matthew, during the week in which he was waiting for Johnny to return to school, told himself that the gift "would have to work. It could not be a trick, done smoothly, mechanically. It could not be a gesture" (331). Even so, Johnny knows immediately that that's what it is; following Matthew's standing up to Mallory, Johnny offers him "no word, no smile, no single gesture to show he knew" (334), although the implication (Matthew's hope?) is that he does recognize the teacher's offer of friendship but won't acknowledge it.

Stark's use of the word *gesture* twice in this crucial scene calls to mind MacIntosh's admonition to Matthew that "the world can't be remade by a gesture." In his down moments, Matthew comes to see the reality of this point. Thinking about a new job his girlfriend has taken with a civil rights organization in Detroit, for example, he wonders whether she thinks "that because she was going to be involved in [the League's] crusade against hate the involvement would liberate her any more fully than his going to the Blackbelt had liberated him. The gesture was never enough" (124). Matthew's gesture clearly doesn't seem to have been enough in the case of Johnny Boston, and the connection is made even more explicit when Matthew's feelings of helplessness and despair are exacerbated at the climax of the novel, in "The Finale" chapter, by the death of Johnny Boston in a gun battle with Mallory. Hearing the news, Matthew questions how much impact he had really had on the lives of the children he taught: "How far, how deep had he nicked into the massive walls of their fear and hate? He had done his best. . . . What was it MacIntosh had said to him four months before? Don't try to remake the world with a gesture. . . . He hadn't remade it" (372). He had gestured, but it had not worked. Johnny Boston is dead and Matthew is left with only the small satisfaction that he was able to kill Mallory on his way out. Claiming Boston as "one of mine" (374) in a conversation with Johnson, he agrees with the assistant principal's assertion that the two deaths represent "poetic justice" (375), although the two educators are interpreting that poet quite differently.

The final scene of the novel takes place on the bridge that has played such an important symbolic role throughout the text. It is here that Matthew and Ben meet to discuss the aftermath of the Boston-Mallory killings. Ben assumes that Johnny's death will mark the end of Matthew's career as a teacher in Harlem, but the younger man surprises him. "'Of course I'm coming back,' Matthew said eagerly. The excitement tingled his body. 'I've got to come back!'" (376). Matthew's exuberant idealism may have given way to the harsh reality of the situation he is trying to remedy, but his belief that it can be remedied remains intact. "Inclined to fight as hard as before for what he believes in," as one reviewer stated,[26] he realizes that changing the world "was like marching up against a stone wall. . . . [I]t would not come tumbling down in a few weeks. There was no single and dramatic answer. But if he pounded on it, if he dug into the mortar between the bricks, day in day out like Ben—What then?" (166–67). As Locke points out, Matthew's "re-dedication to a teaching–social service career in Harlem, even after the disillusionments of the failure of Johnny Boston, his test protégé, gives a moral twist to the end of the story that is far from defeatist."[27] Matthew comes to see Johnny Boston less as a victim than as a hero—he replaces the word *deceased* on Johnny's personnel card with the word *murdered* in a symbolic gesture of defiance—and vows to carry on the good fight against the Mallorys of the world, chastened a bit, "scarred by the stigmata of conscience and compassion" (374), but still forging ahead.[28]

This sounds good for Matthew, and the reader is seemingly meant to identify with him and cheer him on as the novel concludes. Still, there are some underlying problems here, particularly in the self-serving nature of some of Matthew's attitudes. If he continues to teach in Harlem because he feels that he owes it to Johnny Boston, and more importantly to himself, to continue to put forth his gesture, then he is likely to be incapable of creating the very bridges that his project is dedicated to erecting. "You turn and look back," Matthew ruminates at the novel's end, standing on the bridge, "and the school is still there, the Blackbelt is still there and so are Johnny, and Mallory, Connors, Johnson, and all the kids. It's all there. And yet it's not the same. . . . You've been through it, it has done something to you, and you've been caught forever in the equation. . . . In a dim and promising way you are beginning to know that whatever you've given has been a necessary offering. And for the first time you want to scream your lungs into the violent inhale and exhale of life" (376). Matthew's do-gooderism has been good for himself, this passage seems to imply, even if it hasn't been of much value to Johnny Boston. The entire arc of *The Invisible Island*, then, as its jacket copy declares, shows the reader "the testing of [Matthew's] democratic faith through his job" in Harlem, a testing that demonstrates that idealistic Jewish liberal teachers can only do so much good in Harlem precisely because of their position as idealistic Jewish liberal teachers. Matthew's failure to see himself as his students see him, to acknowledge that from their perspective he is part of the problem rather than part of the solution, ultimately leads to his inability to fulfill his mission. Thinking of Johnny Boston, Matthew notes the "iron[y] that they could not cross over to each other and bridge the gap of skin, position, age, understanding and knowledge" (177), but these gulfs turn out to be too wide to traverse, even if Matthew himself never seems to understand fully the significance and practical ramifications of this situation and the role that he plays in it. Although his ostensible mission had been to achieve identification with the stranger, his innate dis-identification had made reaching this goal an impossible task.

SHEILA SOLOMON KLASS'S *COME BACK ON MONDAY*

Like *The Invisible Island*, Sheila Solomon Klass's *Come Back on Monday* opens on a March day with a panoramic description of Harlem, narrowing down to look at a particular school, in this case the all-female Thoreau Junior High, "bottom school in Negro Harlem."[29] That Klass should have named her fictional school Thoreau while Stark had designated his Emerson is one of the odder and more striking parallels between the two texts, and it is a telling connection, since the names conjure up images of self-reliant rebels who set out to correct a system that they feel has become dysfunctional.[30] The kind of idealistic optimism that we associate with the Transcendentalists—as opposed to, say, the brute power that we associate with General Grant, the eponym of Matthew's white school—is an important component in the background of Stark's main character, and it will be for Deborah Lieb, Klass's protagonist, as well. Indeed, Deborah does share many traits with Matthew and experiences many similar situations. In the novel's opening chapter, for example, Deborah explains "how [she] came to teach in Harlem" (22), much as Matthew had explained his rationale to Assistant Principal Johnson. "I requested [the assignment]," Deborah says. "You have to understand my background. I was a refugee kid. I had one haven in those displaced childhood years—the school. There I learned that life didn't have to be so grubby. So I chose teaching and I came to Harlem. Negroes had nothing to do with it. I looked for a school where the kids would want what I had to offer" (22). Negroes may have nothing to do with it for her, which is her awkward way of trying to explain that skin color has no significance for her, as it did not for Matthew, but if Harlem was not black then she likely would not be teaching there because it would not be so full of children in need of her help. This is only one of several parallels between Deborah and Matthew, summed up by their obvious membership in the club of Jewish liberal reformers determined to fix the world, with all of the problematic self-referentiality that is implicit in that brother- or sisterhood of do-gooders. Her mother, afraid for Deborah's welfare in Harlem, is close to the mark when she derisively refers to her daughter as Albert Schweitzer (23). As in Stark's novel, though, in Klass's, too, we find that the Jewish teacher is ultimately unable to form the bridge that would truly earn her Dr. Schweitzer's level of distinction.

The significance of the Jewishness in her background is more obvious to Deborah than it was to Matthew, as evidenced by her reference to being "a refugee kid" and to the importance that the public school had played in her life. "[T]he only child of orthodox Jews who had fled from Austria in 1936 and found haven in Brownsville, Brooklyn" (33–34), where they had stressed to their daughter that "education was everything," Deborah in many ways kept their "poor Jew's point of view" despite being "college educated" and "liberated from Brownsville" (34). Later in the novel, when Deborah is facing a potential disaster, her boyfriend, David, encourages her to stay strong by bringing up this heritage. "I don't want you to just sit around hoping like your Dachau cousins did," he says to her. "Don't let them cut your hair" (199). The reference is to a story Deborah had told of watching the Nazis cutting off her mother's luxurious hair while she had silently urged her to resist, and it is precisely this image of fighting back, of refusing to succumb to power, that impels Deborah forward. There is undoubtedly a strong connection between her experiences in Europe and her work in Harlem, just as Matthew's decision to teach in Harlem stemmed in part from the battlefield death of his friend Howard. In both cases, the protagonists seem to want to make up for some situation earlier in their lives when they were unable to help those closest to them. They clearly see a connection between themselves as outsiders and African Americans, thus linking their liberal do-gooderism to their Jewishness, without having any understanding of how truly fraught this identification can become.

Partly because of the important role being Jewish plays in her life, Deborah's adherence to liberal values is also more obvious at first than was Matthew's. Thinking about her black students at one point, for example, she notes that "she did not allow herself the luxury of prejudice. Memories of the Hitler era had made her a conscientious, puritanical liberal" (55). Her boyfriend, David, also speaks of her "nice liberal adult mind" (63), albeit with a less than entirely positive tone. His condescending attitude is one reflection of Deborah's idealism, which is every bit as pronounced and obvious to everyone around her as was Matthew's.[31] Here, too, one of her fellow teachers warns her: "Be careful. . . . You get a reputation among the teachers as a do-gooder and they'll think you're queer" (67). Even so, Deborah perseveres, presenting herself as a Jewish avenger for her black students much as Matthew did, with equally problematic, and equally unacknowledged, results.

As in Matthew's case, Deborah soon faces real obstacles that she must overcome in order to make her plan a reality, and the same ones: some of her fellow teachers and administrators, on the one hand, and her students on the other. Although Deborah does find a best friend in her African American colleague Ruby,[32] most of her fellow teachers, black and white, are beneath contempt. Even worse is the administration.[33] Deborah's Connors is Sybil Knox, an aging but upwardly aspiring Jewish principal (her husband's original surname was Nussbaum) whose probationary period in Harlem is up, causing her to look forward to being relocated to a better (i.e., white) school. "We served our time," she tells her assistant. "Now it's our turn for parole—let someone else be missionary to the savages" (14). Her primary goal is to make sure that nothing happens at the school that will put a negative mark on her record and threaten her transfer; actually educating Thoreau's students is far down her list of priorities. This naturally marks her as one of Deborah's enemies, and vice versa. In particular, Sybil is put out precisely by Deborah's missionary zeal. "Why was it her rotten luck to always draw these freaks, these crank Samaritans on her staff?," Sybil thinks with regard to Mrs. Wong, the hygiene teacher who had been observed actually talking to her students about the problems of head lice, but the sentiment applies to Deborah as well. "They seemed to pour into Harlem. Why couldn't she get normal, disinterested teachers who followed the Syllabi and didn't make trouble?" (74). This is clearly not what Deborah has in mind and, as a result, she finds Sybil to be not only insufferable but almost dangerous.[34]

With regard to her students, Deborah tells of experiencing much the same reaction on her first day of actual teaching in Harlem that Matthew Stratton felt, a sense that the reality of the situation might be other than what her liberal idealism had led her to expect. "She remembered . . . her panic when she confronted her first class, forty Negro girls. *They all look alike*, she'd thought," betraying her fear. Looking back, she is "ashamed" (55) of her attitude, but it certainly affected her first days as a teacher in Harlem. After a few years in the system, though, Deborah has acclimated herself; just as the students stopped calling her "*the white teacher with the nice hair*" after they got to know her, so "[s]he, in turn, had stopped thinking of them as Negro children. They were just children now" (107). Although some of the students remain wary of her as a white authority figure, despite her claim that this designation does not apply, others come to regard her as a kind of surrogate mother. This would seem to be exactly the kind of bridge building that the Jewish liberal do-gooder project calls for, and indeed Deborah's attempts to befriend her students are portrayed as positive and desirable, but there are also certain indications that the gulfs between them cannot fully be bridged. Perhaps unconsciously, Klass is showing, as did Stark, that the differences that separate Jews and blacks in Harlem cannot be so easily transcended. Deborah identifies at least philosophically with these students, but this proves not to be enough to overcome the factors that simultaneously and inherently dis-identify her from them.

Nowhere is this failure more apparent than in Deborah's relationship with Barbara Jonas, one of the school's toughest cases and Deborah's pet project. Just as Matthew became particularly concerned about his student Johnny Boston, so Deborah becomes especially attached to the idea of saving Barbara, the daughter of an alcoholic prostitute who has lived with her abusive grandmother since the age of fourteen, when she was raped by one of her mother's clients. Although Ruby warns Deborah that "you can't carry that kid as your cross" (41), it's clear that that is exactly what she is going to do. She provides extra time to meet with Barbara, time when they "talked or read a story together" (69). Like Matthew, Deborah laments that all she can really offer Barbara is "the inadequacy of words" (71), but she tries her best to shelter her young protégé. Occasionally she gives Barbara small presents as a token of her feelings, but, as with Matthew's outreach to Johnny Boston, Deborah is not really sure how the gifts have been received. Even so, she is determined at the very least to "show Barbara that in this world where no one had cared for her, her teacher now cared" (73). She even takes the unusual step of loaning her student a dollar, trusting her word that the debt will be repaid and shaking hands on the deal. It does seem that Barbara is becoming more responsible under Deborah's tutelage, a sign of the kind of bridge building that Deborah has been longing to create.

During the week in which the novel takes place, however, Deborah has her own personal issues to deal with and is forced to push Barbara's concerns to the side temporarily, saying to her, in the haunting phrase that gives the novel its title, "Come back on Monday" (229). Specifically, Deborah is tipped off in the opening chapter that a Harlem newspaper is planning to run a story about her that accuses her of being antiblack, a story that she spends the rest of the week trying to quash. The irony that the controversy has arisen over an assignment for Negro History Week, of which Deborah is one of the few supporters, is particularly galling to her. Ruby's boyfriend Marc, who leaks her the information, encourages her to resign, since she could " 'get another teaching job like that—' He snapped his fingers smartly. 'The suburbs and the private schools are crying for teachers' " (21). Deborah maintains her innocence, however, and refuses to give in to false innuendo. "I'd rather stay here," she responds (21), again showing the value that she places on working in Harlem and her resolve to fight back. David encourages her in this path, but being out of town at that particular time he is of little practical assistance. She gets no help from Sybil Knox, not surprisingly, who refuses to allow the students' papers to be released to the reporter (the papers that Deborah are sure will clear her name), lest something untoward be printed about the school. Nevertheless, she is determined to clear her name and save her reputation. She is sure that she would be cleared of the charges if only people could look into her heart and see her true motivation. The idea that Harlem is putting her liberalism and idealism to the test is summed up in David's reflection on the situation, that "it was marvelous, he thought, the sureness with which gratuitous evil battered the innocent. Hundreds of Harlem teachers worked carelessly, ineptly, and no one challenged them. And she—who tried—she was threatened. . . . Even to do good, one needed a phalanx for protection" (64). Deborah has no such phalanx, yet she takes the situation as a chance to prove the worthiness of herself and her liberal ideals. As with Matthew, the self-referentiality of the do-gooder shows itself here, the way in which part of her reason for teaching in Harlem involves not only helping the students but also proving something about herself and thereby building her own self-esteem.

When she finally tells Ruby about the potential newspaper publication, despite Marc's pleas, having failed in all other attempts to stave off the appearance of the article, the two women confront the editor. Echoing David's thoughts, Ruby asks the editor, "Why do you want to destroy a teacher who is helping *our* children—helping *us?*" (244). He tries to explain that his "racial obligation, particularly at present, is primary," but the women refuse to accept this rationale. "You have a human obligation that's primary," Deborah counters (245), showing herself to be a product of her liberal Jewish upbringing. Although the reporter had tried to placate Deborah, telling his editor that "she convinced me that she had given the assignment in good faith—that the whole incident was merely a blunder in liberalism" (242), it is only upon Ruby's threats that the editor finally tells his reporter to tear up the story. Deborah is relieved that the affair is going to end quietly, but she is still very upset with the newspaper. As the week comes to an end, Deborah is no longer the idealistic Harlem teacher that she had been when it began; she appears to be moving away from "her own natural optimism" and succumbing to "the systematic disillusionment of Thoreau" (133).[35] The reader is even left to wonder whether she will be able to continue teaching in Harlem, whether her whole career there hasn't been, to use the reporter's apt phrase, merely a blunder in liberalism. What Deborah cannot see is the way in which liberalism itself may have been the blunder, interfering with the very goals it is ostensibly trying to achieve. What began as identification has, at this crucial juncture, given way to dis-identification.

Deborah's faith in her ability to effect change is handed another dramatic blow when, at the end of the novel—again offering a striking parallel with *The Invisible Island*—her special student, Barbara Jonas, is killed in a scuffle over a club jacket. Barbara had been saving money to buy such a jacket, and Deborah's dollar loan had sealed the deal. However, on Thursday, the day before Barbara is due to turn over the money, her grandmother discovers the cache, assumes that Barbara has gotten it in improper ways, and gives her a beating before leaving with the loot. The next day, Friday, Barbara comes to see Deborah in a distraught manner, but Deborah is preoccupied with her own problems and puts the girl off until Monday. She even offers to give Barbara enough money to buy the jacket, but this gesture is received as poorly by Barbara as Matthew's gift of a necktie was by Johnny Boston, and for the same reason. "I don't want your money, teacher," Barbara says. "I want my money. I didn't come to you for money. I came—I came to you—I came to you for help!" (230). Of course Deborah, like Matthew before her, cannot offer the kind of existential assistance that the student requires, and her gesture can only be seen as paternalistic. Later on, ironically at the same time that Deborah and Ruby are talking with the editor of the newspaper, Barbara meets up with her running-mate, Audrey, who is sporting one of the new jackets, and ends up with her head getting smashed into a car antenna. Deborah arrives at the scene shortly after the catastrophic event has taken place, but there is nothing she can do to help. Worrying so much about saving herself, she has lost her chance to prevent her young student, the symbol of her very purpose in teaching in Harlem, from being destroyed.

In the novel's concluding lines, David plays the role of Assistant Principal Johnson, who asked Matthew whether the dead Johnny Boston was "[o]ne of yours," by asking Deborah, "It was your Barbara, wasn't it?" (252). Whereas Matthew accepted the connection, "Yes—one of mine," thereby cementing his place in Harlem, Deborah responds very differently: " 'It was nobody's Barbara,' she cried bitterly. 'That's the whole trouble. It was nobody's Barbara at all' " (252). Here she seems to be acknowledging the fact that the gesture she had made in reaching out to Barbara was not enough to save her, let alone to effect change in Harlem as a whole. Klass appears to be presenting the same point that one reviewer found to be prominent in *The Invisible Island*, that "trouble . . . dog[s] the footsteps of those who try to stem the mighty tide of prejudice and injustice, and such fighters had better get used to 'lost battles.' "[36] What the novel also shows us, however, perhaps without realizing it, is that the fighters themselves are part of the reason that the battles are lost. Despite her idealistic do-gooderism, and in part because of it, Deborah has failed to build a bridge to the black community, as represented symbolically by Barbara Jonas. She may indeed come back on Monday, that is to say continue her teaching at Thoreau, as Matthew vows to return to Emerson, but doing so will perhaps be more for her own sake than for that of the students. Deborah, like Matthew, despite having so recently escaped from her own ghetto, has come to be seen as a member of the white liberal establishment, even if she doesn't view herself in that light. She wants to identify with her black students, as did Matthew, but finds it difficult to do so because she, again like Matthew, doesn't realize the privileged position that she holds as a white person, albeit a Jew, in the United States. Her own sense of identity is in many unacknowledged ways dependent on the very divide that she is so desperately trying (and therefore failing) to bridge.

ALICE CHILDRESS'S *A HERO AIN'T NOTHIN' BUT A SANDWICH*

A similar portrayal of the problematic position of the Jewish reformist teacher in Harlem emerges, if in considerably less detail, and from a decidedly different perspective, in Alice Childress's *A Hero Ain't Nothin' but a Sandwich*. Here the main character is a thirteen-year-old Harlem boy, Benjie, who has begun using heroin. While much of the novel is told from Benjie's point of view, in the first person, there are also many chapters told from the points of view of other characters involved in the situation, Benjie's family, friends, and teachers. In this way, Childress is able to show us the characters both as they perceive themselves and as they are perceived by others, two perspectives that often do not completely align.[37] One chapter is told from the point of view of one of Benjie's teachers, Bernard Cohen, a Jew who had, along with the black teacher Nigeria Greene, reported Benjie to the principal for being on drugs. Here Cohen shows himself to have many of the tendencies of the Jewish teachers that we saw in *The Invisible Island* and *Come Back on Monday*. He explains that he had begun his teaching with high spirits, "hopes of ignoring the race business, functioning at full speed and forging the way for better education,"[38] but that he has been beaten down by the system. The tone of his narrative is a mixture of lost idealism and defensiveness. He laments the fact that he has been put in the position of "whitey,"[39] explaining that he "go[es] out to work every morning, like a lamb to slaughter" (34), even though he is not personally responsible for any of the acknowledged wrongs that have been committed against African Americans throughout American history. Nevertheless, he has decided to continue teaching at that particular school, partly to spite Nigeria Greene, his fellow teacher and Black Power advocate whom Cohen blames for turning the students against him, and partly, he argues, for the educational good of his students: "Is it healthy for kids to learn nothing but Black history, Black supremacy, and Black power?," he asks (35). He is more than willing to include black studies in the curriculum, but not to make it exclusively black, understanding that doing so would render his position untenable. Ultimately, it is his worry about his own standing that dominates Cohen's section; near its conclusion he explains that "I'm afraid to run and afraid to stay. Everyone is for sale on a new auction block, which is the ground underfoot, wherever we stand" (38).[40] He presents himself as a dedicated teacher trying to better the lives of his students, but he also unwittingly shows us his own true motivations and insecurities.[41] While the novel "reveals the helplessness of parents to rescue their children from forces outside the home," Trudier Harris notes, it also "illustrates how political and personal goals of those in the school system intensify the detrimental effects of those forces," as in the case of Mr. Cohen.[42] His empathy with his students only goes so far when his own position is in jeopardy.

It is precisely these tender spots that are constantly being challenged by Nigeria Greene, as Cohen indicates and as Greene himself spells out in his own narrative. Here he not only complains that Cohen's position at his school is merely a result of the board's wanting white representation throughout the system, but he also argues that Cohen's "whole mission in teaching is to convince Black kids that most whites are great except for a 'few' rotten apples in every barrel" (41), a message with which Greene vehemently disagrees. He would prefer that the black students were taught the truth of institutional racism. He particularly objects to Cohen's attempts to show the students that "[s]kin color has nothing to do with social wrongs,

[that] all groups have been enslaved" (44–45); Greene sees this as Cohen's peddling a liberal line that might sound good but does not actually help the black community in any way, even if it does make the liberals who say it feel better about themselves. Greene's general attitude toward Cohen is summed up in the expression he uses several times, that he "is not to be believed" (41, 44), an ambiguous statement that refers both to the things that he says and to his attempts at expressing identification with his students.

Still, their relationship is not as cut and dried as Greene tries to make it sound. On the one hand, Greene shows himself to be similar to Cohen in many ways. He also began his teaching career in quite an idealistic fashion. He had been a very good student, he tells us, because he was good at repeating the lies that his white teachers had taught him as history. "But I had me a plan," he says. "Nigeria Greene was gonna be the Black Messiah of the classroom, gonna light the way with Blackness" (44). Interestingly, his wife gives him the same kind of advice that Matthew Stratton and Deborah Lieb received, "to cool it and don't try to change the world all at once" (47). On the other hand, Greene also shows himself to have some admiration for Cohen, not only because "he teaches hard, [so that] when kids leave his room, they take something with them, even if it's a lie,"[43] but also because "he has a tough hide to take what some-a these roughs can put on you" (44). He also remembers that Cohen did not join in a complaint that several other faculty members had put forth about Nigeria's creating a hostile work environment. It is certainly significant that Greene approaches Cohen when he becomes concerned about Benjie's drug use. At first Cohen puts up several arguments against getting involved—that he'll be seen as Whitey once again condemning black youth, that "[t]he parents get upset, the principal gets upset, the kid feels betrayed" (48). Here, as Harris points out, we see Cohen putting Benjie's drug addiction "in the context of his status as a martyr going against the odds to teach children in the ghetto."[44] Nevertheless, Greene convinces him that they must act together for Benjie's sake. The principal is somewhat surprised by this joint venture[45]—"Those two men who have never seen eye to eye on anything got together to bring one more straw to this poor camel's back," he says (57)—but he also acknowledges that, from a pedagogical point of view, "Bernard Cohen and Nigeria Greene do not get along very well, but the kids fare a bit better because they're both here" (55). Here we come close to realizing the kind of black-Jewish bridge building that the Jewish liberal reformist project is all about.

Nevertheless, this moment is undercut by several other factors in the novel. First of all, this is a bridge built between a Jewish teacher and a black teacher, not between a Jewish teacher and a black student, as Stark and Klass were envisioning. Secondly, there is the very real question of whether their action actually has had any effect on Benjie himself, whether they aren't merely offering another empty gesture.[46] Just as the efforts of Matthew Stratton and Deborah Lieb to "save" Johnny Boston and Barbara Jonas could not prevent the youths from being killed, there is no guarantee that Benjie has been rescued by the intervention of his teachers. His initial reaction to their turning him over to the principal had been anger, as we would expect. He calls Nigeria "a traitor" and objects to Cohen's paternalistically encouraging him to "be somebody," as that implies that "he think he somebody and I'm not" (48, 89). In general, he lumps the teachers with other do-gooders, social workers, and counselors, who act like they care but who are objects of derision in the Harlem community.[47] Benjie may assert that "I don't mind too much when parents and schoolteachers, social workers and head shrinkers tag names on me and go to generalizin," since "[t]hey old and it's parta they nature to be saying things like they know facts and you don't know nothing!" (10–11), but the rest of the novel shows him trying to break free of these judgmentalizations. At the end of the novel we stand with Butler Craig, Benjie's stepfather, waiting for Benjie to show up for a recovery meeting, unsure whether he will arrive or not. Childress deliberately leaves the ending open, but in doing so she again raises questions about the true position of the Jewish reformers in Harlem. Because she presents Cohen not only from his own perspective but also from those of other members of the Harlem community, we are able to see these problematic aspects of Cohen's project more readily than he himself can perceive them. Along with *The Invisible Island* and *Come Back on Monday*, then, *A Hero Ain't Nothin' but a Sandwich* seems to indicate the difficulty of truly building bridges between Jewish liberal reformers and Harlem communities, at least through the actions of the Jewish reformers themselves.

Matthew Stratton, Deborah Lieb, and Bernard Cohen go into Harlem with the best of all possible intentions—to help better the lives of children by providing them with a quality education. Their sense of empathy for the downtrodden compels them to try to fix the endemic problems in Harlem through such educational acts. Nevertheless, they find themselves beset with a variety of difficulties in carrying out their plans. What all three fail to realize is that their shared background as liberal Jewish reformers is itself part of the problem, that their own actions actually make it harder for them to achieve their objectives. In all three cases, the Jewish teachers complicate the situations rather than ameliorating them by the way in which they approach the black students. Trying too hard, perhaps, they allow their dis-identification with the environment to come to the fore, although they fail to see their own complicity in the failures that they encounter, the way in which their pedagogical projects get lost amidst their efforts to prove the validity of their ideals. While all three novels thus show us the problematic position of the Jewish liberal do-gooders who used Harlem as a proving ground for their idealism in the post–World War II period, they also—perhaps unwittingly—show us the reasons why these missionaries so often failed the test. Not only did they face a myriad of problems provided by the external environment, but they also suffered from a series of self-inflicted wounds. Ultimately, their gestures were never enough to effect significant change in Harlem, no matter the extent to which the experience might have changed the protagonists themselves. They continue to feel a strong sense of identification with the outsiders in Harlem, but the novels show that it is their dis-identification that is most significant for Harlem itself. As a proving ground, Harlem has demonstrated primarily its resistance to the reforms that these reformers are offering, in large part because of the way in which they are being offered.

NOTES

1. Murray Friedman notes that these Jews "sustain[ed] Harlem's economic infrastructure as landlords, shopkeepers, and merchants." *What Went Wrong: The Creation and Collapse of the Black-Jewish Alliance* (New York: Free Press, 1995), 75. The largest department store in the area, for example, remained Blumstein's for many years. Gilbert Osofsky, *Harlem: The Making of a Ghetto* (New York: Harper and Row, 1966), 121.

2. The Harlem Guild of the University Settlement was founded in 1903, for instance, and a second settlement was started by one of Wald's disciples in 1906 (See Osofsky, *Harlem*, 88), with such institutions remaining even after Jewish Harlem had given way to black Harlem.

3. Friedman notes that "efforts to relieve the suffering of blacks became part of the broader Jewish social agenda to build a new and better world" (*What*, 108).

4. See Ruth Wisse, *If I Am Not For Myself . . . : The Liberal Betrayal of the Jews* (New York: Free Press, 1992), 21, and Seth Forman, *Blacks in the Jewish Mind: A Crisis in Liberalism* (New York: New York University Press, 1998), 9.

5. Stuart Svonkin, *Jews Against Prejudice: American Jews and the Fight for Civil Liberties* (New York: Columbia University Press, 1970), 6.

6. Marc Dollinger, *Quest for Inclusion: Jews and Liberalism in Modern America* (Princeton: Princeton University Press, 2000), 7, 104; Michael E. Staub, *Torn at the Roots: The Crisis of Jewish Liberalism in Postwar America* (New York: Columbia University Press, 2002), 57.

7. In addition to Friedman, *What*, and Svonkin, *Jews*, see Hasia Diner, *In the Almost Promised Land: American Jews and Blacks, 1915–1935* (Westport, CT: Greenwood, 1977) and Cheryl Greenberg, *Troubling the Waters: Black-Jewish Relations in the American Century* (Princeton: Princeton University Press, 2006), among many others.

8. Nathan Glazer and Daniel P. Moynihan, *Beyond the Melting Pot: The Negroes, Puerto Ricans, Jews, Italians, and Irish of New York City*, 2nd ed. (Cambridge: MIT Press, 1974), 293.

9. Svonkin, *Jews*, 17.

10. Ibid., 18.

11. Friedman points out that, "[s]ince Jews were seen to profit from black patronage of Jewish stores and businesses in Harlem, the idea took hold among some blacks that Jews were responsible for their problems in the first place and only posed as friends" (81), leading to "rent strikes, business boycotts, and other forms of economic pressure" (92), up to and including the riots of 1935 and 1943 (94, 214), all of which were "tinged with anti-Semitic feelings" (Glazer and Moynihan, *Beyond*, 293).

12. Glazer and Moynihan, *Beyond*, 73; David Rogers, *110 Livingston Street: Politics and Bureaucracy in the New York City Schools* (New York: Random House, 1968), 160.

13. Friedman, *What*, 76.

14. Irwin Stark, *The Invisible Island* (New York: Viking, 1948), 24. Subsequent references to this text will be parenthetical.

15. Alain Locke, "Dawn Patrol: Review of the Literature of the Negro for 1948: Part I." *Phylon* 10, no. 1 (1949): 9.

16. Although the word *Harlem* does appear a half-dozen times in the novel (128, 197, 198, 240, 242, 349), which might seem to indicate that it is a different area than the "Blackbelt," there are other indications that the two terms are synonymous. In any event, James de Jongh includes *The Invisible Island* in his "Checklist of Black Harlem in Novels." *Vicious Modernism: Black Harlem and the Literary Imagination* (Cambridge: Cambridge University Press, 1990), 247.

17. The idea that Emerson is Matthew's battleground is emphasized when, awaiting his students on the first day of class, he asks himself, "against what in Howard's life was this to be balanced? The gray troopship moving into the Atlantic perhaps, its bow trimmed for England?" (5).

18. When he tells Ben that he has finally decided to transfer to Emerson, Ben somewhat humorously replies, "'Hallelujah! . . . Let the walls come tumblin' down!'" (356).

19. Ben's remarks to Matthew in this regard—"'The reality's always confusing, isn't it?' Ben asked. 'And when you don't have to touch it, when you can make up words about it and stay pure, it's easier to handle, isn't it?'" (242)—are reminiscent of the comment by the Jewish teacher Herbert Kohl in his memoir *36 Children* (New York: Signet, 1968), written about his first year in Harlem, that "It is one thing to be liberal and talk, another to face something and learn that you're afraid" (13).

20. Henry Geiger, "Review: 'The Invisible Island.'" *Manas* 6, no. 25 (1953): 7.

21. With regard to race, Matthew sees the significance not in terms of skin color but in terms of racial memory: "Matthew went back to the kids, and as he looked into their faces he knew it wasn't merely a problem of his skin and theirs. It was something else, deeper than a few years or their experience of those years. Skin color was a barrier, for the time an insurmountable one. But it did not explain fear. It did not explain hate. These ran back into the ragged warp of their lives, twisting through the dark alleys, the streets of the jungle, through the tenements, the lung blocks, the roofs on summer nights, back into the fields of the Carolinas,

the Mississippi Delta, the flatlands of Arkansas, the swamps, bayous, back into the hunger, anger, the lynchings, auction blocks, slave ships, into death and the long dim night of the African past" (169).

22. Locke, *Dawn*, 9.

23. Once again, he is criticized, in this case by Connors, for making a situation out of "something disturbingly and needlessly mixed up with his ideals" (330).

24. This action is also an attempt to correct an earlier mistake, when he *had* allowed Mallory to conduct an inspection in the class, an event which caused Johnny's attitude toward his teacher to change from "suspect[ing]" him to "despis[ing]" him (176).

25. That Stark describes the oppressive silence that marks the distance between Matthew and Johnny with the adjective "white" should not be passed over here. It is clear that it is Matthew's whiteness that is causing him to be viewed with such skepticism by Johnny Boston.

26. Geiger, "Review," 7.

27. Locke, *Dawn*, 9.

28. The earlier, shorter version of the novel, the short story "The Bridge," ends on a very different note: "Behind him the jungle lay quiet under the gentle haze of the June afternoon. He did not glance back at it. He was leaving it, he thought, cutting it out of his tissues with the glowing radium of his brain. He was going back to his own, the pure, the white and radiant city across the bridge. But as he left the ramp, and felt the iron floor of the bridge underfoot once more, he knew that he would never get there. The radium was failing, and his eyes were bright. There was no need to look back. The jungle was still there." *The Best American Short Stories 1946*. Ed. Martha Foley (Boston: Houghton Mifflin, 1946), 399. Here Matthew acknowledges the effect that Harlem has had on him personally but seems to have abandoned the idea that he can have any similar effect on Harlem itself, a much less optimistic viewpoint than that with which Stark ends *The Invisible Island*. The fact that Matthew refers to the portion of the city where he feels that he truly belongs, i.e., not Harlem, as "white and radiant" is again a marker of his unacknowledged position of privilege, even as he asserts that he will never entirely be able to return to the way he had been before his experiences in the Blackbelt.

29. Sheila Solomon Klass, *Come Back on Monday* (New York: Abelard Schuman, 1960), 65. Subsequent references to this text will be parenthetical.

30. Along the same lines, it is not insignificant that Matthew Stratton's best friend is named Howard *Whitman*.

31. In this way, both of them are clearly coming from a different position than are those with whom they will be interacting, since "cynicism is consistent with one of the main characteristics of ghetto psychology—suspiciousness and doubt concerning the possibility that anyone, either white or Negro, can be motivated by other than self-serving interests. According to the laws of the ghetto, everyone has an angle." Kenneth B. Clark, *Dark Ghetto: Dilemmas of Social Power* (New York: Harper and Row, 1965), 159.

32. Glazer and Moynihan note that, "[o]n the whole . . . relationships between teachers . . . whose training and work tend to develop a high degree of

tolerance and insight, have been productive of some of the healthiest and most satisfying interracial relationships that one may find anywhere" (73), and that seems to hold true for Deborah and Ruby.

33. Indeed, Klass has said that "the callous opportunism of the white administrators" she experienced while teaching in Harlem was something that drove her to write the novel in the first place ("Quick Facts," Macmillan Books, accessed June 8, 2010, http://us.macmillan.com/author/sheilasolmonklass), and she pulls no punches in showing this.

34. The conflict here between two views of the proper kind of Jewish adjustment to American life, Sybil Knox's assimilationism versus Deborah Lieb's liberalism, is fascinating, but somewhat beyond the scope of this essay. That this confrontation between these two women also involves issues of gender role stereotyping is also quite interesting, but even farther off the current track.

35. This disillusionment had already been present—witness Tuesday's interior monologue where Deborah asks herself, "*Why should you stay here? You work so hard and then they betray you. Why stay? Think of all the teachers here who hate kids, who hate Negroes, who sit on their asses and collect checks because this is Harlem and all that's required is that you keep the kids quiet—no use teaching them anything. No one accuses these teachers*" (65)—but it has certainly been exacerbated dramatically by the week's events.

36. Geiger, "Review," 7.

37. Miguel A. Ortiz points out that the use of multiple narrators "enables the author to clearly show the discrepancy between what one character thinks he or she is doing and what is perceived by others, without violating the integrity of any of them." Quoted in La Vinia Delois Jennings, *Alice Childress* (New York: Twayne, 1995), 8.

38. Alice Childress, *A Hero Ain't Nothin' but a Sandwich* (New York: Coward, McCann and Geoghegan, 1973), 38. Subsequent references to this text will be parenthetical.

39. Here again, as with Matthew Stratton and Deborah Lieb, we note the Jewish teacher being seen by his students as being part of the white authority structure while he does not see himself in that way.

40. La Vinia Delois Jennings argues that Cohen's "[s]elf-absorption in his own victimization—the resentment he receives from his students—eclipses [his] sympathetic acknowledgement of the racial contempt that every black American experiences from the day they are born" (93).

41. In this way Cohen may be one of the characters John Oliver Killens had in mind when he noted that "there are times in the book . . . when the characters, the victims, in this novel are their [own] worst enemies. They appear unable to get out of their own way." "The Literary Genius of Alice Childress," in *Black Women Writers (1950–1980): A Critical Evaluation*, ed. Mari Evans (New York: Doubleday, 1984), 132.

42. Trudier Harris, "Alice Childress (12 October 1920–)," in *Afro-American Writers After 1955: Dramatists and Prose Writers*, ed. Thadious M. Davis and Trudier Harris-Lopez. *Dictionary of Literary Biography*, Vol. 38. (Detroit: Gale Research, 1985), 72. For a much less forgiving analysis of Cohen's character see Jennings. She

refers to him first simply as "Benjie's white reading teacher" (92) and then introduces him in more detail as "a liberal but racist Jewish instructor" (92), in opposition to the "fiery black nationalist" (92) Nigeria Greene. She charges Cohen with fighting harder to keep his own job than to educate his students and comes down hard on him for his initial reluctance to come to Benjie's aid (93).

43. Jimmy-Lee Powell, Benjie's friend, concurs, reflecting that "[a] white teacher named Mr. Cohen is the one who taught me to read good and fast" (27), while the principal notes that "the highest percentage of good readers come out of Cohen's class" (55).

44. Harris, "Alice Childress," 72.

45. Although a very minor character, the unnamed principal here is reminiscent in some ways of Klass's Sybil Knox; three years away from retirement, he doesn't want to acknowledge Benjie's drug use because it will make his school look bad and that might hurt his standing with the board (54–57).

46. Jennings, not surprisingly, takes the negative, asserting that Cohen and Greene "portray two distinct warring political factions whose unification for the good of the students appears doubtful" ("Literary Genius," 92).

47. A number of characters in Childress's novel express their detestation of social workers, including Butler Craig, Benjie's stepfather (21), and Walter, Benjie's pusher (59). Interestingly, both Benjie and his friend Jimmy-Lee have contemplated becoming social workers, since it seems like an easy way to make money (11, 25).

SEVEN

HARLEM STREETS CAN TALK

Engendering Affective Disorders of Characterization in James Baldwin's Works

Magdalena J. Zaborowska

> This was a complex matter, for I was *not* living with my family in Harlem, after all, but "down-town," in the "white world," *in alien and mainly hostile territory*. On the other hand, for me, then, Harlem was almost as alien and in a yet more intimidating way and risked being equally hostile, although for very different reasons . . . .
>
> The fact that this particular child had been born when and where he was born had *dictated certain expectations*. The child does not really know what these expectations are—does not know how real they are—until he begins to fail, challenge, or defeat them. . . . I became a kind of *two-headed monstrosity of a problem*.
>
> —James Baldwin, *The Price of the Ticket*

In "The Harlem Ghetto" (1948), James Arthur Baldwin (1924–1987) reflects on the oppressive atmosphere of his native New York City neighborhood, which "has changed very little in my parents' lifetime or mine." A child of black migrants from Louisiana and Maryland, who came seeking better jobs and economic stability in the industrial North, he grew up keenly aware of their desperate efforts to keep the large family housed, clothed, and fed in the city that could offer only badly paid domestic work to some women of color and equally badly paid menial jobs to the men. Baldwin was born at the Harlem Hospital, grew up around the projects, and kept returning to the area no matter how famous and successful he became in his later years. He speaks about a specific local optic he developed as someone who knows more than "the white man walking through Harlem [who] is not at all likely to find it sinister and no more wretched than any other slum . . . [because] Harlem wears to the casual observer a casual face."[1] No Promised Land by any stretch of imagination, no primordial world of childhood encased in the golden glow of nostalgia like the one immortalized by Vladimir Nabokov, to Baldwin, his neighborhood is, I will argue, both a liberating source of artistic inspiration and a prison for his body as a black American: "All of Harlem is pervaded by a sense of congestion, rather like the insistent, maddening, claustrophobic pounding in the skull that comes from trying to breathe in a very small room with all the windows shut."[2]

Baldwin's visceral depiction of Manhattan's uptown reflects his ambivalent affective location as a writer born and raised in Harlem, but made famous by straddling the divide between black and white Americas.[3] "The Harlem Ghetto" emphasizes his preoccupation with the sensory perceptions of his environment and anticipates the focus of his later works on the ways in which race and gender intersect with the politics of sexuality and social space.[4] A black queer writer and civil rights activist who championed liberation from racism as equally important as liberation from homophobia and sexism—a position that turned many black militants against him in the 1960s and 1970s—Baldwin reconsiders his liminal location in his community of origin in the introduction to his last volume of essays, *The Price of the Ticket* (1985). In the epigraph that I have chosen for this chapter, he perceives himself to be viewed by others as doubly troubled, the "two-headed monstrosity of a problem."[5] A son of Harlem, he found himself in between uptown and downtown, from but not of his native ground. Having achieved fame and notoriety, he came back as a visitor, usually in a hired limo because, as he ironically remarks in *No Name in the Street* (1971), "I have . . . been forbidden to expose myself to the quite tremendous hazards of getting a cab to stop for me in New York."[6]

Astute and ironic, frank and fearlessly honest, "The Harlem Ghetto" is a useful lens through which to read Baldwin's works that came in its wake and that offer a literary jigsaw puzzle of this iconic African American neighborhood. In all of his literary productions—from the early essays and book reviews, first novel *Go Tell It on the Mountain* (1953), and play "The Amen Corner" (1954), through later novels, *Another Country* (1962), *If Beale Street Could Talk* (1974), a children's story, *Little Man, Little Man* (1976), to the later essay collections, *No Name in the Street* (1971), *The Devil Finds*

Work (1976), and last novel, *Just Above My Head* (1979)—Harlem remains a site of ethnic and racial divisions, the nation's representative ghetto under perpetual siege. Part of the "city that kills," as one of Baldwin's characters refers to it in *Another Country*, it is the place where blacks discover time and again that their lives are shaped by historical and social forces bent on their destruction.

And yet, despite the claustrophobic and foreboding depictions of Harlem in these works, Baldwin's narrators and characters are able to glimpse this neighborhood as a place for unexpected new beginnings. Art, friendship, and queer love blossom within and without the area and on its peripheries, while its black inhabitants—many of them migrants from the American South like Baldwin's parents—are able to transcend their sense of entrapment through meaningful encounters with other people: immigrants, Jews, and artists. This paradoxical juxtaposition of hard social realities with possibilities of a better, racially and ethnically mixed future is somewhat of a pattern, if seldom noted by critics, in Baldwin's later fiction.[7] An important trope to consider, given this writer's exilic trajectory among New York City, Paris, Istanbul, and Provencal St. Paul-de-Vence, such contradictory representations of Harlem and its dwellers in Baldwin's key works seem to prove his point from the essay, "A Fly in Buttermilk" (1958): "You can take the child out of the country . . . but you can't take the country out of the child."[8] Baldwin's works demonstrate that the mixed blessings of one's origins do not diminish the power of, and in fact testify to the transformative potential that a writer's native ground holds over, his or her imagination, no matter how much of that imagination may have been forged, if not forced, in exile.[9]

This essay examines the ways in which Baldwin's changing representations of Harlem as a synecdoche for the whole country blend metaphorical and material representations of American urban space to engender a novel concept of mid-twentieth-century national identity. While glimpsing Baldwin's ambivalent representation of Harlem in his oeuvre, I argue that his fifth novel, *If Beale Street Could Talk*, is a particularly fertile fictional site to consider these representations. My reading of this novel's pivotal role in Baldwin's literary journey from Harlem and into the international worlds that he later occupied focuses on its portrayals of Harlem as a space of oppression and liberation that frames Baldwin's black characters' affective relationships with other Americans, and especially Jews and European immigrants. The first-person narrator and main character of *If Beale Street Could Talk*, Tish Rivers, offers valuable gendered insights into the late-twentieth-century U.S. national identity as spatially contingent, multidimensional, and inflected in powerful ways by race, ethnicity, and sexuality. Baldwin's representations of Harlem and of the United States as the "house of bondage" put a new spin on what Raymond Williams terms the "structures of feeling" by both revealing and challenging the constructedness and spatial underpinnings of the black-white divide at the heart of the twentieth-century American literary imagination.[10]

In the three sections that follow, I first briefly locate Baldwin's Harlem as a site of the "disorders of characterization" in his earlier works, paying close attention to "The Harlem Ghetto." I then explore Tish's journeys within and without Harlem and her encounters with various inhabitants of New York City in *If Beale Street Could Talk*. Finally, I show that, as a text that engenders a deliberate unmaking of the male-centered narratives in Baldwin's earlier urban novels, such as *Giovanni's Room* and *Another Country*, this one enables productive rereadings of his later works, such as his last novel, *Just Above My Head*. Eclectic in approach and method, my analysis relies on Baldwin's texts as both primary material and sources of theoretical insights on gender, race, sexuality, and social space, while also engaging scholarship from the fields of literary and cultural, as well as urban and visual culture studies.[11]

ETHNIC ENCOUNTERS AND AUTHORIAL AFFECTS FROM "THE HARLEM GHETTO" TO *THE FIRE NEXT TIME*

Baldwin's nonfictional texts have often been used as frames and rhetorical devices by means of which to read his novels. Written when its author was just twenty-four years old and published in the February 1948 issue of *Commentary*, the essay "The Harlem Ghetto" provides a useful introduction to his early works, and, as I will show later on, a rather surprising introduction to his fifth novel, *If Beale Street Could Talk*, which Baldwin published more than two decades later. The essay crafts a series of detailed representations of the African American's other in Harlem—the Jew—and locates the discussion of the conflicted relationship between New York's Jews and blacks within the sometimes overlapping, and sometimes discreet, realms of religious, popular, and news media discourses. In a brilliant move that anticipated what interdisciplinary scholarship in literary and cultural studies would theorize only decades later, Baldwin saw these discourses as key sites for articulating the conundrums of gendered, racialized, and sexualized American identity.[12] His essay moves between the local and the national, between his native ground and the larger landscapes of American imaginary that were profoundly affected by the racist fallout of World War II at home and abroad.

"The Harlem Ghetto" proceeds from a gripping opening that locates the writer's family in Harlem—"the buildings are old and in desperate need of repair, the streets are crowded and dirty, and there are too many human beings per square block"—through sections criticizing its "perpetually embattled" black leadership whose "dramatic and publicized battles are battles with the wind." Then comes a hard look at the "Negro press," which "supports any man, provided he is sufficiently dark and well-known—with the exception of certain Negro novelists accused of drawing portraits unflattering to the race." Next, "The Harlem Ghetto" offers a glimpse of the black churches in the area, which Baldwin sees as dishing out religion that operates "as a complete and exquisite fantasy revenge: white people own the earth and commit all manner of abomination and injustice on it; the bad will be punished and the good rewarded."[13]

This indictment of black religious institutions for their role in maintaining and perpetuating rather than fighting poverty and ignorance of the area dovetails into a frank examination of what Baldwin calls the "Negro's ambivalent relation to the Jew." That he brings up this divisive issue at all at the time when American culture is struggling to combat anti-Semitism in the wake of the Holocaust is a confirmation of his disorderly conduct as a self-described "[aspiring] Negro novelist."[14] By pointing an accusing finger at his fellow African Americans, he is drawing a portrait that is "unflattering to the race" and thus risking hostility of some of his readers and critics.[15] The "Jew" in Harlem, Baldwin explains, is a discursive concept whose roots are both religious and secular and whose uses illustrate the irreconcilable political purposes, multivalence, and omnipresence of American racism. On the one hand, the term *Jew* is meant to "include all infidels of white skin who have failed to accept the Savior," while on the other, it is a powerful symbol of black unity and resilience, as "the wandering, exiled Jew . . . [is] a fairly obvious reminder of the trials of the Negro." In the latter approach, the Jew is someone to identify with, as "[t]he more devout Negro considers that he *is* a Jew, in bondage to a hard taskmaster and waiting for a Moses to lead him out of Egypt."[16]

Ambivalent and powerful, the concept of the "Jew" thus perceived serves Harlem preachers as a handy rhetorical and emotive device. It can be used to shape the ways their flock see themselves and their neighbors, if not the whole country in exclusionary and always racialized terms. Like the casual face mask worn by Harlem for the sake of a white passerby, the mask worn by the "Jew" imagined and discursively circulated throughout Harlem's black churches conceals and obscures a painful paradox. For while a devout churchgoer knows that "[t]he image of the suffering Christ and the suffering Jew are wedded with the image of the suffering slave, and they are one: the people that walked in darkness have seen a great light," the same churchgoer will also "wear anti-Semitism as a defiant proof of [his/her] citizenship" outside of the church because s/he needs to hate the "infidels" and "taskmasters" and because the darkness of "hatred must have a symbol."

Caught in the "American crossfire," or the economics and politics of race and class, the relationship between Jews and Blacks in cross-ethnic Harlem reflects and refracts the racialized relationships on the national scene: "the Negro, facing a Jew hates . . . the color of his skin" and enacts a fantasy revenge inspired by what s/he has heard in church. At the same time, black anti-Semitism is yet another symptom of the all-American way of positing an identity of a majority by means of scapegoating a minority. Hence, national attitudes affect local practices: "Georgia has the Negro and Harlem has the Jew." Moving in the opposite direction at the end of the essay, from the local to the national, Baldwin's sweeping panorama of his neighborhood and its main players becomes an indictment of "the American white Gentile . . . [whose] structure of the American commonwealth has trapped both these minorities into attitudes of perpetual hostility."[17]

Speaking against "the social and political optimists," or those whom in his later works he will brand simply as "white liberals," "The Harlem Ghetto" mocks a naive belief that suffering makes anyone a better human being: "Oppression . . . does not imbue a people with wisdom or insight or sweet charity: it breeds in them instead a constant, blinding rage. . . . [T]here seems no hope for better Negro-Jewish relations without a change in the American pattern."[18] Baldwin's depiction of the American nation in "The Harlem Ghetto" hinges on a triangle of symbolic personae locked in perpetual struggle—a white American, an African American, and a Jew—that is key to understanding both his earlier and later works, and especially his novels.[19] And while it can be said that his essays make it clearer and in some cases sooner than his novels, Baldwin's creed that no one, not even its victims, is immune from the virus of exclusionary and ethnocentric identity politics, is at the heart of all his works, regardless of their genre.[20] In the world depicted in Baldwin's novels, the main subject of this chapter, no one is exempt from the seductions of power, envy, and rage; Harlem is one of the locations where the consequences of these potent emotions on the lives of literal and literary characters are played out most poignantly.[21]

Filled with the rage of the oppressed, the 1943 Harlem riots took place just days before Baldwin's father's funeral: "The day . . . had also been my nineteenth birthday. As we drove him to the graveyard, the spoils of injustice, anarchy, discontent, and hatred were all around us."[22] Published two years after his first novel drew critical attention to Baldwin as the bard of Harlem, the essay recording these images, "Notes of a Native Son" (1955), depicts his neighborhood both as a wasteland of destruction and as his primary, and primal, literary inspiration. Similarly to "The Harlem Ghetto," the place he describes in "Notes of a Native Son" is stunted in temporal terms—"Infected by waiting" and "violently still"—and reflects "racial tensions throughout the country." Everywhere there is reinforced police presence, "on foot, on horseback, on corners everywhere, always two by two." The violence of the riots is destructive, but it also serves a social purpose because in its aftermath the least likely people band together in ways that defy stereotypes of class, gender, and status that had ruled the area until World War II. United by a "common vision" and fear, they appear in "strangest combinations" that disorient even the keenest of observers: "large, respectable churchly matrons standing on the stoops or the corners with their hair tied up, together with a girl in sleazy satin whose face bore the marks of gin and the razor, or heavy-set, abrupt, no-nonsense older men, in company with the most disreputable and fanatical 'race' men, or these same 'race' men with the sharpies, or these sharpies with the churchly women."[23]

This topsy-turvy vision of Harlem's population is already present in Baldwin's first novel whose composition took place between Harlem and Greenwich Village in New York City, Paris, and a Swiss mountain village where it was finished. Besieged by poverty, temptations of the street, and his budding sexuality, the protagonist of *Go Tell It on the Mountain,* fourteen-year-old John Grimes, finds partial solace in the storefront Pentecostal church he attends with his family. His choices as to what and who to become are narrowed down to an impossible juxtaposition of social spaces and forces that seem to cleave Harlem in half: either the "church" or the "street," either the company of those who follow a religious calling and become "saved" or the company of those who follow a secular calling and embrace crime, drugs, sex, and violence.[24] Withering under the gaze of his religiously fanatical and sometimes violent stepfather—in whom it is easy to see the autobiographical shades of Baldwin's own—John makes an uneasy truce between what can be called performances of a closeted black queerness and an official religiosity that entails an official "salvation" and inception into the community of the church. His balancing identity act requires acceptance of this duality, and of his own "two-headed monstrosity" as someone who "walks disorderly" or who is both within and without the church due to his gender and budding sexuality. John's identity conundrum is sketched in ways that echo the rhetoric used to construct the conflicted discursive figure of the "Jew" that Baldwin first articulated in "The Harlem Ghetto."[25]

Harlem's ability to interweave social circumstances of oppression with uncanny chances for spiritual and artistic liberation reverberates as well in "The Amen Corner" (1954), Baldwin's first play. David Alexander is a conundrum incarnate as a preacher's and jazz musician's son, a gifted young man who discovers that he must choose between holy and secular music, indeed, between the church and the street. He can play either within the stifling religious framework preferred by his "saved" mother or forge his own future in the scary and sinister world on its outside that has both inspired and ruined his estranged bohemian father. At the end, David embraces the messy and terrifying life of an artist who will be an outcast in the eyes of respectable Harlemites, a decision suggesting that "the street" and not the church is the place where blacks must embrace and test their creativity. Baldwin's biographer and long-time assistant and friend, David Leeming, states that the writer's approach to Harlem in these early works made it into "a place where people still clung to the possibility of a normal life. It was dilapidated, but it had not yet given up."[26] A veritable cauldron of identities, spaces, and possibilities, the neighborhood bred both success and failure, while its streets and churches harbored saints and sinners in equal measure.

This view of the neighborhood also holds in Baldwin's later publications, some of them offering rather gloomier visions, though they are not without glimmers of hard-won hope. For example, like John Grimes and David Alexander, jazz musician siblings Rufus and Ida Scott of *Another Country* struggle to get out from, yet, unlike him, cannot shake off the powerful influence of their social and cultural roots in Harlem. Their challenges overlap with the key political and personal issues that emerged during America's "greening" in the 1960s: erotic desire, cross-racial unions, betrayal of the younger generation by the state, wars abroad, racial and gender discrimination, homophobia and sexism, as well as class and racial segregation of mid-twentieth-century New York City. The lives of Rufus and Ida resonate clearly with the plight of Peter and Ruth from the short stories "Previous Condition" and "Come Out the Wilderness" that Baldwin collected in the volume *Going to Meet the Man* (1965).[27] In all of these texts the neighborhood is pitched against the rest of the city as a location where either a conventional middle-class and religious life, or poverty, crime, or untimely death are the only options for young people. At the same time, love and resilience and especially ties within black families that are not bound by religiosity provide hope and saving grace, no matter that these families' values often fly in the face of the politics of respectability that Baldwin rejected so clearly in "The Harlem Ghetto."

Rufus's suicidal leap from the George Washington Bridge in *Another Country* makes it clear, however, that only the few lucky ones make it out of the ghetto. Rufus can be seen as a synecdochic character, standing for the multitudes of invisible black men who perish in the American city. And yet, he is also singular, for Baldwin's characterization makes it clear that Rufus is no Richard Wright's Bigger Thomas, as he portrays his protagonist as both a victim of a racist society and an agent in his own destruction. Having abused and destroyed his "poor white trash" lover, Leona, and having rejected his family and friends—among them Eric, a white gay man from the South who loved him and whom he once used and brutally tossed aside—Rufus realizes that neither his music nor the love he glimpsed and destroyed were enough to save him.[28] After his death, his sister Ida sleeps her way to a jazz singer's career by cynically deciding to "become the biggest whore" in Harlem; she does so by having an affair with a powerful white impresario and while being involved with Irish Italian Vivaldo, Rufus's best friend, who feels he can somehow expiate his guilt toward his dead friend by becoming Ida's lover.

A descendant of European immigrants who became white in America, Vivaldo used to visit brothels and clubs in Harlem in hopes of acquiring an imaginary blackness that would make him a better writer and a more manly man. Ida thinks that Vivaldo's investment in his whiteness, masculinity, and his efforts as a would-be novelist may have made him blind to his friend's suffering and hence contributed to Rufus's decision to take his life. Her attempt to take revenge on Vivaldo, and on the whole white world that has wronged her brother, ruins her reputation in her community of origin. And yet Ida is a survivor, for while she may be seen by some as having "walked disorderly"—as she is by her brother's musician friends who cast her out of Harlem as a "white man's whore"—her awareness that she is partially responsible for her fall from grace enables her to go on. Though not entirely successful, as some critics noted, Ida's character continues a lineage of resilient black women that Baldwin initiated in *Go Tell It* and *The Amen Corner*, while also anticipating the growing interest in women and gender that appears in his later works.

As Baldwin wrote about his own coming of age in Harlem in *The Fire Next Time* (1963), local and individual dramas have national dimensions: "[T]his innocent country set you down in a ghetto in which . . . it intended that you should perish."[29] As all of his Harlemite characters realize, any attempt at survival is an escape artist's feat;[30] the trick is to get out by means of a "'thing,' a gimmick to lift [one] out, to start [one] on [one's] way."[31] Baldwin's gimmick was writing and a prodigious intellect. As Baldwin's works published in the wake of *The Fire Next Time* demonstrate, women become more and more central to his literary visions of Harlem, African America, and the nation, and nowhere else is it presented more clearly than in *If Beale Street Could Talk*.

DISORDERLY AFFECTS IN *IF BEALE STREET COULD TALK*

> The other places in Harlem are even worse than the projects. You'd never be able to start your new life in those places, you remember them too well, and you'd never want to bring up your baby there. But it's something, when you think about it, how many babies were brought into those places, with rats as big as cats, roaches the size of mice,

> splinters the size of a man's finger, and somehow survived it. You don't want to think of those who didn't; and, to tell the truth, there's always something very sad in those who did, or do.[32]
>
> —James Baldwin, *If Beale Street Could Talk*

Thinking about her birthplace and its inhabitants, Tish recognizes that in Harlem there are only two kinds of people: those who do not make it and leave scary memories in their wake, and those who do and offer tales of survival and sorrow. Tish's first-person narrative, much like David's in Baldwin's acclaimed second novel *Giovanni's Room*, is a retrospective that loops back and forth between past and current events. It consists of two books whose titles, in ways familiar from Baldwin's other works and especially *No Name in the Street*, evoke black spirituals and biblical references: "Troubled about My Soul" and "Zion." Interestingly, these titles evoke two unlikely bedfellows, or African American and Judeo-Christian female figures that Baldwin might have had in mind as providing symbolic contexts for his portrayal of Tish: the performer Lillie Knox, whose gospel song may have inspired the title of the first book of his novel, and the New Testament's "Daughter of Zion," a symbolic incarnation of his Church and bride of Christ, who may have inspired the title of the second. Against the background thick with references to the bible, black music, the blues, gospel, and spirituals, Tish sings her Harlem blues. At the same time, as a pregnant woman and Fonny's savior, she also embodies hope, faith, and possibilities for new life; she is a survivor whose gender, Baldwin seems to indicate, has something to do both with her power to get out of Harlem and her ability to engage other people.

Dedicated to his friend and collaborator, the illustrator Yoran Cazac,[33] and published when Baldwin's star was waning in the eyes of his critics, *If Beale Street Could Talk* marked his return to Harlem and intensified focus on the dynamics in urban, mid-twentieth-century black families. At the same time, and to the degree that has not been sufficiently explored, it offered a mix of realistic and allegorical ways to read Americanness as complexly gendered, racialized, and localized. In short, it can be called a feminist, or better yet, a womanist urban novel. Its epigraph, "Mary, Mary,/What you going to name/That pretty little baby?" echoes a line from a spiritual, but also the story of Mary giving multiple names to her divine son: Jesus, Emmanuel, Savior. When Tish begins her narrative, the analogy with the spiritual is clear: she is a symbolic, black, Harlem-born mother who names herself and her lover, while leaving her yet-to-be-born child nameless. Having been given the name Clementine, she comments, "people call me

Tish," whereas Fonny was "christened Alonzo . . . but, no, we've always called him Fonny."[34] The naming process reflects Tish's role as a storyteller and nurturer of her community. She is also a Harlem ambassador of sorts who shuttles between her neighborhood, where she resides with her family, and the world of prison, where her lover awaits trial for a crime he did not commit.

Received with mixed responses by reviewers, some of whom rejected its narrator as "improbable" for the reasons of her age, race, and class, and few of whom received it enthusiastically, such as Joyce Carol Oates who proclaimed it "economically, almost poetically constructed," "quietly powerful, never straining or exaggerating for effect," and "timeless," this novel has become a beloved text of adolescent readers and is garnering attention from a new host of scholars.[35] In his biography of Baldwin, Leeming defines it as a "prison parable,"[36] a "fictionalization of [Baldwin's] prison concerns" during 1968–1973, a result of the writer's "long meditation on psychological, emotional, and intellectual imprisonment."[37] Focusing on its references to black religious culture and gender, Trudier Harris claims that it also marked "Baldwin's progression away from the church" and a conscious move on his part to shift "positive black women characters . . . beyond active participation in the church," to the realm where the "questions of morality are no longer simplistically two-sided," where they "no longer believe themselves guilty beyond redemption."[38] The rich history of the reception of this novel signals not only that this book warrants a fresh rereading by literary scholars, but also that it may have been underestimated as a pivotal text in Baldwin's later career.[39]

The pivotal nature of *If Beale Street Could Talk* has foremost to do with its depictions of Harlem, and with Tish's narrative voice and specific vantage point on her native ground. At first, her comments echo young Baldwin's voice from "The Harlem Ghetto," as she too thinks of her birth place as a dead-end space, "You'd never be able to start your new life in those places . . . you'd never want to bring up your baby there."[40] She considers New York City the "ugliest and the dirtiest city in the world," with the "nastiest people," and "worst cops." It is "so close to hell that you can smell people frying,"[41] she remarks one day. One another occasion, while on the subway, she discovers that the crowd around her reminds her of the "drawings . . . of slave ships."[42] When she recalls her first and only visit to the church with Fonny and his family, she is struck by the fact that they both realize their exclusion from the sanctified Harlem at the precise moment when the spirit possesses other people: "Whoever loved us was not here. It's funny what you hold on to get through terror when terror surrounds you." When she visits Fonny in jail, the memory of the church, "that awful place," and of prison blend together in a radical juxtaposition, "when I first had to go and see him in the Tombs, and walked up those steps and into those halls, it was just like walking into church."[43]

The penitentiary spaces remind her not only of the imprisonment she and her lover felt inside the church, but also seem to represent the bowels of the U.S. justice system that is based in Western Christian values. Tish is a weary traveler by the time the story opens. Her every trip to visit Fonny in the Tombs entails a crossing of a deathly expanse whose description mocks the happy stories of American settlers' westward progress. A literary and literal urban space, it represents her misery and loss; it is the representative space of her journeys, crossings, and rites of passage as a daughter of her people: "these big, wide corridors I've come to hate, corridors wider than all the Sahara desert. The Sahara is never empty. . . . If . . . you fall, by and by vultures circle around you, smelling, sensing, your death. . . . The poor are always crossing the Sahara."[44] Tish's thoughts also reverberate with unequivocal references to the Book of Exodus, and align, once again, the African American and Jewish stories of exile and passage through American urban wilderness.

These stark visions, however, do not doom Tish. She learns to accept herself as a young woman entering full bloom: she is happily in love with Fonny and is carrying his child; she has the support of her family and of Fonny's father; she embraces her out-of-wedlock pregnancy without shame. She is able to cope with her situation because, like her mother, father, and sister, she does not fall prey to the "fantasy revenge" offered by the church—the view that is embraced, unfortunately and destructively, by Fonny's "sanctified" light-skinned mother, Mrs. Hunt, who denies her dark-skinned son once he has been locked up. Like Eric in *Another Country*, Tish chooses to live by her own and Fonny's set of recognizably, though not always unproblematic, Baldwinian morals. Among them, being loyal to one's kin is at the top of the list, hence "lifting from the Jew"[45] to provide money for Fonny's bail is fine, along with celebrating erotic love for its spiritual and transformative properties—it is referred to as "some strange anointing."[46] If the Hunt women are all about the church in this novel, Tish's family, the Riverses, are all about the street, but in a new sense, that is, they are street-smart and savvy about the world rather than being corrupted, trapped, or victimized by it.

As Tish's journey progresses, she engenders a new way of seeing herself and her fellow Americans.[47] She becomes a sharp observer and commentator on her reality, having found out that her trouble has taught her to "see people like . . . [she] never saw them before. They shine as bright as a razor. . . . This makes them very strange to you."[48] A female extension, as it were, of John Grimes, that first teenage protagonist in Baldwin's fiction,

Tish comes to terms with her body and her family, and embraces her ability to feel the "strangeness" in others. She is the "despised black mother" and carrier of the new world, who is "kicking in the belly of its mother . . . ready to be born," amidst the "global, historical crisis" that Baldwin identified in the Epilogue to *No Name in the Street*.[49] Serving as Baldwin's porte-parole, as a character/narrator Tish is a lens through which we can reconsider other key figures from his earlier and later works. Immersed in her emotions, often contradictory and confusing, Tish also offers a powerful optic on American race relations through gender and affect, the optic that helps to explain why she is fascinating to today's readers, why Baldwin's early critics saw her characterization and narrative as unreliable, and why her disorderly characterization was both deliberate and necessary.

That Tish's narrative resembles David's in *Giovanni's Room* and opens in exactly the same way as his is no coincidence: "I look at myself in the mirror. . . . I'm tired, and I'm beginning to think that maybe everything that happens makes sense. . . . But that's really a terrible thought. It can only come out of trouble—trouble that doesn't make sense."[50] Baldwin uses her to offer a powerful rewriting of David's white male American vantage point from a black female American perspective. Unlike David, who hopes to escape his troubled sexuality and family by going to France, Tish is stuck in Harlem, in the midst of the segregated heart of the American house of bondage. Her coming-of-age story can thus be read as much as an allegorical retelling of the nation's story as David's.[51] Written at the time when blacks were becoming disillusioned with the results of the civil rights movement, when Black Power postulated sexist and heterosexist machismo, and when many of the Black Arts Movements proponents advocated ethnocentric identity politics, Baldwin's novel offered glimpses of a different world. That new world appears in Tish's narrative and interior monologues, which combine sorrow songs about hard reality with dreams about a utopian, multicultural, egalitarian society of the righteous. It is a world in which women are as important, if not more important, than men.

Indeed, Tish's Harlem is a space populated by African American women; it is the new world of gender equality advocated by Angela Davis, Audre Lorde, and Nikki Giovanni, all of whom Baldwin knew and admired.[52] As Tish assesses the situation in the scene when she reveals her pregnancy to her family—her father Joseph, mother Sharon, and sister Ernestine—and to Fonny's family who came to listen to her—his father Frank, mother Mrs. Hunt, and sisters Adrienne and Sheila—she realizes that, "these six women [in the room] . . . had to deal with each other."[53] Although the fathers are there, she realizes that it is their story as a group of women, who are either supporters (Sharon, Ernestine, and Tish) or enemies of men (Mrs. Hunt, Sheila, and Adrianne). Baldwin's female characters in this novel reflect the changes in gender and race relations and in their literary representation that he not only witnessed but also helped to bring about. They are not only victims of but also agents struggling against the social forces beyond their control. Such an approach to gender and race was novel, especially coming from a male writer who was included in the trinity of the great twentieth-century black novelists alongside Ralph Ellison and Richard Wright. Baldwin's representations of his hometown and its dwellers highlight the roots and consequences of gendered riffs as much on the American literary scene as in the black communities in the late 1940s and 1950s, the riffs that cast a long shadow over the civil rights movement and its aftermath. Writing about gendered strife, not to mention colorism, whose destructive effects are blatantly evident in the Hunt family, was nevertheless a risky proposition.

By emphasizing confusion, anger, and frustration in his characterization of Tish, Baldwin shows that she is only beginning to realize her feminist possibilities and embrace the burdens of political agency. When she learns that it will not be easy, or even possible, to get Fonny out of jail, she understands that "time could not be bought" because "the only coin time accepted was life."[54] It is by embracing and trusting her feelings and by accepting who she is, by opening up to other people despite color lines and racial stereotypes, and by appreciating her origins and community that she is able to forge new relationships that help her to cope with her situation. Tish learns to cross black and white racial lines, and to do so she ventures outside of Harlem and beyond the bipolarity of the church-versus-street spaces that have so far delineated her possibilities as a black woman. Her story records her growing self-reflexivity and awareness of her body, and in that sense makes it possible, again, to read Baldwin's novel as wrestling with the racialized, gendered, and located deployments of affect.[55] In several instances, Tish learns to step back from and course-correct her negative feelings, which enables her to form important affective relationships with nonblacks.

For example, when Mr. Hayward, the white leftist lawyer her family has hired, tries to console her, she initially resists his kindness, having appraised his elegant office and family photos as a white space, and hence automatically alien to her—"There was no connection between this room, and me."[56] Yet she soon recognizes Hayward's dedication and conviction as a civil rights lawyer, and learns to look beyond the whiteness of his face,[57] thinking that "something really human happened between us, for the first time."[58] On another occasion, when she remembers her and Fonny's search for a loft in Greenwich Village, she recalls "this cat, whose name was Levy," a young Jewish landlord with a wife and two small children, who "dug us . . . [who] dug people who loved each other." Levy, who, in

Tish's parlance, "wasn't full of shit," and whom she saw as not exactly white, "was an olive-skinned, curly-haired, merry-faced boy from the Bronx, about thirty-three . . . with big, kind of electrical black eyes,"[59] and agreed to rent them his place, a loft that was ideal for their needs. Tish and Fonny's suspicion about Jewish landlords, voiced earlier by their friend Daniel, was that "this country really do not like niggers . . . so bad . . . they will rent to a leper first."[60] Baldwin remarks on the same phenomenon in the essay written in 1967: "When we were growing up in Harlem our demoralizing series of landlords were Jewish, and we hated them . . . because they were terrible landlords, and didn't take care of the building."[61] However, this stereotype crumbles in the case of Levy, as Tish experiences a moment of strong connection with him, one that anticipates her later[62] contact with Hayward: "[Levy] didn't make either of us feel self-conscious." He is not only egalitarian but also supportive of their love and, sensing their sexual passion, gives them what amounts to a brotherly blessing by urging them to make "some beautiful babies . . . the world damn sure needs them." But Levy is not naive about living in America. He tells them, too, as if anticipating the trouble to come, to watch out for the cops in the Village because "they're murder."[63] Later, he keeps the place reserved for them, no matter that Fonny has been sent to jail.[64]

Another moment of contact and understanding that defies color lines and expands Tish's affective possibilities takes place after she has been attacked by an Italian "greaser" while shopping at a vegetable stand in the Village. The elder immigrant Italian woman, "the Italian lady" who runs the establishment, defends Tish against the "miserable urchin" who attacked her, and when Fonny comes to Tish's aid and knocks down the attacker, she defends the couple in front of a white police officer who is about to take Fonny in for beating up a white man.[65] Informed by an immigrant story about whose contents we can only wonder, the Italian lady's reaction includes an aside meant only for Tish that suggests her sense of gendered kinship with the young African American woman: "You have a good man. . . . Take him home. Away from these diseased pigs. . . . I have been in America a long time. . . . I hope I do not die here."[66] Coming from an immigrant who was not born an American and directed to an African American whom the dominant culture still refuses to see as an equal, this comment links women across generations, ethnic groups, neighborhoods, and nationalities.

Taking place in the Village, this encounter suggests that, beyond Harlem, the world is teeming with ethnics and newcomers. Fonny's friends include Spanish and Mexican immigrants, among them vivacious Pedrocito, who runs a restaurant and feeds the couple on numerous occasions. When Fonny is in jail, Pedrocito continues to take care of Tish and drives her home on the day when she goes into labor. When Tish's mother, Sharon, travels to Puerto Rico to seek out the rape victim and beg her to change her testimony, she relies on the kindness of a young man, Jaime, who becomes her chauffer and chaperone. Ernestine, Tish's feisty sister who might be the only character in the novel that is queer-identified, takes advantage of her friendship—and possible romance—with a liberal white actress, who helps the family raise the money for Fonny's bail.

But some cross-racial encounters turn lethal in their brutal application of the illogic of racialization and discrimination that Baldwin signaled already in "The Harlem Ghetto." Following the run-in with the white police officer, Bell, who intervened at the vegetable stand, Fonny and Tish realize that they have acquired a mortal enemy. Seeing in their blackness the cause of his perceived victimization as a white man and police officer, Bell vows to destroy Fonny. His threat to the couple that he would "see" them later materializes when Fonny is taken in for a police lineup as a suspect in a rape case and, as the sole black man, is pointed out as the perpetrator by the traumatized Puerto Rican victim, Mrs. Victoria Rogers. As with the ambivalent vision of the "Jew" in his early essay, Baldwin makes it clear in this novel that he does not want his readers to think of the world in simple black and white terms. There is no solidarity based only in skin color, just as there is no gender solidarity based only in social roles and identity constructions. Even after Sharon has traveled all the way to Mrs. Rogers's *favela* in Puerto Rico—a slum much worse than Tish's mother could have imagined having seen the worst of Harlem—the rape victim refuses to take back her accusation. In a flash, the black American woman from Harlem realizes her advantage, as the "black" American woman from Puerto Rico tells her: "One thing I can tell, lady—you ain't never been raped. . . . It looks like him. But he wasn't laughing."[67] The verbs to "look" and see" point at the issue of black bodies being interchangeable, not only in the eyes of the U.S. justice system, but also to the victim who knows her own invisibility all too painfully: "They didn't see him when—when *I* saw him—when he came to *me*! They *never* see that. Respectable *women*—like you!—they never see that."[68] Victoria's accusation against Fonny guarantees her importance and visibility as a witness, albeit tragically; it makes her somewhat "respectable" because victimized, a status that she clearly does not want to give up, no matter Sharon's attempts to elicit her sympathy and understanding.[69]

Seen from another vantage point, however, Victoria's insistence casts a shadow on the novel's romance. Was Fonny capable of hurting another woman if he loved Tish so much? Was Sharon right to assume him incapable of rape only because she knew him "all his life"? Doubt and fear never leave the women characters in this novel and they muddle Tish's perceptions and her narrative to some degree. These characters' emotions cast a shadow on the reader's perceptions as well. Should we distrust Tish's account, perhaps?

And yet, like her mother who returns home to Harlem weary but not defeated, Tish learns to live with her feelings and perceptions, even though they are disorderly and unreliable, even though they may show her that things often, if not always, are not what they seem. Her maturing perspective and growth as a character mark the end of the novel: Fonny is back, out on bail, and the baby has been born happily. Still, it is clear that the hope such a conclusion offers to the main characters, who are still caught up in the ambivalences of their native ground, is at best tentative.

"THIS STREET LONG"

> Because the responsibility of a writer is to excavate the experience of the people who produced him, the act of writing is the intention of it; the root of it is liberation. Look, this is why no tyrant in history was able to read but every single one of them burned the books.[70]
>
> —James Baldwin

Following *If Beale Street*, the theme of young Harlemites dreaming of a better future reappears in a little-known book for children that Baldwin wrote in collaboration with the illustrator Yoran Cazac, *Little Man, Little Man: A Story of Childhood* (1976). Using Black English and vivid descriptions of the neighborhood, Baldwin offers a unique view of Harlem's everydayness through the eyes of the five-year-old narrator/character, TJ. Somewhat similar to Tish, TJ's occasional lapses in reliability call the reader's attention to the gravitas of the events he is relating as a black male child of Harlem.[71] TJ starts his story on a joyful note, while bouncing his ball against the sidewalk and hearing "music all up and down this street,"[72] but soon seems to echo the perceptions of the area that Baldwin signaled in "The Harlem Ghetto" nearly three decades earlier.[73] TJ knows about dangers lurking in Harlem streets: drugs—that the boys who "shoot that dope in their veins" will not survive long, and omnipresent violence—he is scared that even his best friend, WT, "he beat on his brother, he slap him all over his face with both hands hard as he can."[74]

Amid brutality and hopelessness, though, there are moments of kindness among the kids and among them and adults, the moments that give the young narrator hope and enable his resilience, his possible future survival, and certainly his creative expression. For example, there is a kind Puerto Rican storeowner with whom the children exchange smiles and greetings in Spanish. There are moments of tough love between children and adults, and moments to marvel at the beauty and pain of the various dwellers of the neighborhood who migrated from the American South, the

Caribbean, Central and South America, and various places in Europe, and whose sad stories the young narrator hopes to understand one day.

Published just three years later, Baldwin's last novel, *Just Above My Head*, takes homoerotic possibilities and attachments between black men as its central theme. Harlem, whose vignettes return in the essay collections published earlier, *No Name in the Street* and *The Devil Finds Work*, is one of this novel's main settings, a place of mixed blessings much like the one described by TJ and Tish. The narrator of *Just Above My Head*, the middle-aged Hall Montana, both tries to escape and cannot live without Harlem. With the passing of time he realizes that he has been as much inextricably rooted in his native ground as in his actual or imaginary flights from it, first as a hip young man who used to frequent clubs in the Village, then as a soldier who was shipped overseas to fight his country's imperial wars, and finally as a middle-aged family man who loves his wife and children. Harlem is the place where Hall has met diverse people,[75] like the child evangelist, Julia who used to preach in a church on 129th Street and Park Avenue, the church where Hall's gay younger brother, Arthur, began his musical career.[76] Arthur is "a nappy headed mother [who] did not know how to protect himself" and who grew up to become an internationally famous gospel and soul singer, thus linking his native ground to places as remote as Paris or Istanbul. At the beginning of the novel, Hall, Arthur, and their parents live at 135th Street, between Fifth and Lennox, and they worry that "they were going to tear down our building to make room for a housing project."[77]

As Baldwin paints its picture in retrospective vignettes throughout the expansive text of his last work of fiction, Harlem comes into focus as a place whose history and social and cultural tensions reflect and refract the crises of his characters' singular lives; the neighborhood becomes the location and lens that focus Baldwin's most extensive examination of black American life as the twentieth century is cresting into its last two decades. Taking its characters from the North to the South in the United States and abroad, as well as offering panoramic and detailed views of several decades in American history, *Just above My Head* succeeds in conveying the state of crisis enveloping the whole country and the ways in which it registers on local and individual levels against the background of the height and subsequent waning of the civil rights movement.

Set in mid-twentieth-century Harlem and Greenwich Village, *If Beale Street Could Talk* preceded and anticipated Baldwin's final novelistic vision by five years. Its disorderly characterization of and narration by Tish can be seen as deliberate, as having in fact made Hall Montana's complex and Harlem-rooted story in *Just Above My Head* possible.[78] This way of reading Hall's voice, as at least an echo if not a direct descendant, so to speak, of

Tish's narrative provides yet another proof for the pivotal nature of *If Beale Street Could Talk*.

FROM GIRLS & WOMEN TO MEN & BOYS

When Baldwin published his last two novels in the 1970s, genre and gender were still seen as delineated rather neatly, in mutually exclusive terms that reflected social and political mores: men wrote "muscular" works and women wrote autobiographically; action and analyses of social processes, such as seen in the works of Baldwin's literary compatriots Wright and Ellison, were the domain of male writers, while describing affect and psychological nuance belonged to the females. As the era of Black Power proclaimed its masculinist and heterosexist vision of race struggle, Baldwin's turn to female characters and his insistence on articulating the nuances of sexuality and gender caused many of the younger generation of African Americans to turn away from him. At the same time, he became an inspiration and friend, sometimes an elder brother-teacher to, and more often than we realize a student of Audre Lorde, Nikki Giovanni, Toni Morrison, and many others. That is why Joyce Carol Oates's review of *If Beale Street Could Talk* is not only astute but also ahead of its time in its attention to Baldwin's gendered and affective transgressions: "Baldwin certainly risked a great deal by putting his complex narrative, which involves a number of important characters, into the mouth of a young girl." Oates praises Tish's voice as "absolutely natural" and her "flights of poetic fancy" and "her articulation of what it feels like to be pregnant" as "convincing," and credits this narrative success to Baldwin's insistence on the primacy of feeling and affect as key forces driving the story.

Although by the end of *If Beale Street Could Talk* Harlem remains largely unchanged as a physical location, much as the nation and the state do in "The Harlem Ghetto," Baldwin's narrative makes it clear that its inhabitants' dynamism and disorderly conduct beyond its boundaries, and especially the affective relationships they forge beyond and against its color and class lines, challenge that fixedness. If, as Baldwin claims in "A Fly in Buttermilk," he confronted his national identity only having left the United States—"I found myself . . . alchemized into an American the moment I touched French soil"[79]—*If Beale Street Could Talk* helps us to see that his Harlem roots, the influence of people he met there, and the power that his native ground held over his literary imagination made this alchemization both possible and necessary in his works.

Baldwin's risky narrative in *If Beale Street Could Talk* develops his earlier approaches to social space, race, ethnicity, gender, and national identity, as well as making his later, complex, even experimental, works possible. That is why he lets Tish embrace an allegorical and parabolic vantage point, one that is nevertheless firmly located in the spaces and places she inhabits, one prone to unreliability and shifting perspectives that reflect the preponderance in this novel of what Kathleen Stewart defines as "ordinary affects," or "an animate circuit that conducts force and maps connections, routes, and disjunctures . . . a kind of contact zone where the overdeterminations of circulations, events, conditions, technologies, and flows of power literally take place."[80] Literary applications of broadly understood "affects" are familiar to readers versed not only in the "third person limited" perspective of Henry James, but especially to those familiar with the works centering on female voices, perspectives, and imaginaries by such writers as Zora Neale Hurston, Gwendolyn Brooks, and Ann Petry. What in these writers' works is seen as natural in Baldwin's is seen as disorderly. His characterizations and narrative voices serve specific purposes of enabling a novel recasting and rewriting, through the lens of gender and social space, of the visions of Harlem that inspired multiple literary incarnations throughout his career.

No wonder then that with the exception of Oates, the vision Baldwin articulated in *If Beale Street Could Talk* puzzled both the 1970s white/downtown and black/uptown critics. Like a congregation imprisoned by its own dualistic rhetoric, they saw in him the "two-headed monstrosity," rather than a revolutionary writer and thinker whose early Harlem visions grew expansive enough for the wider world. They saw in him a gender- and genre-transgressor, a new incarnation, perhaps, of that other, who, like the "Jew" whom Baldwin first sketched in "The Harlem Ghetto" decades earlier, was a product of both affective religious rhetoric and racist national imaginary.

Walter Mosley, born to a blended African American and East European Jewish family, sums up the painful legacy of twentieth-century black-Jewish relations in a recent vignette. First, he echoes his family's instructive history: "I was reared around peoples who knew each other without having to speak the same language. . . . We understood the signs and scars and signals and the segregation, racism and hatred piled upon each other's souls." But then, like Baldwin has done, he realizes that his folks' history reflects that of the nation's: "As we, the hated and feared and used peoples, were torn apart from the outside and in . . . I felt the forces of history pulling apart the sides of my family . . . [when] modernity had eschewed any kind of history that didn't turn a profit." Again like Baldwin, whose 1974 novel yearned for more familial ties among blacks, Jews, and other Americans, Mosley bemoans in 2011 the crumbling of the possibility of that yearning's fulfillment: "[T]hat delicate bond, so beautiful and so revealing, is scarring over with antipathy that derives from ignorance and a brand of self-hatred that identifies the me in you and hates you for it. A hatred that disguises itself as self-love but it's really its own opposite."[81]

NOTES

1. The lore of white writing on Harlem is vast, so let me refer to one notorious example: Norman Mailer's "The White Negro: Superficial Reflections on the Hipster," (*Advertisements for Myself*, 1957) which Baldwin brilliantly critiqued in the essay "The Black Boy Looks at the White Boy" (*Esquire*, May 1961), and which Lorraine Hansberry discusses in *To Be Young, Gifted and Black* (New York: A Signet Book, 1970) as a piece on "Harlem" and "an absurdity" that Mailer "locked himself in" (208).

2. James Baldwin, *The Price of the Ticket: Collected Nonfiction 1948–1985* (New York: St. Martin's Press, 1985), 1.

3. Baldwin was also straddling the contentious divide between race and sexuality, or blackness and queerness. See Zaborowska, "Mapping Transcultural Masculinities: James Baldwin's Innocents Abroad, or Giovanni's Room Revisited," in *Other Americans, Other Americas: The Politics and Poetics of Multiculturalism*, ed. Magdalena J. Zaborowska (Aarhus and Oxford: Aarhus University Press, printed in the UK, 1998), 119–31. And Zaborowska, *James Baldwin's Turkish Decade: Erotics of Exile* (Durham: Duke University Press, 2009).

4. For an extensive treatment of this theme, see E. Patrick Johnson, *Appropriating Blackness: Performance and the Politics of Authenticity* (Durham: Duke University Press, 2003); Robert Reid-Pharr, *Once You Go Black: Choice, Desire, and the Black American Intellectual* (New York: New York University Press, 2009); Dwight McBride, *James Baldwin Now* (New York: New York University Press, 1999); and Zaborowska, *Turkish Decade* (2009).

5. Baldwin, *Price of the Ticket*, xvi.

6. Ibid., 456.

7. For a review of how Baldwin's essays engage motifs of the immigrant narrative, see Zaborowska, " 'In the Same Boat': James Baldwin and the Other Atlantic," in *Historical Guide to James Baldwin*, ed. Douglas Field (Oxford: Oxford University Press, 2009).

8. Baldwin, *Price of the Ticket*, 161.

9. I refrain from discussing Baldwin's status as a writer who lived most of his career abroad. For an extensive treatment of this theme, see Zaborowska, *Turkish Decade* (2009).

10. What I am arguing as well is that Baldwin, as Harlem's native son, was not only deeply versed in local and international literary pasts, but also he was well ahead of his time in applying theoretical concepts of identity in his works, e.g., what Eve Kosofsky Sedgwick terms "nondualistic" approaches to identity. See, Eve Kosofsky Sedgwick and Adam Frank, *Touching Feeling: Affect, Pedagogy, Performativity* (Durham: Duke University Press, 2003). See especially her discussion of "affect and texture" (13–22).

11. I refer here to the term that Williams deployed in *The Long Revolution* (1961) in which he talks about "methods of analysis which, over a range from

literature to social institutions, can articulate actual *structures of feeling*—the meanings and values which are lived in works and relationships—and clarify the processes of historical developments through which these structures form and change" (emphases mine). I am particularly interested in how in Baldwin's works we can interpret the focus on what Williams refers to as the "created and creative meanings—which our inherited reality teaches and through which new reality forms and is negotiated" (Ontario: Broadview Press, 2001), 319. I'm aware of the long discussion of this concept across various disciplines in the humanities and social sciences, a recounting of which is well outside the scope of this chapter. My approach here has been also influenced by how Stuart Hall approaches the term *structures of feeling* as referring to "interactions between all these practices and patterns [and how they] are lived and experienced as a whole, in any particular period." I also found useful to my project the deployment of Williams's term to understanding the impact of social space and locality in Ian R Taylor, Karen Evans, and Penny Fraser's *A Tale of Two Cities: Global Change, Local Feeling, and Everyday Life in North of England* (London: Routledge, 1996), 5–6. Particularly useful is their focus on the "impact of local place on individual personality formation, personal biography, and 'orientation to the world' or 'affect' (all of which contribute to what we mean by 'local identity')." For further discussion on how structures of feeling are carried by "documentary culture," such as literature and the arts, see also Williams, in *Cultural Theory and Popular Culture: A Reader*, Ed. John Storey (Athens: University of Georgia Press, 1998), 53.

12. Baldwin will come back to this theme multiple times throughout his career, and especially in the 1967 essay published in *The New York Times*, "Negroes are Anti-Semitic Because They're Anti-White," collected in *Price of the Ticket*, 425–33.

13. Baldwin, *Price of the Ticket*, 165–68.

14. I use the phrase "disorderly conduct" fully aware of its gendered implications and its historical and disciplinary roots in the studies of nineteenth-century white women's culture. Carroll Smith-Rosenberg's *Disorderly Conduct: Visions of Gender in Victorian America* (New York: Oxford University Press, 1995) provides a useful context for how I deploy this term along others, and especially "affect" and "structures of feeling." For shedding light on the ways in which gender intersects with race in the making of a national history and literary culture, I am also indebted to Mary Kelley's *Private Woman Public Stage: Literary Domesticity in Nineteenth-Century America* (Chapel Hill: University of North Carolina Press, 2002) and " 'The Need of Their Genius': Women's Reading and Writing Practices in Early America," *Journal of the Early Republic* 21, no. 8 (2008): 1–22.

15. See also Catherine Rottenberg's discussion on black-Jewish encounters in *Performing Americanness: Race, Class, and Gender in Modern African-American and Jewish-American Literature* (Hanover: Dartmouth College Press, 2008). Her discussion of "the ways in which the black-and-white divide has operated" and the "uncertainty surrounding the racial position of the Jew at the turn of the century" (74) are especially helpful to situating the historical and literary historical contexts for my argument in this chapter.

16. Baldwin, *Price of the Ticket*, 166–69.

17. Ibid., 169–70.

18. Ibid., 170.

19. Baldwin's interest and investment in the complicated relationship between African Americans and Jews stemmed also from his close personal friendships with artists and intellectuals he met at the DeWitt Clinton high school in the Bronx—friendships that were opposed by his devout father, and that Jimmy cultivated until his death, especially with Sol Stein and Richard Avedon. See Baldwin's and Avedon's famous collaboration, *Nothing Personal* (New York: Atheneum, 1964) and the one, posthumously published, with Stein, *Native Sons: A Friendship that Created One of the Best Works of the Twentieth Century:* Notes of a Native Son (New York: Ballantine, 2004).

20. See Harold Bloom's assessment of Baldwin's rhetoric: "Like Carlyle (and a single aspect of the perspectivizing Nietzsche), Baldwin is of the authentic lineage of Jeremiah, most inward of prophets" in *James Baldwin*, ed. Harold Bloom (New York: Chelsea House Publishers, 1986), 1.

21. His early study of black-Jewish-white relationships in Harlem of the 1930s and '40s echoes especially powerfully in the racialized portrayals of characters in *Another Country* (New York: Dial, 1962) and *If Beale Street Could Talk* (New York: Dial, 1974), which depict both blacks making anti-Semitic comments as well as Jews who exhibit racist and sexist behavior, e.g., Steve Ellis in the former and Fonny's friend Daniel in the latter.

22. Baldwin, *Price of the Ticket*, 127.

23. Ibid., 136–37.

24. For a thorough examination of the in-between street/church queer spaces, see E. Patrick Johnson's magisterial *Appropriating Blackness* (2003).

25. "Walking disorderly" is a church idiom signifying straying off the path in both spiritual and sexual terms; Baldwin uses it to describe Ella Mae's and Elisha's erotic friendship that was publicly exposed and squelched by the church elders.

26. David Adams Leeming, *James Baldwin: A Biography* (New York: Knopf, 1995), 11.

27. In an earlier work, Baldwin's first play, *The Amen Corner* (1954), which followed immediately in the footsteps of *Go Tell It on the Mountain* (New York: Knopf, 1953), we encounter a family whose lives are dominated and severely tested by their Harlem storefront church and we also confront another young artist struggling between the sacred and secular callings. See also Sarah Blair on Baldwin's photographic collaborations on Harlem in *Harlem Crossroads: Black Writers and the Photograph in the Twentieth Century* (Princeton: Princeton University Press, 2007).

28. This portrayal brought about the vitriolic wrath of homophobic and sexist Eldridge Cleaver in *Soul on Ice* (New York: McGraw-Hill, 1968).

29. Baldwin, *Price of the Ticket*, 335.

30. Like to Baldwin in his teens, to John Grimes in *Go Tell It*, a gimmick that changed his life was becoming a youth preacher, an endeavor in which he was aided by community members: his elder friend, Elisha, and his paternal aunt, Florence. To Rufus and Ida, however short-lived, it was jazz, the black music adored by white America. But to Peter and Ruth, who may be read as companion characters

to the siblings from *Another Country*, an escape route seems unattainable. Similarly to the young protagonist of another short story set in Harlem, "The Rock Pile," (1965) they dream of places to run away to, but are held back by realities of race, class, and gender that they feel curtail their dreams and aspirations.

31. Baldwin, *Price of the Ticket*, 341.

32. Baldwin, *Beale Street*, 38.

33. For references to Baldwin's collaboration and friendship with Cazac, see Nicholas Boggs, "The Critic and the Little Man: On African American Literary Studies in the Post–Civil Rights Era" (PhD diss., Columbia University, 2005). See also Boggs's "Of Mimicry and (Little Man Little) Man: Toward a Queersighted Theory of Black Childhood" in *James Baldwin Now*, 122–60.

34. Baldwin, *Beale Street*, 3.

35. See for example, Thomas A. Edwards, "Can You Go Home Again," *New York Review of Books*, June 13, 1974. See also Joyce Carol Oates's review in *The New York Times*, May 19, 1974.

36. Leeming, *Biography*, 323.

37. See Zaborowska, *Turkish Decade* (2009), for an extensive treatment of these concerns related to his stays in Turkey and to the works he drafted there, such as *No Name in the Street*, as well as the play, John Herbert's *Fortune and Men's Eyes* (1964), which he directed in Istanbul as *Düşenin Dostu* in 1969.

38. Trudier Harris, *Black Women in the Fiction of James Baldwin* (Knoxville: University of Tennessee Press, 1987), 128–30.

39. More recently, Randall Kenan has assessed this text as concerning primarily "the precariousness of American judicial system for black men and . . . love," as well as Baldwin's "mounting anger toward his homeland" in Douglas Field's *Historical Guide* (2009), 54. Like Harris, Clarence E. Hardy III sees it as another proof of Baldwin's commitment to demonstrating the spiritual and redemptive power of erotic love in challenging and transcending social divisions and norms. Like to Baldwin, to Tish and Fony "sex holds a sacramental power over lovers, bodily cementing various partners across sex and gender." Hardy III also sees Baldwin's deployment of religious language in this novel as "suggest[ing] the mystery at the core of all human relationships and the instability that marks all sexual (and racial) identities" (*Historical Guide*, 64–65). Darryl Pinckney wrote about *If Beale Street Could Talk* as echoing Balzac in its hatred of oppression and as Baldwin's unequivocal "return to the Harlem family" to celebrate its bonds and survival (in "James Baldwin: The Risks of Love," *New York Review of Books*, April 13, 2000, accessed June 9, 2010 at http://www.nybooks.com/articles/archives/2000/apr/13/james-baldwin-the-risks-of-love). Like Pinckney's, assessments published in the last decade tend to distance themselves from the often angry and emotional reactions of critics in the 1970s, such as, for example, Mary Fair Burks's, whose religious sensibilities and notions of literary decorum were offended by the book's explicit sex scenes (in "James Baldwin's Protest Novel: *If Beale Street Could Talk*," *Negro American Literature Forum* 10, no. 3 [1976]), or Thomas A. Edwards's, who felt unconvinced by the descriptions of Harlem only because they did not correspond to his own perceptions of social realities of race, not to mention his conceptions of literary realism: "I unhappily

suggest that an important and honorable writer has failed to make us believe in his vision of horrors that surely do exist, but outside his book" ("Home Again," 1974).

40. Baldwin, *Beale Street*, 38.

41. Ibid., 10–11.

42. Ibid., 141. Despite this view, much like Gwendolyn Brooks illuminates Chicago and the domestic spaces of lower-class blacks in *Maud Martha* (New York: Harper, 1953), Baldwin sometimes shows Harlem as a place of new beginnings, and especially so for his female narrators and characters, of whom Tish is the most resilient. Like Brooks's Chicago or even Anne Petry's New York in *The Street* (Boston: Houghton Mifflin, 1946), Baldwin's representations of his hometown as the "house of bondage," reveal the roots of the pre–civil rights movement's gendered riffs in the black community in the late 1940s and 1950s.

43. Baldwin, *Beale Street*, 32.

44. Ibid., 7.

45. Ibid., 212.

46. Ibid., 101.

47. This novel also illustrates Baldwin's preoccupation with music, social justice, and the intersections of the sacred and secular black cultures—themes that by then he had honed well in *Another Country*, *Tell Me How Long the Train's Been Gone* (New York: Dial, 1968), and *No Name in the Street*.

48. Baldwin, *Beale Street*, 9.

49. Baldwin, *No Name in the Street*, 196–97.

50. Baldwin, *Beale Street*, 3.

51. I discuss this feature of *Giovanni's Room* in detail in "Mapping Transcultural Masculinities: James Baldwin's Innocents Abroad, or *Giovanni's Room* Revisited," 119–31. It is tempting, albeit well outside the scope of this chapter, to consider *Giovanni's Room* as a "gay novel" in contrast to the blatantly heterosexist *If Beale Street Could Talk*.

52. Baldwin told Giovanni that she served as an inspiration for the character of Tish. Interview with the author, Blacksburg, VA, December 2009.

53. Baldwin, *Beale Street*, 85.

54. Ibid., 117.

55. After Patricia Ticineto Clough in *The Affective Turn: Theorizing the Social* (Durham: Duke University Press, 2007), I refer to affect as relating not only to the human body but also to the technologies of representation that that body might produce, i.e., to Tish's production of her narrative.

56. Baldwin, *Beale Street*, 115.

57. Burks chastised Baldwin for this portrayal and racializes Hayward as "the liberal Jewish lawyer" calling him "a new Baldwinian stereotype" (1976, 86).

58. Baldwin, *Beale Street*, 120.

59. Ibid., 163.

60. Ibid., 123.

61. Baldwin, *Price of the Ticket*, 423. Baldwin also mentions other hated establishments in Harlem run by Jews, "The grocer was a Jew . . . the butcher was a Jew. . . . We brought our clothes from a Jew . . . and the pawnbroker was

a Jew—perhaps we hated him most of all. . . . Not all of these white people were cruel—on the contrary, I remember some who were as thoughtful as the bleak circumstances allowed—but all of them were exploiting us, and that was why we hated them" (*Price of the Ticket*, 425–26).

62. Chronologically, the meeting with Levy precedes the one with Hayward given that it has taken place before the meeting with the racist cop and Fonny's subsequent conviction, but Tish's narrative, interweaving recollections and current events, places them in a reversed order.

63. Baldwin, *Beale Street*, 164–66.

64. Baldwin makes this encounter reflect his views on black-Jewish relationships, which he expressed in the essay, "Negroes Are Anti-Semitic because They're Anti-White" (*The New York Times*, April 9, 1967) in which, as if echoing DuBois's local-to-global perspective on the "color line" from *The Souls of Black Folk* (1903), he states: "The root of anti-Semitism among Negroes is, ironically, the relationship of colored peoples—all over the globe—to the Christian world. This is a fact that may be difficult to grasp, not only for the ghetto's most blasted and embittered inhabitants, but also for many Jews, to say nothing of many Christians" (*Price of the Ticket*, 427).

65. Baldwin, *Beale Street*, 166–71.

66. Ibid., 171.

67. Ibid., 205.

68. Ibid., 208.

69. The lack of affective connection between Sharon and Victoria in this scene points at Baldwin's skepticism concerning the limits of cross-ethnic sisterhood.

70. James Baldwin and Nikki Giovanni, *A Dialogue* (Philadelphia: Lippincott, 1973), 82.

71. The more accurate term to describe the narrative point of view here would be the "third-person limited," which one of Baldwin's literary forefathers, Henry James, used to deliberately mix the narrative consciousness of a character with that of the author. Listing all the examples of TJ's narrative unreliability is beyond the scope of this essay, but let me cite a couple: TJ seems to know how to read complicated construction site signs (71); his psychological interpretation of Mr. Man in the post-accident basement scene (85).

72. James Baldwin, *Little Man, Little Man, A Story of Childhood* (New York: Dial, 1976), 4.

73. Ibid., 14–19.

74. Ibid., 27.

75. Harlem is also the place where Arthur gets sexually assaulted as a child in *Just Above My Head* (New York: Dial, 1979), the event that launches his brother's narrative of his life as a black queer artist.

76. Baldwin, *Just Above My Head*, 9.

77. Ibid., 72.

78. The novel is impressively reread by two Baldwin critics extraordinaire: Lynn Orilla Scott, in *James Baldwin's Later Fiction: Witness to the Journey* (East Lansing: Michigan State University Press, 2002) and Robert Reid-Pharr, in *Once You Go Black* (2009).

79. Baldwin, *Price of the Ticket*, 161.

80. Kathleen Stewart, *Ordinary Affects* (Durham: Duke University Press, 2007), 3.

81. Walter Mosley, "What Is It Like to be Both Black and Jewish?" *The Nation*, October 17, 2011.

79. Baldwin, *Price of the Ticket*, 161.
80. Kathleen Stewart, *Ordinary Affects* (Durham: Duke University Press, 2007).
81. Walton Muyumba, "What Is It Like to Be Both Black and Beautiful?" *The Nation*, October 17, 2011.

EIGHT

TEXTS OF MEMORY

Romancing the Past

Hasia Diner

In 1951 the Lower East Side broke into the mainstream of American culture. That year Follett Publishing Company, a New York trade house, published Sydney Taylor's *All-of-a-Kind Family*, the first commercially published, widely distributed children's book with a Jewish subject. The book also had the distinction of providing the first postwar mass-market depiction of the Lower East Side. Nearly fifty years later, it, as well as the later volumes in the series, remains in print and is still stocked on the shelves of public libraries and general bookstores as well as Jewish ones.

All-of-a-Kind Family received rave reviews and won Follett's three thousand dollar prize as the outstanding book for children in 1951.[1] *Publishers Weekly* speculated that the judges decided to choose this book "not only on the [basis of the] story but also on the fact that it would portray New York's teeming East Side, an unusual setting for a juvenile, to children throughout the country."[2] Advertisements noted that the book's drama centered on "five little girls who live with their parents in a four-room apartment in New York's lower East Side."[3] *All-of-a-Kind Family* received the accolades of the Jewish world as well. The book won the first Isaac Siegal Memorial Award for Jewish children's books, bestowed by the Jewish Book Council of the Jewish Welfare Board. This book, and those that followed—*More of All-of-a-Kind Family* (1954) and *All-of-a-Kind Family Uptown* (1958) essentially made up the entire corpus of children's literature in the 1950s that identified the lives of American Jews as fit reading material for American children.[4]

The Lower East Side setting did not play an incidental role in the book's warm reception and its achievement of canonical status. Nor did the author consider the setting as a mere vehicle to tell a family story. The lives of these girls developed as they did precisely because they lived on the Lower East Side, a throbbing, bustling place. The centrality of place in the book, in turn, helped establish the Lower East Side as American Jewry's sacred center.

Published at a moment when American Jews were moving to the suburbs of the nation's largest cities, this book for the first time in the history of American publishing presented ordinary American Jews to their non-Jewish neighbors.[5] A "heartwarming bit of Americana. Delightful," commented *Library Journal*.[6] Describing *All-of-a-Kind Family* as "Americana" allowed the experience of Jews to be enshrined in the rhetoric of American national culture, like Laura Ingalls Wilder's *Little House on the Prairie*[7] or Esther Forbes's *Johnny Tremaine*,[8] which themselves placed the experiences of children in America's sacred soil and sacred time.[9] The author was born in 1904 on the Lower East Side, the back of the dust jacket revealed, and had created the story of this immigrant Jewish family to recapture the texture of life in the "old" neighborhood for her own daughter. The adventures of Ella, Henny, Sarah, Charlotte, and Gertie—"Mama's girls"—reflected the stories that Taylor's parents had told of their immigrant childhoods earlier in the century.

Like the girls in the book, Taylor came from a family of five girls, and she initially wrote these stories just for her daughter. When her husband read about a contest sponsored by Follett, he submitted the manuscript without her permission. Taylor won, and the book launched her career.[10]

Taylor had moved beyond the Lower East Side. American-born, American-educated, the product of cleaner, quieter neighborhoods, she was an actress and a playwright and had also spent time as a dancer in Martha Graham's company. She had traveled far from the Lower East Side of her parents.[11]

In *All-of-a-Kind Family*, however, we hear the voice of longing for a space where everyone helped everyone else; where warmth, religious ritual, home, love, noisy streets, and a throbbing public culture made life for these Jewish girls seamless and laden with meaning. Families got along, and those families were large, noisy, and demonstrative. Neighbors cared about each other and shared generously. The senses operated at a sharper level, and even the food tasted better than in the suburbanizing world where Taylor's readers found themselves.

Taylor herself noted in an interview years later that she had only one child, her daughter, Jo.

> When she was a little girl she would say: Mother, I hate going to bed. It's so lonesome. Won't you stay a while?
>
> I would look around the room with its solitary bed, and my mind would go back to my own childhood. Once again I would be living in the flat on New York's lower East Side where five little girls shared one bedroom—and never minded bedtime. Snuggled in our beds we would talk and giggle and plan tomorrow's fun and mischief.[12]

She could not have presented the contrast more clearly: the warmth and the shared lives of the Lower East Side with the privacy of affluence. The remembered Lower East Side stood for the jumble of family and fun, of camaraderie and togetherness, in sharp contrast to the loneliness of success.

The narrative line and rhetorical style of *All-of-a-Kind Family* attested to the emerging sanctity of the Lower East Side and the particular ways in which American Jews after World War II remembered it. First, Taylor contrasted the "meanness" of the neighborhood's physical appearance with the sweetness of its people—all immigrant Jews—and their intense relationships with each other:

> The East Side was not pretty. There was no grass. Grass couldn't very well grow on slate sidewalks or in cobblestoned gutters. There were no flowers except those one saw in the shops of the few florists. There were no tall trees lining the streets. There were tall gas lampposts instead. There was no running brook in which children might splash on hot summer days. But there was the East River. Its waters stretched out wide and darkly green, and it smelt of fish, ships, and garbage.[13]

Unlike suburbs, which boasted lawns and wide-open spaces, the place where "Mama's girls" lived was one where personal relationships, rather than landscape, defined values.

In this neighborhood, Jews lived in a universe of almost total Jewishness. With the exception of Miss Allen, the librarian, the mysterious but handsome Charlie, who worked with Papa in his junk shop and turned out to be Miss Allen's boyfriend, and the one reference to "Joe, a swarthy Italian" ragpicker, everyone and everything here was Jewish. "Only one tongue," Taylor asserted, could be heard in the noisy marketplace. "Yiddish. It was like a foreign land right in the midst of America. In this foreign land, it was Mama's children who were foreigners since they alone conversed in an alien tongue—English."

The world of that marketplace, of loud peddlers, of obtrusive hucksters who hawked and screamed and shouted out their wares, offered a portrait of life unlike that which children born right after World War II, the book's original readers, would ever know, particularly if they joined the stream of migrants to the outlying areas of the cities and to suburbia, touted by developers for the quietness of private space and the green stretches of lawn. In this marketplace, the heart of the Lower East Side, Taylor took her readers on a sensory journey to a realm of distinctive sounds, smells, tastes, and sights:

> Heaped high with merchandise, they [pushcarts] stretched in endless lines up and down the main streets. . . . They were edged up close to the curb and wedged together so tightly that one could not cross anywhere except at the corners. The pushcart peddlers, usually bearded men in long overcoats or old women in heavy sweaters and shawls, outdid each other in their loud cries to the passers-by.[14]
>
> The sweet potato man stopped before her [Ella] and pulled open one of the drawers of his oven. There arose on the air such a delicious smell that Ella smacked her lips expectantly. Inside she saw the plump sweet potatoes in their gray jackets. . . . For her penny, Ella got a large half and as she bit into it, she wondered why sweet potato baked at home never tasted half so good.[15]

(In a subsequent volume when the family moved to the Bronx, Mama comforts her daughters by telling them, "We'll still be able to buy *bagel* and lox for Sunday morning breakfast"[16]—an amusing anachronism, since no accounts of *real* life on the Lower East Side ever mention lox as a commonly eaten food, or Sunday mornings as a day that merited a special breakfast ritual, or lox and bagels as a particular combination.)

In at least *this* Jewish home of the Lower East Side, traditional practices, holidays and Sabbaths in particular, caused no one embarrassment. In no place did Mama, Papa, and the girls (and, by the last chapter of the first book, little brother Charlie) suffer any personal inconveniences in order to fulfill ritual practice, nor did the demands of acceptance into the American mainstream rub up against the inherited, cherished ways of marking off time or eating. The girls' Aunt Lena, in *More All-of-a-Kind Family*, observed the commandment of immersing herself in a *mikvah* (ritual bath) before her wedding. Although Taylor did not explain Lena's act in sexual terms, she, unlike almost all other Jewish writers of the era, including rabbis writing for adults, included this element of the Judaic repertoire in her depiction of immigrant life.[17]

Taylor portrayed an imagined cultural moment in which no conflict separated home and street. The central public institution for this family was the public library, where the girls made a weekly pilgrimage, fittingly, as they prepared for the Sabbath. "No, not Sarah, nor any of the girls could forget that Friday was library day," Taylor told her readers on the book's first page. Avid readers, the girls connected to the American world primarily through the library, where they went after school every Friday afternoon to stock up with armloads of books.[18]

The joys of Sabbath suffused the family's apartment, without any intrusions from the outside world: "At home, the kitchen was warm with the smell of fresh-baked white bread. The room sparkled with cleanliness. The table, which wore only an oilcloth covering all through the week, now had on a snowy white tablecloth. . . . They were just in time to see Mama saying the prayer over the candles. . . . A lovely feeling of peace and contentment seemed to flow out from Mama. . . . Thus was the Sabbath ushered in."[19] After the inevitably tasty meal, everyone sat around the table, with the Sabbath candles flickering, reading: "the children with their books, Mama with her magazine, and Papa with his Jewish newspaper. . . . So they would continue reading until the candles burnt low. Then they would . . . go to bed. . . . There could be no light struck on the Sabbath. That was the law."[20]

Finally, on Taylor's Lower East Side, American patriotism cozily existed side by side with Jewish life, uncontested by conflicting demands. So, the Fourth of July came to the Lower East Side: "The streets were full of excitement. Everybody was expressing their joy in freedom today. From tenement house windows and from store fronts flew American flags. . . . The air was filled with the clang of cowbells and the blasts of horns." Mama prepared a special meal for the Fourth, as befitted this sacred moment. "What a wonderful meal it was! . . . Mama took the kugel out of the oven and bore it triumphantly to the table. It looked very festive in all its crusty brown deliciousness on Mama's best company platter." Mama's special Fourth of July meal had as its centerpiece a kugel, a dish that surely graced her Sabbath table as well.[21]

So, this early artifact of the memory of the Lower East Side, written by a Jewish woman a generation removed from it, offered post–World War II readers a glimpse of a world where food tasted better, where grass and trees did not make the good life possible, where families could be observant Jews and enthusiastic Americans at one and the same time. Taylor's Lower East Side, an almost hermetically sealed world of Jewishness and love, existed without contest over culture or generational conflict.

However, conflict deeply informed three earlier Lower East Side texts that were "rediscovered" and reissued in the postwar period: Abraham Cahan's *The Rise of David Levinsky*, Henry Roth's *Call It Sleep*, and Anzia Yezierska's *Bread Givers*. Published originally in 1917, 1934, and 1925, respectively, these tense novels about the discord of immigrant Jewish life on the Lower East Side reached new audiences in turn by 1960, 1962, and then 1975. They achieved canonical status after their reissues, becoming standard fare for college literature and ethnic studies courses. Scholars around the world turned to them for access to what they defined as the authentic voices of the immigrant era of the late nineteenth and early twentieth centuries.[22] They also ushered Americans, particularly the grandchildren and great-grandchildren of East European Jewish immigrants, "back" to the Lower East Side.

All these novels, as well as a number of other works written during the heyday of the Lower East Side as an immigrant Jewish neighborhood, had a common fate, of sorts. Published, reviewed, and read at a time when immigrant Jews were defined as a problem and when American Jews pondered the fate of their poor, newly arrived coreligionists, the books then fell into obscurity. They ceased to be actively discussed, since the condition of the Jews had ceased to be an American concern. Notably they were revived, republished, and reread in the emerging culture of Lower East Side memories.

These novels, as well as other texts written about the East European Jewish immigration to America, shared a common fate. Written, reviewed, and discussed during the years of immigration, these works attested to the degree to which Jewish immigrants were considered to be both a novelty and a problem. As their immigrant era came to an end, as Jews entered increasingly into the middle class, and as they ceased to be a problem, these works lost their readership. But when Lower East Side memory culture surfaced after World War II and when it became particularly powerful in the 1960s as an element in American Jewish culture, these works achieved a new lease on life as they provided voice and texture to the place now defined as the heart of the American Jewish historical experience.

All these novels, written for general as opposed to Jewish readers particularly, dealt in uncompromising terms with class, gender, and religious conflict. Two involved coming-of-age stories that demonstrated repeatedly the chasm between the youth, who intimately knew the American streets, and their parents, who could never achieve that knowledge. (The Cahan novel posed the crisis somewhat differently in that the young David came to America alone, and in essence the parent-child conflict over Jewishness took place within himself.) In all, the Lower East Side served as the powerful locus of conflict, maturation, and the inevitability of the generational gulf.[23]

The three books likewise had a similar history. They received various levels of positive acclaim, but then were truly lost. Since being reissued in the post-1960s era, they have entered into the realm of the canon.

Call It Sleep, described by the literary critic Leslie Fiedler as "the best single book by a Jew about Jewishness written by an American,"[24] underwent the most dramatic example of this trajectory. First published in 1934 when the author was twenty-eight years old,[25] *Call It Sleep* focused on a young child, David Schearl, who came to America with his mother to join his father, who had preceded them there. It depicted a bleak life of poverty, violence, and family discord, embedded in the noise, dirt, foul smells, and vermin of the neighborhood.

Critics greeted the novel favorably, lauding its literary strength, the power of its language, and the tension in its structure. Likened to James T. Farrell's *Studs Lonigan*, it emerged on the mid-1930s American literary landscape both as *the* Jewish proletarian novel of the decade and as a deep, complex novel laced with Freudian insight, akin to the writings of James Joyce, particularly *Portrait of the Artist as a Young Man*.[26] It went into an immediate second printing and then died.[27]

After the mid-1930s, *Call It Sleep* faded into obscurity. According to one literary scholar in a postscript to the 1962 paperback reissue, "Until recently, no one I met, American or British, seemed to have heard of it, much less to have read it." Before the 1960 reissue, the novel figured in literary criticism only twice, and then as an interesting text that, despite its merit, had no audience to speak of. When, in 1956, the literary scholar Walter Rideout included—and praised it—in his study *The Radical Novel in the United States, 1900–1954: Some Interrelations of Literature and Society*, he discussed it as a book that no one else would have been familiar with.[28] Both Alfred Kazin and Leslie Fiedler cited it in a 1956 symposium, appropriately entitled "Neglected Books," in the *American Scholar*.[29]

In 1960, a small publishing house, Cooper Press, saw fit to reissue the Roth novel in hardback, and two years later a bigger concern, Avon, purchased the paperback rights, due in part to the efforts of literary agent Harold Ribalow. Within two years the book had gone through twenty editions, and nearly nine hundred thousand copies had made their way into circulation.[30] It brought the Lower East Side into the American literary landscape. Repeatedly reissued with new introductions, it became the focus of international critical inquiry.[31]

In the same year that *Call It Sleep* got its new lease on life, so, too, did Abraham Cahan's *The Rise of David Levinsky*, reissued by Harper Brothers with an elegant introduction by John Higham, an eminent scholar of both immigration and American intellectual history. Initially, Cahan had tinkered with the basic idea for his novel in a multipart series in 1913 in *McClure's Magazine*, entitled "The Autobiography of an American Jew." Four years later the fully developed novel, *The Rise of David Levinsky*, appeared. Initially it enjoyed only modest success, even in the face of the quite positive reviews it earned in such publications as the *New Republic*, which hailed it as "one of the most impressive novels produced in America in many a day."[32] Cahan had hoped for literary acclaim among American readers, but despite the close relationship between him and the author William Dean Howells, *Levinsky* did less well in terms of sales and literary fame than Cahan expected.

Higham rightly concluded in his essay that the book, which "has received more respect than attention," did not fit the Zeitgeist of American Jews before the 1960s, and therefore it had fallen into disuse. The book, he noted, had made upwardly mobile Jews uncomfortable. Its portrait of the "Jewish East Side" (Higham, like many early commentators, did not use the name "Lower East Side") did not shy away from the unflattering and the coarse. "Readers," Higham noted, presumably for the most part Jews, "thought he had perversely documented all the anti-Semitic stereotypes." They, as they were "escaping from confinement" in their "immigrant ghettos," found the novel embarrassing. They preferred texts that had "decontaminate[d] Jewish life from the color and flavor of the Ghetto."[33]

More importantly, however, *The Rise of David Levinsky* did not endure. After its brief surfacing, it drowned in obscurity. It was reissued once in 1928, as "a cheap edition," but by 1943, "the book went out of print."[34] In 1952 critic Isaac Rosenfeld published a piece in *Commentary* testifying to the seeming irrelevance of *David Levinsky* and the Lower East Side genre: "I had long avoided *The Rise of David Levinsky* because I imagined it was a badly written account of immigrants and sweatshops in a genre which—though this novel had practically established it—was intolerably stale by now."[35] Rosenfeld, who died a few years after writing these words, ones that reflected a deep disinterest in the immigration experience and by extension the Lower East Side as "stale" subjects for engaging literature, could not have known that these topics—immigrants and sweatshops—would resurface in the next decade and beyond as central metaphors of American Jewish memory.

Since the novel's reissue and the emergence of the Lower East Side as a central focus of historical interest, numerous historians have drawn from Cahan's life and his observations in *David Levinsky* to describe the nature of that community and to document its life and demise.[36] They have taken Cahan and his fictional immigrant, Levinsky, to be the paradigmatic and defining characters of the Lower East Side, which in turn defined the immigration experience of the Jews to America.[37]

Anzia Yezierska's *Bread Givers* (1925) received wide acclaim in its initial incarnation, although, like *The Rise of Levinsky* and *Call It Sleep*, it then went into a tailspin of neglect. In the 1920s this book and Yezierska's other works, such as *Hungry Hearts*, garnered stellar reviews in major American publications. The reviewer for *International Book Review* in 1925 compared Yezierska to no less than Henry James and Tolstoy, while Samson Raphaelson (author of the short story "The Day of Atonement," on which *The Jazz Singer* was based) declared that "Miss Yezierska has accomplished for the Yiddish what John Synge has done for the Gaelic," oblivious to the fact that *Bread Givers* had been written in English.[38] In general, critics hailed the book as realistic and authentic, offering readers an "almost barbaric tapestry of the east side . . . raw, uncontrollable poetry."[39] (*Hungry Hearts*, published five years earlier, had been reviewed in the *Nation* alongside D. H. Lawrence's *Women in Love* and Knut Hamsun's *Hunger*.[40] It caught the attention of Samuel Goldwyn, who purchased the rights to the book, transformed it into a movie in 1922, and briefly brought Yezierska out of the Lower East Side to the sunshine of California.)[41]

In the 1920s, Yezierska mingled with George Bernard Shaw, Gertrude Stein, and the cream of American and European literary society.[42] But by the 1930s, her career devolved from frame to obscurity, and her work, including *Bread Givers*, went out of press and merited no notice from literary scholars or historians.

But that all changed in a new cultural era. In 1975, with the rise of the women's movement, the efforts of feminists to reclaim a women's past and culture, and the flowering of a specifically Jewish feminist movement, *Bread Givers* and Yezierska emerged from the shadows, and, in a way, so did the Lower East Side. The rediscovery of *Bread Givers* was due in large part to the efforts of labor historian Alice Kessler Harris, who in the early 1970s was writing about Jewish women's lives on the Lower East Side in the context of their trade union activism.[43] Kessler Harris played a pivotal role in Persea Press's 1975 reissue of the book. In her introductory remarks, the historian thanked a number of individuals who had played a role "in rescuing this novel from the world of 'out of print' books." Since then, *Bread Givers* has been in print continuously and never far from the reading public. It finds its way into general bookstores, Jewish bookstores, synagogue libraries, and the required reading lists of college courses.

The three books described here—so unlike *All-of-a-Kind Family*, with its depictions of family warmth, love of Jewish ritual, and deep harmonious community bonding—presented grim portraits of Lower East Side life. Poverty and prostitution show up here. Gangsters, criminal violence, husbands and wives who shout at each other and who treat their children with brutality seem to bear little resemblance to Mama and Papa and their girls. Crass materialists devolved out of Old World Talmud scholars.

But as with the children's books, *The Rise of David Levinsky*, *Call It Sleep*, and *Bread Givers* could not have been written about other places. For all their anger and disgust at aspects of immigrant Jewish life in America, they posited the Lower East Side as the incarnation of Jewishness, the intensity of life, and the essence of authenticity.

Sara Smolinsky, the heroine of *Bread Givers*, despised everything about the neighborhood, whose narrowness is encapsulated in her feelings about her father, a cruel man who spent his time, energy, and very limited money on himself. As the representative of Judaism, Sara's father, with his disregard for his wife and daughters, his blend of self-centered concern about money and "fanatical adherence to his traditions," made Sara question her relation to that tradition. Yet every time Sara left the Lower East Side, she found herself inexorably drawn back to it, just as ultimately she could not abandon her father. In the novel's final scene, as she confronted her father on his deathbed in his Lower East Side tenement apartment, Sara "walked on. But I felt a shadow there, still over me. It wasn't just my father, but the generations who made my father whose weight was still upon me."[44]

Place also shaped David Levinsky's life and Cahan's narrative. The entire "I Discover America" section of the book played itself out in "the heart of the Jewish East Side." A place of scurrying and bustle, of old-timers who derided the greenhorns, and the greenhorns who initially tried to retain tradition, Levinsky's East Side thrived on the endless contradictions within its boundaries. It was on the Lower East Side that Levinsky lost his soul. As the neighborhood and the city forced him to accommodate to modernity, he made a bargain that success should come at any price. By the book's end, when the unbelievably successful cloak maker returned to the streets of his youth, he felt sadness, not triumph:

> One day I paused in front of an old East Side restaurant that I had often passed in my days of need and despair. The feeling of desolation and envy with which I used to peek in its windows came back to me. . . . On another occasion I came across a Canal Street merchant of whom I used to buy goods for my pushcart. I said to myself: "There was a time when I used to implore that man for ten dollars' worth of goods. . . . Now he would be happy to shake hands with me." . . . And yet in all such instances I feel a peculiar yearning for the very days when the doors of that restaurant were closed to me and when the Canal Street merchant was a magnate of commerce in my estimation. Somehow encounters of this kind leave me dejected.[45]

In *Call It Sleep*, place shaped David Schearl's life and Roth's narrative as well. In an unusual twist, the Schearl family first lived in Brooklyn, but a quarter of the way into the book, he and his parents moved to the Lower East Side, a "world as different from Brownsville as quiet from turmoil."[46] Roth offered little in the way of Brownsville street life to explain the boy and his family, and the action of the early part of the book took place largely within the confines of the apartment. On the other hand, the Lower East Side as lived out-of-doors space shaped the boy's development, and the neighborhood functioned as a key element in the narrative.

If the polyglot Lower East Side seemed different from almost exclusively Jewish Brownsville, it stood even more radically apart from the non-Jewish sections of America. On an excursion uptown to the Metropolitan Museum of Art with his aunt, a "greenhorn" who followed David and his mother to America, he witnessed that world through a Lower East Side lens. "The further they got from Third Avenue," Roth narrated, "the more aloof grew the houses, the more silent the street. David began to feel uneasy at his aunt's loud voice and Yiddish speech." To David's aunt the most obvious difference between real life, that is, the Lower East Side, and Fifth Avenue involved the absence of children. "Not a single child on the street. Children, I see, are not in style in this portion of America," she commented.[47]

But the streets of Roth's Lower East Side teemed with children, good ones, bad ones, noisy ones, studious ones, but children everywhere. They, and the crowds of adults shouting, pushing, running, selling, buying, became the central element in the Lower East Side landscape of memory. People, rather than buildings or nature, endowed the Lower East Side with its distinctive quality. As such Roth, through David's aunt, early expressed a key element in the memory of the Lower East Side, the image of masses of people moving about at a frenetic pace.[48]

Such rhetoric about the Lower East Side as quintessentially Jewish, decidedly not American, throbbing with life, people, and conflict, informed these novels, which were canonized in the 1960s and 1970s. Their very history of loss and retrieval functioned as a ritual act and, as with the Lower East Side narrative itself, had clear parallels in the history of Jewish sacred texts, namely, the finding of hidden books such as the Dead Sea Scrolls and the discovery of the Cairo *genizah* (a trove of hidden books). Once found, these texts became objects of both intense study and deep veneration, in part because of their histories.

The canonization of these "classic" Lower East Side novels did not, however, preclude the production of new fiction that foregrounded the neighborhood and its people. The late 1970s saw the emergence of a particular genre within American popular literature, the Lower East Side romance novel. Novels such as Belva Plain's *Evergreen* (1978),[49] Gloria Goldreich's *Leah's Journey* (1978),[50] Meredith Tax's politically charged *Rivington Street* (1982) and its sequel, *Union Square* (1988),[51] and Janet Robertson's *Journey Home* (1990)[52] all conformed to the formula of the highly popular style of romance fiction and simultaneously reflected peculiarly Jewish and decidedly Lower East Side memories.

Like the corpus of romance novels that take up whole sections of American bookstores, all of the Lower East Side romance novels were written by women authors and tell their stories through the voices of female protagonists.[53] Like the genre as a whole, its Jewish variant explored women's emotions set against some very specific turbulent location.

However much the Lower East Side romances conform to the genre, they appealed to Jewish audiences in particular ways. Goldreich won the National Jewish Book for Fiction for *Leah's Journey*, a sure sign of the novel's endorsement by Jewish literary tastemakers. These books appeared in Judaica gift shops, synagogue libraries, and Jewish book fairs, bearing witness to at least the tastemakers' assumptions that Jewish audiences would receive such books warmly.

Publishers must have sensed a fertile market for this type of book. In 1994 Zebra Books, a major romance house, advertised three Jewish books at the end of Emily Maxwell's *An Easter Disguise* ("A daring masquerade could bring her ruin . . . or romance"). One, *Heritage*, involved the Holocaust, but the other two, *The Lion's Way* and *Tiger's Heart*, used the Lower East Side as the locus for love and adventure. A brief description of *Tiger's Heart* linked the rhetoric of romance writing and Jewish history:

> A family held together by tradition—and torn apart by love! As beautiful . . . as the natural gem she was named for, Pearl Resnick always stood out in the crowded world of New York's Lower East Side. And as she blossomed into womanhood, she caught the eye of more than one man—but she vowed to make a better life for herself. In a journey that would take her from the squalor of a ghetto to the elegance of Central Park West, Pearl triumphs over the challenges of life—until she must face the cruel twisted fate of passion and the betrayal of her own heart![54]

These Lower East Side books shared certain characteristics with each other and with their non-Jewish romance counterparts, the ubiquitous "bodice rippers." Place mattered a great deal. The drama could not have occurred just anywhere, and the feel of the setting crucially informed the characters' behavior. They derived their motivation and intensity from the very essence of the Lower East Side, whose noisy streets and constricted apartments, the intensity of relationships, shaped their lives and their fantasies. When they moved to other places, the quality of their lives altered dramatically. The sights, sounds, and smells of the remembered Lower East Side endowed these books with the authenticity so necessary to the romance genre in general, and to Lower East Side texts in particular.

The Lower East Side romances depended on early and repeated descriptions of place to draw readers into the intimacies of the characters' lived world. To feel for the heroine in the romance genre requires that the reader be in her world. Goldreich and Plain placed their characters in tenements on Hester Street, while Tax used the Levys' Rivington Street address as her book's title, and Robertson's Klugerman family made its home on Orchard Street. Indeed, Robertson included the specific house number, 40 Orchard Street, leading us right up the stairs into the dark, problematic space the characters occupied.

The characters of romance novels expressed the realities of the world around them through their senses. Thus, Belva Plain's Anna of *Evergreen* experienced the five-story tenement on Hester Street as crowded and noisy. "The stench surged from the street door . . . cooking grease; onions; an overflowing toilet . . . the sickening steam of pressing irons; a noxious drenching of tobacco from the front apartment where the cigar-makers lived." Leah Goldfeder began her American journey in a bleak apartment on that same street, where "the narrow panes . . . were covered with soot minutes after they had been scrubbed," while the "stairway smelled of ammonia and urine." Conditions were horrible, and Meredith Tax's Hannah and her family lived in a "dark hole." "Where was the sun? How could it get in? And where were the trees?" Hannah's husband asked, humiliated by his failure to support his family in the American style he had expected. Through the narrator's voice we learn that on the Lower East Side, "colors glowed more garishly, dirt was greasier, people grew bigger, and all the latent exaggerations in their characters flowered. Hannah heard her own voice come out louder than before."[55]

As with all romance novels, these books hinged on a plot of forbidden sex between the heroine and a dashing man, often in contrast to a steady but boring husband. The inner worlds of the Lower East Side heroines involved the turmoil of secret lovers, either past or present. Leah's affair with the union organizer Eli Feinstein, for example, reverberated with passion, as opposed to the heavy silences between her and her husband. "We never pretended to love. Never," she convinced herself. Anna of *Evergreen* chose to marry Joseph Friedman, steady and reliable, when she found herself pregnant with a child fathered by Paul, the dashing but callous son of the wealthy, uptown, German Jewish family she had worked for as a domestic servant. Sarah Klugerman, in *Journey Home*, carried a deep, dark secret, and despite her *shitel* (the head covering worn by married Orthodox women), she was a woman with a past. In that past she had an illicit affair. She fulfilled her halakic ritual duties of immersing herself in the mikvah, but at times, when her husband came to her bed, "she thought of David Nathan and wondered."[56] Her need to confess that affair informed the book's basic plot.

Although these Jewish tales conformed to the basic romance outline, they should not be seen as mere imitations. Their authors did not just replace the Scottish Highlands with Hester Street's *chazzer mark* (the so-called pig market, a sarcastic comment, implying that one could buy anything on Hester Street except for pork). As pieces of fiction they balanced the romance formula with the post–World War II American Jewish narrative. With the exception of *Journey Home*, all these books began in Eastern Europe. (In *Journey Home*, Sarah went back to Hungary to see her dying mother and got caught up in the horrors of World War I, thus still allowing the author to pose the contrast between America and "back home.") They all rely on the pogrom story to bring the family to America, and they all focus on the challenges to tradition posed by American realities. Leah, of *Leah's Journey*, confessed that in the course of beginning her affair with the handsome, fiery labor organizer, she also began to eat non-kosher food. After a passionate night in bed, Leah and Eli went off to eat. "It was the second time," she recounted to herself, "in as many days that she had eaten meat that was not kosher. But now, in this holiday interlude in her life, all things were permitted just as all things had been forbidden."[57]

The novels all focused on the details of Jewish life, highlighting the home rituals and focusing on those involving Sabbath preparations and cooking, highlighting female-based activities. The heroines, before or after their affairs, braid challah and light candles. They cook traditional meals of soup, gefilte fish, kugel, roasted chicken, and compote. Indeed, the details of food, depicted so sensually that the reader might whiff the aromas and hear the sizzling in the pans, defined these romance novels as particularly Jewish. In the more general books of this genre, heroines *never* engage in such corporeal acts as eating. Remembering food also functioned as a particularly salient element of most Lower East Side narratives, and as a fundamental element in American Jewish memory culture.[58]

These post–World War II Jewish novels contrasted America and its possibilities with the violence and destruction of Eastern Europe. The pogrom scenes play a crucial role in establishing the reason for migration and in heightening the vast distance between America and "back there." Thus, in the aftermath of the pogrom in "Proskurov, in the Ukraine," which opens *Rivington Street*, we see the horror through the eyes of a little child:

> Lev was only five. When he saw what the soldiers were doing, he hid in a hole under the stairs, stuffing his shirt in his mouth, covering his eyes.
>
> Mama was still lying where they had left her, her clothes ripped off, blood dried, horror frozen on her face. She was cold and had begun to smell. Tentatively he [Lev] touched her cheek. A tear rolled down his face. . . . They had ripped off her skirt, and an envelope had fallen out of the torn pocket, onto the floor. He squinted and picked it up. That was it. The letter from their cousin in New York, and the picture of her family.[59]

The frequency of rape in the Russian episodes of the Lower East Side romances moved these books further away from the conventional romance genre, which assiduously avoids this disturbing subject. But Lower East Side novels must have rape or its specter as the peculiarly women's take on the exodus from Russia. The emphasis on rape established for the women, both protagonists and readers, the horrors of Europe as the place that must be fled. The relationship between Eastern Europe and America could have not been more obvious. Jews migrated to America because of pogroms. America loomed in their consciousness as the beacon of hope and salvation; Eastern Europe signified murder, rape, violence. This formulaic understanding of Jewish immigration ran through *all* the Lower East Side romances, as well as the entire sweep of post–World War II American Jewish culture.

Thus, America functioned as a hope and a dream, in contrast to the evils of Eastern Europe. Belva Plain's Anna remembered about her migration: "Keen American air. Beautiful America, more wonderful, painful, generous, difficult and kind than she could have dreamed when she had been a child and longed so much to see it."[60] Even the most politically leftist of the books, Meredith Tax's *Rivington Street*, could not avoid the theme of ultimate success, the leitmotiv of American Jewish history. Although the book's dust jacket touted it as not like the American Jewish success story ("*Rivington Street* is the story of the Jews who didn't move to the suburbs or strike it rich"), it still allowed one of the Levy girls to become a world-renowned clothing designer and another to mimic the Rose Pastor Stokes story of the Lower East Side radical young woman who married the gentile American millionaire.[61]

Mobility and the achievement of their material dreams drove the novels' heroines and their men. As Anna's cousin told her when she first arrived in America from the countryside of Russia—symbolized by the evergreen—"It is not beautiful here, God knows. . . . But one has a future here."[62] That future, its expectation and fulfillment, provided another distinctively Jewish element to the romance fiction. Goldreich structured the chapters of *Leah's Journey* to chart Leah's physical and economic mobility. The chapters and the heroine go from "Russia 1919" to "Lower East Side, 1925," "Brighton Beach, 1933," and "Scarsdale, 1939." (A final section, "Home, 1956," took place in Israel, at the fictional Kibbutz Shaarai HaNegev. In the book's brief epilogue, Leah returned to Russia, only to find her village obliterated. She learned, as "gentle ghosts travelled at her side," that Russia could no longer figure in her memory as back home.)[63]

In *Evergreen*, Anna and Joseph moved uptown and finally out to tonier and tonier suburbs with their increasing wealth. We know, however, from the beginning of their moves to comfort and affluence, that all will not be well, and emotional trouble will overtake them as they get farther and farther away from the Lower East Side. Success had been their goal, comfort their dream, but that trajectory as depicted in these Jewish novels did not come without a sense of loss. In *Evergreen* and *Leah's Journey*, once the families have left the Lower East Side, we no longer read about Jewish ritual observances other than funerals. No more Sabbath dinners or flickering candles. No more descriptions of food preparation, hearty meals, and good fellowship. Indeed, the juxtaposition of the Lower East Side, as life lived intensely and fully, with the loneliness and sterility of success brought both of these novels to a close. In both novels, wealth may have brought material comfort, but it also brought suicides, intermarriages, conversions to Christianity, lovelessness, and loneliness.

Joseph's mother in *Evergreen* (like Henry Roth's real mother) probably knew this would happen. "More than once," Plain informed the readers, "he [Joseph] had urged her to sell the store and move uptown to the Heights [Washington Heights]. But she would not. She had made one great move in her lifetime, across the ocean, had put down tentative roots on Ludlow Street and that was enough."[64]

But staying put had not figured into their calculus. The reader cannot ultimately be sure who made the better decision. Anna and Joseph became very wealthy, but the quality of their lives deteriorated, and their children and grandchildren lived lives disconnected from the past and from Jewishness.

Evergreen ended with Anna's grandson bringing out a tape recorder to take down her life story. Anna looked at her very American grandson and mused: "He has my father's pale eyes . . . he moves like him, clumsily. How can he understand what life was like for his great-grandfather, maker of boots and harness? For him it's a story, picturesque and touching."[65] Anna knew better. Leah, too, understood the losses that came with success. If the Lower East Side had overwhelmed these women with its smells, noises, and the press of people crowding in on them from every direction, success brought emptiness. The bittersweet endings of Lower East Side romance novels moved these books farther out of the romance category, as perfected by the Harlequin and Silhouette publishers, and made them a distinct Jewish genre. More than anything, readers of the immensely popular books demanded a happy ending, but Lower East Side tales involved as much loss as gain, and the endings could not avoid mixing the happy with the sad.[66]

NOTES

1. According to Althea K. Helbig and Agnes R. Perkin's *Dictionary of American Children's Fiction, 1859–1959: Books of Recognized Merit* (Westport, CT:

Greenwood Press, 1985), only one children's book on an American Jewish topic predated *All-of-a-Kind Family*. That book, John R. Tunis's *Keystone Kids* (New York: Harcourt Brace, 1943), has not had the same longevity as *All-of-a-Kind Family*.

2. Mary Arbuthnot, review of *All-of-a-Kind Family*, *Publishers Weekly*, October 13, 1951, 1577.

3. *Library Journal*, October 15, 1951, 172.

4. Other 1950s titles include Nora Benjamin Kubie, *Joel*; Mina Lewitin, *Rachel and Herman*; Leota Harris, *Freckle Face Frankel*; Arbuthnot, review of *All-of-a-Kind Family*.

5. The same year Gladys Malvern published, "*Behold Your Queen!*" (New York: Longmans, 1951) a juvenile fictional rendition of the story of Queen Esther.

6. *Library Journal*, October 15, 1951, 78.

7. Laura Ingalls Wilder, *Little House on the Prairie* (New York: Harper, 1935).

8. Esther Forbes, *Johnny Tremaine: A Novel for Old and Young* (Boston: Houghton Mifflin, 1943).

9. For the wide appeal of *All-of-a-Kind Family*, see Mary Hill Arbuthnot, *Children and Books* (Chicago: Scott, Foresman, 1957), 420–21. Arbuthnot, a specialist in children's literature, recommended it for use at Sunday school and summer camps, as well as home reading.

10. See the entry "Children's Literature," in *Jewish Women in America: An Historical Encyclopedia*, ed. Paula E. Hyman and Deborah Dash Moore, vol. 1 (New York: Routledge, 1997), 220.

11. See "Taylor, Sydney (1904–1978)" in *Jewish Women in America: An Historical Encyclopedia*, vol. 2, 138–39.

12. "TAYLOR, Sydney (Brenner)," in *Something about the Author: Facts and Pictures about Authors and Illustrators of Books for Young People*, vol. 28, ed. Anne Commire (Detroit: Gale Research Company, 1971), 203.

13. Sydney Taylor, *All-of-a-Kind Family* (New York: Follett, 1951), 34.

14. Ibid., 67–68.

15. Ibid., 73–74.

16. Sydney Taylor, *More All-of-a-Kind Family* (New York: Follett, 1954), 158.

17. Ibid., 144–45.

18. Ibid., 1.

19. Ibid., 77–78.

20. Ibid., 80–81.

21. Ibid., 135–38.

22. See, for example, Jianhua Yu, "Immigrant Life and Its Cultural Implications in the Fiction of Jewish Immigrant Writers of New York's Lower East Side, 1890–1930" (PhD diss., University of East Anglia, 1991); K. Dittmar, "Jewish Ghetto-Literature: The Lower East Side, 1890–1924," *Amerikastudien* 26 (1981): 170–292.

23. A fourth novel of the historic Lower East Side had a somewhat different history. Mike Gold's *Jews without Money* (New York: Horace Liveright, 1930) had actually never gotten lost. It became a popular book among left-wing leaders from the time of its initial publication, and although it changed publishers a number of times, it never went out of print. It is the case, however, that it was reissued in 1965 by a mainstream publishing company, Avon, and as such became available,

or at least acceptable, to a wider audience. See also Eric Homberger, "Michael Gold, Ethnicity, and the Left in the 1930's," *Revue Françoise d'Etudes Americaines* 16 (1993): 31–41.

24. Leslie A. Fiedler, *Love and Death in the American Novel* (New York: Criterion, 1960), 463.

25. Henry Roth, *Call It Sleep* (New York: R. O. Ballou, 1934).

26. The *New York Herald Tribune* focused on its "crude bitterness," which "makes Erskine Caldwell's work monotonous" by comparison. See *New York Herald Tribune*, February 16, 1935, 9.

27. Bonnie Lyons, *Henry Roth: The Man and His Work* (New York: Cooper Square, 1977).

28. Walter Rideout, *The Radical Novel in the United States, 1900-1954: Some Interrelations of Literature and Society* (Cambridge: Harvard University Press, 1956), 186–90.

29. Alfred Kazin, "Neglected Books," *American Scholar* 25 (Autumn 1956): 478, 486; Leslie Fiedler, "Henry Roth's Neglected Masterpiece" (1960), in *The Collected Essays of Leslie Fiedler*, vol. 2 (New York: Stein and Day, 1971), 271–79.

30. Walter Allen, "Afterword" to Henry Roth, *Call It Sleep*, 442.

31. Since the initial reissue, editions of *Call It Sleep* have been published in 1963 (in England), 1966 (in Spanish, published in Barcelona), 1991, 1995, and 1996. See *New Essays on* Call It Sleep (New York: Cambridge University Press, 1996); Horst Immel, *Literarische Gestaltungsvarianten des Einwanderromans* (Frankfurt am Main: Peter Lang, 1987); and Mario Materassi, *Rothiana: Henry Roth nella critic italiana* (Florence: Giutina, 1985).

32. *New Republic*, February 2, 1918, 31.

33. John Higham, "Introduction," in Abraham Cahan, *The Rise of David Levinsky* (New York: Harper and Brothers, 1960), xi.

34. Likewise, Cahan's short stories saw life, died, and then were revived in the late 1960s. Thus, *The Imported Bridegroom and Other Stories* was first published in 1898 by Houghton Mifflin; *Yekl* had been published in 1896 by Appleton. In 1968 a small press, Garrett, released *The Imported Bridegroom*, and in 1970 Dover published a volume of Cahan stories as *Yekl and The Imported Bridegroom*.

35. Isaac Rosenfeld, "The Fall of David Levinsky," in *Preserving the Hunger: An Isaac Rosenfeld Reader*, ed. Mark Schechner (Detroit: Wayne State University Press, 1988), 152.

36. It is virtually impossible to cite the number of places where Cahan is quoted and the number of scholarly articles that have referenced *The Rise of David Levinsky*. Ronald Sanders, *The Downtown Jews* (New York: Harper and Row, 1969), is subtitled *Portraits of an Immigrant Generation*. It is, however, a loosely constructed biography of Cahan. In the index to Irving Howe, *World of Our Fathers: The Journey of the East European Jews to America and the Life They Found and Made* (New York: Harcourt Brace Jovanovich, 1976), no name appears more often than Abraham Cahan, no newspaper more frequently than the *Jewish Daily Forward* nor any novel more than *The Rise of David Levinsky*. Moses Rischin, *Grandma Never Lived in America: The New Journalism of Abraham Cahan* (Bloomington: Indiana University Press, 1985), has brought together Cahan's English newspaper writings, while Isaac

Metzker's *A Bintel Brief: Sixty Years of Letters from the Lower East Side to the Jewish Daily Forward* (Garden City, NY: Doubleday, 1971) transformed Cahan's advice column in the *Forward* to canonical status. See also Sanford E. Marovitz, "The Lonely New Americans of Abraham Cahan," *American Quarterly* 20, no. 2, pt. 1 (1968): 196–210.

37. A similar story might be told of Hutchins Hapgood's journalistic treatment of the neighborhood in *The Spirit of the Ghetto: Studies of the Jewish Quarter*. Published in part in a number of magazines (*Atlantic Monthly*, *The Critic*, *The Bookman*, and others) and then brought out in book form in 1902 by Funk and Wagnalls, *Spirit of the Ghetto* was intended to offer a fresh look at the immigrant Jews of New York's East Side. Rather than presenting any single Jew as typical of the immigrants, Hapgood sought to show that many Jews lived there, expressing diverse views about Jewishness and America. He offered portraits of "the old and new woman," rabbis, poets, radicals, "submerged scholars," and many others. After its 1902 publication, *The Spirit of the Ghetto* lay on library shelves. In 1965 Funk and Wagnalls reissued it, with Schocken paperback editions coming out in 1966 and 1967.

38. *International Book Reviews*, October 1925, 719; *New York Tribune*, October 25, 1925, 20.

39. *New York Times*, September 13, 1925, 8.

40. Blanche H. Gelfant, "Introduction," in Anzia Yezierska, *Hungry Hearts* (New York: Penguin, 1997), xvii.

41. Joyce Antler, *The Journey Home: Jewish Women and the American Century* (New York: Free Press, 1997), 27.

42. Yezierska, *Hungry Hearts*, xix.

43. Alice Kessler Harris, "Organizing the Unorganizable: Three Jewish Women and Their Union," *Labor History* 17 (Winter 1976): 14–28; Harris, "Where Are the Organized Women Workers?" *Feminist Studies* 3 (Fall 1975): 92–110.

44. Yezierska, *Bread Givers*, 297.

45. Cahan, *Rise of David Levinsky*, 525–26.

46. Roth, *Call it Sleep* (New York: Avon, 1962), 138.

47. Ibid., 147.

48. Just as the retrieval of these novels represented a new and different interest in America in the Lower East Side so, too, did some memoir literature. Rose Cohen's *Out of the Shadow* was first published in 1918 by G. H. Doran. This autobiography of a young woman growing up on the Lower East Side was reissued in 1971, and then again in 1995 by Cornell University Press with an introduction by the labor historian Thomas Dublin.

49. Belva Plain, *Evergreen* (New York: Delacorte, 1978).

50. Gloria Goldreich, *Leah's Journey* (New York: Harcourt Brace, 1978).

51. Meredith Tax, *Rivington Street* (New York: William Morrow, 1982); Tax *Union Square* (New York: William Morrow, 1988).

52. Janet Robertson, *Journey Home* (New York: Simon and Schuster, 1990).

53. On the romance genre and its formulaic nature, see Janice Radway, *Reading the Romance: Women, Patriarchy, and Popular Literature* (Chapel Hill: University of North Carolina Press, 1991).

54. Emily Maxwell, *An Easter Disguise* (New York: Zebra Books, 1994).

55. Plain, *Evergreen*, 29; Goldreich, *Leah's Journey*, 27; Tax, *Rivington Street*, 80.

56. Goldreich, *Leah's Journey*, 103; Robertson, *Journey Home*, 62.

57. Goldreich, *Leah's Journey*, 102.

58. For this see my book *Memories of Hunger: Immigrant Foodways and Ethnic Identities* (Cambridge: Harvard University Press).

59. Tax, *Rivington Street*, 9.

60. Plain, *Evergreen*, 587.

61. On Rose Pastor Stokes, see Herbert Shapiro and David L. Sterling, eds., *"I Belong to the Working Class": The Unfinished Autobiography of Rose Pastor Stokes* (Athens: University of Georgia Press, 1992).

62. Plain, *Evergreen*, 18–19.

63. Goldreich, *Leah's Journey*, 449.

64. Plain, *Evergreen*, 30.

65. Ibid., 587.

66. Roadway, *Reading the Romance*, 74.

CONTRIBUTORS

Hasia Diner, Paul S. and Sylvia Steinberg Professor of American Jewish History and Professor of Hebrew and Judaic Studies, New York University.

Henry Louis Gates Jr., Alphonse Fletcher University Professor and director of the W. E. B. Du Bois Institute for African and African American Research, Harvard University.

Meredith Goldsmith, Associate Professor of English, Ursinus College.

Cheryl Greenberg, Paul E. Raether Distinguished Professor of History, Trinity College.

Adam Meyer, Associate Professor of Jewish Studies, Vanderbilt University.

Catherine Rottenberg, Assistant Professor of Foreign Literatures and Linguistics and Gender Studies, Ben-Gurion University of the Negev.

Cherene Sherrard-Johnson, Professor of English, University of Wisconsin, Madison.

Magdalena J. Zaborowska, Professor of American Culture, University of Michigan.

INDEX